Half a century
of British politics

edited by
Lynton Robins
and
Bill Jones

Manchester University Press
Manchester and New York
distributed exclusively in the USA by St. Martin's Press

Published by Manchester University Press
Oxford Road, Manchester M13 9NR, UK
and Room 400, 175 Fifth Avenue, New York, NY 10010, USA

Distributed exclusively in the USA
by St. Martin's Press, Inc., 175 Fifth Avenue, New York,
NY 10010, USA

British Library Cataloguing-in-Publication Data
A catalogue record for this book is available from the British Library

Library of Congress Cataloging-in-Publication Data
Half a century of British politics / edited by Lynton Robins and Bill Jones
        p. cm.
    ISBN 0-7190-4839-7 (cloth). — ISBN 0-7190-4840-0 (pbk.)
    1. Great Britain–Politics and government–1945–   I. Robins, L. J.
(Lynton J.)   II. Jones, Bill, 1946–
JN231.H35   1997
320.941'09'045—dc21   96-51815
                                                          CIP

ISBN   0 7190 4839 7 *hardback*
       0 7190 4840 0 *paperback*

First published 1997

01 00 99 98 97   10 9 8 7 6 5 4 3 2 1

Printed by Biddles Ltd, Guildford and King's Lynn

For Carolyn Vibert (1946–65)

Contents

Contributors

Martin Burch is Senior Lecturer in Government at the University of Manchester, where he teaches courses on British politics, policy analysis and European Union politics. He is the author of numerous books and articles, including *British Politics: A Reader* (with Michael Moran); *Public Policy in Britain* (with Bruce Wood); and *The British Cabinet System* (with Ian Holliday).

Philip Cowley is a temporary lecturer at the University of Hull. He has published extensively on aspects of the Conservative Party, party leadership contests and parliamentary elites. His articles have appeared in *Political Studies*, *The Journal of Legislative Studies*, *Party Politics*, *Public Law*, and *Politics*, as well as in the teaching and political press. He has a chapter in the *British Elections and Parties Yearbook 1996* and in the forthcoming *The General Election of 1997*.

David Denver is Reader in Politics at Lancaster University. He is the author of the widely used textbook *Elections and Voting Behaviour in Britain* and of *Modern Constituency Electioneering*. He is co-convenor of the Elections, Public Opinion and Parties Group of the Political Studies Association and is a popular speaker at sixth-form conferences.

Wyn Grant is Professor of Politics at the University of Warwick. His books include *Pressure Groups, Politics and Democracy in Britain* and *The Confederation of British Industry* (written with David Marsh).

Stephen Ingle is Professor of Politics at the University of Stirling. He has written widely in the areas of British party politics and politics and literature. His most recent book was a political life of George Orwell and he is currently working on the third edition of *The British Party System*.

Bill Jones, who is a Research Fellow at the Department of Government, University of Manchester, has authored, co-authored or edited twelve books, mostly on British politics. He edits the Politics Today series for Manchester

University Press and co-edits the Political Analysis series. He was Director of Extra-Mural Studies, 1987–92, and retired from full-time university work in 1994.

Roger Levy is Professor of Public Policy and Head of the School of Public Administration and Law at the Robert Gordon University, Aberdeen. He has published extensively on nationalism and devolution in the UK, including *Scottish Nationalism at the Crossroads*, plus numerous articles and book chapters. He also researches the management and accountability of European Union programmes.

Kenneth Newton is at the Department of Government, University of Essex, and is Executive Director of the European Consortium for Political Research. His research interests cover media politics, mass political opinion, and comparative politics. Recent books include *The Political Data Handbook*, *The Politics of the New Europe* (with Ian Budge *et al.*), and *Beliefs in Government* (with Max Kaase), which was one of a five-volume series, Beliefs in Government.

Philip Norton is Professor of Government at the University of Hull. His publications include more than twenty books, among them *The Constitution in Flux*, *The British Polity* (now in its third edition), *Does Parliament Matter?* and *The Conservative Party*. He is presently working on a book on the role of senior ministers in British government.

Lynton Robins is editor of *Talking Politics*, co-author of *Contemporary British Politics* and co-editor of *Public Policy in Britain, Governing the UK in the 1990s* and *Britain's Changing Party System*. He teaches politics at the Leicester Business School.

David Sanders is Professor of Government at the University of Essex. His work in the British foreign policy field includes *Losing an Empire, Finding a Role: British Foreign Policy Since 1945*. He has published numerous articles on British domestic politics, focusing particularly on the effects of the economy on party support. He is editor of the *British Journal of Political Science*.

John Street is a Senior Lecturer in Politics at the University of East Anglia. He is the author of *Politics and Technology*; *Rebel Rock: The Politics of Popular Music*, and *Politics and Popular Culture*. He is co-author, with John Greenaway and Steve Smith, of *Deciding Factors in British Politics*.

Paul Wilding has been Professor of Social Policy at the University of Manchester since 1981. He has written widely about social policy. His most recent book (with Vic George) is *Welfare and Ideology*.

Bruce Wood is Senior Lecturer in Government at the University of Manchester, where he teaches courses on British politics, health policy and comparative health care. He is the author of numerous books and articles, including *The Process of Local Government Reform*; *Public Policy in Britain* (with Martin Burch); and *States, Regulation and the Medical Profession* (with Michael Moran).

Preface

In September 1990 a conference was convened at the University of Manchester to commemorate twenty-one years of the Politics Association – the UK's professional body for politics teachers in schools and colleges. The papers delivered at the conference by the Association's founder, Bernard Crick, and others were subsequently augmented by other academics active in the Association and published as *Two Decades in British Politics* (Manchester University Press, 1992). The book was well received and sold very well and it was no real surprise when MUP's Richard Purslow agreed to commission a follow-up book, this time addressing the longer time frame of five decades. So much has happened in British politics since the Second World War it was obvious there would be no lack of things to analyse and comment upon.

In 1945 Britain was triumphant but broke, with large pockets of poverty; it was a nation close to the breadline. Fifty years on the country is much wealthier – it can even boast over 100,000 millionaires – but poverty remains and arguably affects a whole new 'underclass' striving to sustain an existence at the base of the social pyramid. What has changed inevitably and irrevocably is the mood of the former period, when a battle-weary population stoically accepted the continuation of rationing and the bleak, grim winter of 1947. They were sustained and buoyed up by memories of a recent heroic victory and the promise of a benign welfare state with free health care plus full employment. The mood in the nineties is much different, with so many achievements of the postwar administration either denigrated or dismantled. There is certainly less hope these days than cynicism as the political culture fully traverses the bitter ground between expectation and experience, aspiration and failure.

The essays in this volume by a number of the country's leading political scientists illuminate themes from this pivotal half century in our history which include: the shrinking role played by Britain on the international stage; the changes in the role of the state in our politics; pressure groups; political leadership and parties; the media; and the welfare state; not to mention the transformations which have removed the former certainties of class, authority and voting behaviour.

Another reason why the idea of the volume appealed to us was the fact that its span almost exactly matches that of our own lives, though not sadly that of an old school friend to whom this book is dedicated, who tragically lost her life with much promise unfulfilled.

We wish to thank MUP for their forbearance in indulging the whim of two half-centurion products of the postwar baby boom; we also thank the authors for their promptness and, most importantly, the high quality of their contributions.

Lynton Robins
De Montfort University

Bill Jones
University of Manchester

Introduction: end-of-war Britain

Bill Jones and Lynton Robins

However it is phrased, whichever words are chosen, L. P. Hartley has already said it. British politicians and public fifty years ago thought and behaved very differently from their contemporary counterparts. The immediate postwar world that they inhabited contained threat and danger, but both at home and abroad there was considerable certainty about what sort of society was to be constructed as well as a robust confidence about Britain's place in the international order. At home, theirs was to be an age of popular socialism established without significant dissent by the collectivist inheritance of the war effort. Abroad, the national interest was served by continuity in policy; Britain chose the open seas rather than Europe.

The first Labour government with a majority in the Commons presided over a social and economic, but not a constitutional, revolution. Beveridge and Keynes, both Liberals, provided the blueprints for reconstruction and it was only elaborations on health and education that came from Labour and the Conservatives, respectively. Parties may have forged similar policies for rather different reasons, but what was created during the war years and immediately afterwards was a political consensus that was to characterise Britain's political culture for three decades. Party conflict, a necessary reassurance that democracy was at work, was commonplace in form rather than content during the immediate postwar Labour and Conservative administrations.

Political consensus seemed to reflect the common values held in wider society. Political scientists frequently commented on the homogeneous nature of British society, in which social class seemed to cause the only fracture, and even class did not run parallel with party politics. Women, young people, the small ethnic minorities, people in the regions, as well as people promoting any form of alternative lifestyle, did not exist in the world of postwar politics. Indeed, as late as halfway into this political survey, research by American academics which found that English school children exhibited an unusually weak attachment to the political system provoked outrage in

1

the British academic community (Dennis *et al.* 1971). Poll data showing a lack of support for political institutions, particularly the monarchy, together with speculation about a possible crisis of legitimacy developing in Britain, punctured the comfortable image of society held then by British political scientists. At the time it seemed ludicrous to describe Britain's political order as anything but well supported and secure.

There was a widely held belief that Britain's political institutions worked well. So well, in fact, that they served as models which could be exported around the world for the benefit of all. They were seen as being free from corruption, if not incorruptible, based on traditions of caution and probity when handling public money, impartiality when dealing with or representing members of the public, and operated always with fairness, decency and integrity. It was easy to believe in the existence of duty and a public service ethos motivated by higher goals rather than by a healthy bottom line or improving performance indicators.

How could it be that postwar Britain was a more confident as well as a more settled society, given the problems of scarcity endured by the public during the war and on into peacetime? For many who experienced the 1930s, wartime and peacetime rationing actually brought improvement rather than austerity. In other words, life for many postwar Britons may have been bleak and shabby in material terms but they had known worse. It did not take a great effort to endure the hard winter of 1947 since ordinary life had been pretty tough by the standards of today. An added bonus was the feeling that government cared about the welfare of its citizens even if actual improvements were small and slow in arriving. Expectations were rising and, more importantly, being met.

Political scientists have put forward other explanations for the stability and order of immediate postwar Britain: the false consciousness of the workers on the one hand, widespread attitudes of deference and effective socialisation of working-class youth to the established order on the other hand. Beyond the remit of political science, it is possible to offer more intuitive accounts of life in postwar Britain. It is, for example, possible to argue that compared with now most Britons led smaller, simpler lives with fewer connecting points with agencies of change. For most people, other than as members of the armed forces, foreign travel had never been experienced. Indeed, for many, domestic, even local, travel was restricted by today's standards. Leisure activities were limited in both scope and frequency by a lack of money once necessities had been paid for, which, for most people, included rent. Radio was more socially conservative than television which followed. Tabloid newspapers were very much less red-blooded in their reporting on the rich and famous. Quite undeservedly many political reputations survived intact, facilitating greater deference, and adding to the belief Britons had that they were the respectable society. Social conservatism, together with a lack of resources necessary for alternatives, resulted in marriages lasting till death did they part and extended families maintaining regular contact as newly married offspring set up home close to their parents.

In short, Britain of the 1940s and 1950s was more disciplined, partly as a result of wartime routines and national service, and partly as a result of more severe punishments in the schools and courts. Prewar austerity fashioned a people who could tolerate considerable adversity and who were grateful for modest social and economic gain. At risk of some exaggeration, the wartime effort of 'pulling together' slid easily into the postwar world of Labour's popular socialism. In this sense, the aura of 1945 was much less the rays of a new dawn than they were the twilight and shadow of Britain's risky war with Germany.

On 8 May 1945, V-E Day was celebrated in Britain with an intensity born of six long and uncertain war-filled years. On 23 May, Churchill disbanded the coalition and set up a caretaker government as the prologue to what most political commentators, not to mention politicians themselves, anticipated would be a rerun of the 'khaki' or 'coupon' elections when governments victorious in war looked for their expected political dividend. Confident expectations of a Churchill victory were, of course, confounded on 5 July when Labour won 393 seats to the Conservatives' 213.

In his book, *Never Again*, Peter Hennessy (1992: 88) quoted the journalist Peregrine Worsthorne, who recalled:

> the panic that hit some of my rich fellow officers – Astors and Barings – when the news of Labour's victory reached our mess in Holland. They thought the game was up there and then, and blocked the 21st Army Group's headquarters communication system telephoning anguished instructions to sell to their stockbrokers.

It was almost as if the upper classes believed the election victory equalled immediate and total socialism, dispossessing the rich and elevating the masses. As mentioned, the transition was neither total nor immediate, yet the more perceptive of Worsthorne's fellow officers must have already known that in many ways the Britain of 1945 was already socialist in political climate and that while the machinery was not yet in place, the underpinnings in terms of public expectations and desires were.

The war had transformed Britain from a divided and fractious society into a more united and confident whole. While some had enjoyed a 'very good' war, made money and rarely, if ever, experienced risk to life or limb, others had shared in the conflict: rich and poor had fought together in the forces, had died or lost loved ones equally; the rich and comfortably off met the poor via the evacuations of city children to the countryside; and everyone looked to the future as a time which would reward everyone, high and low, for the effort of war and danger so heroically survived. During the depression the suffering had been borne unequally; memories of this fuelled the egalitarianism of wartime arrangements where, black markets apart, notions of 'fair play' prevailed. The prewar suggestion that pregnant women should receive milk and vitamins, for example, was painlessly introduced in June 1940 and a month later the school meals scheme was vastly extended. Some of this was functional, to create young replacements for those killed in conflict, but it was also to provide treatment that was fair and equal for all. Later in the war, in April 1941, income tax was increased to 10s 6d; for the rich it was 19s 6d in the pound. But as David Vincent writes in *Poor Citizen*:

> The real message of the budget ... was not that the balance of wealth was being tipped towards the common man, but rather that the privileged were being forced to participate in its sufferings. The ration book, with its new system of points stood as a symbol and a guarantee of the commitment to equal protection and shared sacrifice which underpinned all the welfare reforms and proposals of the period. (Vincent 1991: 116)

It is not too fanciful to discern at this time the forging of a species of social contract between citizen and government, a new relationship whereby substantial contribution to the national effort entitled one to a new range of privileges. Part of this contract was the acceptance of a new centralised economic system almost analogous to that of the Soviet Union. Ernest Bevin as Minister of Labour was able to conscript workers for any necessary economic function, from factory work to the mines. The necessities of war elevated the role of government for everyone, but with so much popular support the relationship worked; at no time in British history can government and people have been so united in common purpose and expectation.

The year 1942 saw the publication of the historic Beveridge report, which recommended a national system of social and health insurance, financed by central taxation, which would provide also for maternity and child benefits plus unemployment insurance and pensions. An austere academic, William Beveridge had sought 'the greatest measure of common agreement in the views of those who have thought most seriously upon its problems' (Vincent 1991: 118). That he succeeded cannot be denied given the plethora of endorsements from the middle-class intelligentsia and a Mass Observation survey in the autumn of 1942 which revealed over 90 per cent popular support for his proposals. In a radio broadcast during the following year, even the prime minister was pledging his government to 'establish on broad and solid foundations ... a national compulsory insurance for all classes for all purposes from the cradle to the grave.' It is ironic that the 'People's William', who achieved so much on his nation's behalf, should have eventually suffered a similar political fate to that of the architect of victory himself: Beveridge was defeated as a Liberal candidate in the 1945 election. But his influence far outlasted the war and its aftermath.

For the average soldier returning home after the war Britain did not offer the most salubrious of settings. Many city centres were devastated; such buildings that escaped war damage were stained by coal smoke and town atmospheres were polluted; the average pay was a mere 1s per hour (compared with the 2s 6d earned by their American counterparts); housing was in desperately short supply; the educational and health services still excluded the poor; food was in very short supply; people were badly clothed, either in baggy demob suits or still in uniform; and motor vehicles were as scarce as the petrol needed to propel them.

Nevertheless, the average British soldier returning home must have felt wonderful. From a moment in history of great national peril when Britain alone held the line against barbarism, the nation had won the support of countries around the world and not just from those with imperial and ethnic connections. The future seemed bleak in those dangerous early years but, thanks in no small measure to Churchill, the nation never fell into total despair; rather it focused its energies to survive its greatest test. To be British in 1945 was to be economically bankrupt but, in Hennessy's phrase, 'morally magnificent'. Yet, even though 1940 may have been historically our 'finest hour', for those who fought in Africa and Europe this description would more properly have suited their return home to their families and grateful country.

Something akin to this enthusiasm certainly infected new Labour MPs who noisily took their places in the Commons singing the 'Red Flag' (much to the embarrassment of the old guard). The country was exhausted by war but its borders had more or less avoided the humiliation of invasion; it was weaker militarily than the United States or even the Soviets but its armed forces had never been stronger or more crowned with glory; the Empire was intact again and Britain held sway in many parts of Europe, not to mention the Mediterranean; its people were impoverished but were wealthy relative to the rest of Europe; its overseas assets were severely depleted but its international reputation never higher. Labour looked confidently to the future, supported by a country united, thanks to the war, and, to adapt Powell's phrase, 'humming a socialist tune'.

In November 1945 Dalton introduced his first budget 'with a song in my heart'. He refused to acknowledge any discordant voices over the ending of the wartime lifeline of lend–lease, which was replaced the following year, in a deal brokered by Keynes, by a £3.75 billion loan repayable over fifty years. Britain's economic position was indeed parlous, as the following wartime and end-of-war data (from Hennessy 1992: 99) demonstrate:

- population, 46 million;
- armed forces (pre-1939, 0.5 million), 5 million;
- civil defence and munitions workers, 5 million;
- deaths (military and merchant navy), 380,000;

- deaths (civilian), 60,000;
- houses destroyed, 500,000;
- houses severely damaged, 250,000;
- gold reserves disposed of, 33 per cent;
- overseas assets sold, 33 per cent;
- debts incurred, £3.5 billion;
- increases in direct taxation, 1939–45, over 300 per cent;
- increases in indirect taxation, 1939–45, over 160 per cent.

The cupboard was bare, the wallet alarmingly empty and the currency itself pitifully fragile.

In retrospect, it seems incredible that the new Labour government reformed with such confidence and apparent blissful unawareness of its underlying bankruptcy. The social security system was set up in accordance with Beveridge's instructions; the National Health Service was legislated for in 1946 and came into existence two years later; the 1944 Butler Education Act with its tripartite provision for grammar, secondary modern and technical schools was implemented in bipartite form; three-quarters of a million new state-subsidised council houses were promised (over a million were actually built by 1952). On top of all this was the bold programme of nationalis- ation – socialism British style. In all, some 20 per cent of the economy was taken into the public sector, including the Bank of England, coal, railways, road transport, civil aviation, gas, electricity, and cable and wireless.

In summary, Britain was not the most comfortable country to live in when peace came in 1945. Yet for a British citizen it was the headiest of times: victorious in war, a nation blessed with spirit, solidarity and possessing a heroic image of itself. A radical government, newly in office, promised exciting and far-reaching reforms; the old country would continue to make history. For any citizen of the country in that watershed year, anything seemed possible and no problem insurmountable.

References

Dennis, J., Lindberg, L. and McCrone, D. J. (1971), Support for nation and government among English children, *British Journal of Political Science*, 1:1, 21–44.
Hennessy, P. (1992), *Never Again*, London, Cape.
Vincent, D. (1991), *Poor Citizen*, Harlow, Longman.

1

Britain and the world

David Sanders

Britain emerged from the Second World War as one of the three 'great powers' which, at Yalta and Potsdam in 1945, had played a decisive role in shaping the postwar settlement. As one of only five permanent members of the United Nations (UN) Security Council, Britain enjoyed the privilege of the right to veto any of the Council's resolutions. Under the terms of the 1944 Bretton Woods agreement, London also found itself acting as Washington's junior partner in a new international economic regime (based on the International Monetary Fund (IMF), the World Bank and the soon to be created General Agreement on Tariffs and Trade (GATT)) aimed at promoting economic stability and growth in the 'western' capitalist world.

The newly elected Attlee government, moreover, had a clear vision of the sort of foreign policy strategy that postwar Britain would follow. In line with the analysis advanced by Churchill in 1945, the British government would seek to preserve British interests in three interlocking circles: in Europe, in the Empire and in the special relationship with the USA. The view of Britain's postwar foreign policy makers was that Britain remained a great power with far-flung global interests that required protection – and that it was likely to remain so for the foreseeable future. By the early 1950s, Britain had acquired its own independent nuclear capability. It was one of the two leading members of the North Atlantic Treaty Organization (NATO), the military alliance which was set to guarantee the security of western Europe and north America for the next five decades. In spite of the loss of India in 1947, it retained control of a still extensive empire. And its share of world trade was well over 20 per cent – not much lower than the share it had enjoyed at the peak of the country's industrial and military pre-eminence in the mid-nineteenth century.

What a difference half a century can make. By the mid-1990s, although Britain retained both its membership of the Group of Seven leading industrial economies and its permanent Security Council seat, its circumstances were considerably reduced. Britain's international ranking in terms of gross domestic product (GDP) per capita had declined, between 1950 and 1990, from seventh position to twenty-second. Its share of world trade had fallen to less than 5 per cent. It was experiencing stubbornly low long-term growth rates of around 2 per cent per year. And, despite having decolonised comprehensively in favour of a foreign policy that focused primarily on Europe, its government remained profoundly uncertain about the extent to which Britain should commit itself to the further development of the European Union (EU).

This chapter considers the way in which the international environment in which Britain was obliged to operate changed during the half century after 1945. It also examines the way in which successive British governments, while seeking to maximise what they perceived to be Britain's national interests, responded to these environmental changes. The main substantive theme of the chapter is that, although there has been a major shift in Britain's postwar foreign policy away from the Empire and towards Europe, the continuing pursuit of a residual world role – the legacy of Empire – has impeded Britain's full and effective participation in the EU. The chapter begins by summarising the main changes that have characterised global politics and economics since 1945. It then outlines the major changes in Britain's international position that have occurred during the same period and reviews the adjustments to Britain's foreign policy that successive governments have made in order to respond to them.

The main changes in Britain's external environment since 1945

Given that one person's profundity is often another's triviality, it is difficult to determine which of the many changes in global politics and economics over the last fifty years have in some sense been fundamental. To complicate matters further, the interconnections among many aspects of change means that simple characterisations of what has changed are always open to challenge. While recognising these limitations, the following discussion addresses the question of change in three areas: changes in observable behaviour and capabilities of state and non-state actors since 1945; changes in the prevailing climate of political and economic ideas since 1945; and changes in the character of the international system since the end of the Cold War in 1989.

Changes in observable behaviour and relative capabilities

Perhaps the most important change in international relations in the last fifty years is that, among the major industrial powers, competition for the control of territory, populations and natural resources has increasingly been replaced by competition for global market share and the ability to repatriate profit. Before 1945, countries with relatively powerful economies tended to use their economic and military muscle to extend their direct political influence beyond their current national boundaries. European imperialism in the nineteenth century and German and Japanese expansionism in the 1930s involved precisely this sort of extension. Since 1945, however, nation states have increasingly recognised that economic security and global influence can be achieved without direct or indirect political control – as the cases of Germany and Japan have so clearly demonstrated. In the late twentieth century, a sustained balance-of-payments surplus appears to be a far more potent weapon in the competition for global influence than either a large standing army or even an independent nuclear deterrent.

A second and related change in the international system has been the massive increase in world trade and financial exchanges. These increases have both reflected and reinforced the revolutions in transport technology and global communications that have occurred since 1945. Although direct comparison is difficult, the available figures suggest that the volume of world trade in goods and services in 1993 was more than twenty times greater than it had been in 1950. The volume of currency exchanges and capital transfers, spurred on by deregulation by western governments in the 1980s, was so great by the mid-1990s that it was beyond the capability of those governments even to monitor them effectively. This expansion of the financial sector, in particular, has served to increase the significance of international markets and market forces. Economists sometimes speak about the permeability of national economies – the extent to which capital, labour, goods and services can be either introduced into or extracted from a given country. There can be little doubt that, over the last fifty years, the average level of permeability has increased considerably. The consequence of this has been a commensurate diminution in the decision-making autonomy of national governments – which have found their economic policies increasingly vulnerable to international market pressures.

A third change has been the decline from economic pre-eminence of the USA. The USA's postwar military dominance was, of course, repeatedly challenged by the Soviet Union throughout the Cold War – a position made even more potentially hazardous for Washington and its allies by the 'defection' of China to the communist bloc in 1949. In the global economic sphere, however, the United States retained a near hegemonic position until the early 1970s, when the US-sponsored Bretton Woods system of fixed exchange rates collapsed. Since that time, the world economy has been characterised by a far more complex, multipolar structure in which Germany and the EU, Japan, the 'Asian tigers' of the Pacific rim and the Middle Eastern oil states have all successfully challenged US economic dominance of global trade and financial markets.

A fourth area of change has been the growth of international regimes. Regimes are sets of international 'rules of the game' that exist when 'patterned state behaviour results from joint rather than independent decisionmaking' (Stein 1993: 31). States are prepared to accept regime-imposed restrictions on their decision-making autonomy on two conditions:

- that the benefits of any cooperation sponsored by the regime more than outweigh the costs entailed by any loss of autonomy;
- that the regime is able to ensure that states that fail to cooperate (or that free-ride on the concessions made by others) are suitably penalised.

In the postwar period, regimes have proliferated to such an extent that it is impractical to attempt to describe them all here. Three examples, however, give an indication of the wide range of contexts in which international regimes have developed. In the economic sphere, GATT (now the World Trade Organisation) has been remarkably successful, through a series of negotiating rounds which culminated in the Uruguay round in the early 1990s, in bringing down trade barriers and in expanding world trade. In the security sphere, the Conference on (now the Organisation for) Security and Cooperation in Europe made an important contribution to the softening of East–West relations in the years immediately before the end of the Cold War. Finally, in the ecological sphere, the Vienna Convention (1985) and the Montreal Protocol (1987) established and extended guidelines for reducing production of chlorofluorocarbons in order to protect the earth's ozone layer.

Ensuring compliance with a regime's rules is always difficult. Nonetheless, the enormous growth of regime-like organisations and practices since 1945 represents an important change in the international environment in which Britain now operates. To a lesser extent, the development of regimes also reflects the commitment of successive British governments to the construction of regimes that would themselves facilitate further international cooperation.

The final set of behavioural changes that British governments were obliged to confront after 1945 concerned the third world. From the mid-1940s onwards, the economic development of the colonies, which European imperialism had actively sought to encourage, started to bring social and political tensions in its wake. The process of urbanisation, together with the expansion of education and mass communications, fragmented old social networks, rendering the indigenous populations of the colonies much more susceptible to new, often radical ideas. As Porter (1988: 322) observed, colonialism bred 'its own antidote'. By developing the colonies, the imperial powers created the very conditions in which anti-colonial oppositions could thrive. Throughout the 1950s and '60s, the demands of indigenous colonial peoples for self-determination grew ever more insistent and difficult to resist. Indeed, indigenous pressures for change had become so strong by the mid-1960s that all the major European imperial territories in Africa, the Caribbean and the Far East had achieved independence. Not only did this rapid decolonisation dramatically increase the number of states in the state system, thereby making international diplomacy a much more complex affair, but it was also accompanied by an increased sense of concern in the west that the Soviets or their allies might make political or military strategic progress in the territories thus vacated.

Changes in the climate of political and economic ideas

Not surprisingly, the changes in global economics and politics were accompanied by changes in the overall climate of ideas. Three of these changes in ideas are worth highlighting. One was that the 'white man's burden' view of empire – in which the colonising powers claimed to be on a civilising mission that would grant independence to colonial peoples 'when they were ready for it' – became increasingly unacceptable. It was replaced by an increased sense of embarrassment about the domination and exploitation of the third world that colonialism implied. Unfortunately for the newly liberated colonial populations, however, this change in attitude was not accompanied by a commensurate willingness or sense of obligation to do much to alleviate their impoverishment.

A second change was the apparently increasing appeal of communism as a mobilising ideology of the dispossessed. Anti-imperialists throughout the third world frequently saw the economic and political difficulties that their countries faced, even after decolonisation, as deriving fundamentally from the operation of the global capitalist system of production, distribution and exchange. Between 1945 and 1975, over thirty countries 'succumbed' to the attractions of Marxist-Leninist ideology. After 1980, however, this seemingly inexorable tide of socialism went into rapid reverse. With the success of the Islamic revolution in Iran after 1979, with Moscow's conflict with Islamic forces in Afghanistan after 1979, and with the collapse of socialism in eastern Europe and in the Soviet Union in 1989–90, communism's appeal as a vehicle for mobilising deeply felt grievances declined significantly. It was replaced in large parts of the third world, and particularly in the Middle East and the Far East, by Islam – though whether Islam will prove any more adept at removing grievances once power has been secured remains to be seen.

A third major change in the postwar climate of international opinion was an increased interest in, and commitment to, the promotion of individual human rights. In part this emphasis reflected a conscious rejection of the sort of 'community rights' that generally accompany the rhetoric of socialism. But it also reflected a genuine humanitarian effort on the part of western governments and non-governmental organisations (such as Charter 88 and Amnesty International) that sought to extend internationally the protective cover of human rights legislation.

The impact of the end of the Cold War

The most obvious change to the global system associated with the end of the Cold War was the disappearance of an ideological bloc in eastern Europe which, since the late 1940s, had represented a constant potential threat to western capitalist interests in both Europe and the third world. It is difficult to overestimate the extent to which the Soviet/communist threat informed western strategic calculations during the Cold War. The need to protect western Europe from possible Soviet aggression was always a first priority. All major foreign policy decisions were undertaken with a view to the Soviet bloc's likely reaction. In these circumstances, the abrupt termination of the external threat that, since 1949, had provided the NATO alliance with its *raison d'être* was bound to create difficulties for western policy makers. In early 1996, with NATO embarking on its first (Bosnian) 'out-of-area' operation, the alliance's unity and resolve seemed undiminished. Such external appearances, however, could not hide the fact that, unless some new threat equivalent to that represented by the USSR were to emerge, NATO's long-term survival would always be in doubt.

An important corollary to the disappearance of the Soviet threat, of course, has been the further spread of 'democracy' based on competitive elections. This process had already been under way in Latin America and in Africa in the 1980s. The end of the Cold War saw the process extend to eastern Europe and the former Soviet Union. The spread of democracy has important implications for the international system. Democracies rarely, if ever, go to war with one another. One reason for this is that democratically elected leaders are far less inclined than their non-democratic counterparts to impose the costs of war on voters whose electoral support may be required in the near future. It follows, other things being equal, that the proliferation of democracy should reduce the chances of international war. We shall see.

A third consequence of the end of the Cold War has been an increase in the international community's ability, acting through the UN, to intervene in local conflicts in order to protect the innocent and defend the interests of victims of aggression. Before 1989, the Cold War ideological divide almost invariably meant that one of the permanent Security Council members (and it was often the USSR) would employ its veto power in order to ensure that the Council was deadlocked. The sort of concerted action that the UN-sponsored multilateral force took in defence of Kuwait against Iraq in 1991, for example, would have been almost unthinkable during the Cold War. Sadly, the Kuwait crisis excepted, greater agreement within the Security Council since 1990 has not been accompanied by conspicuous success on the ground. As events in Bosnia between 1992 and 1995 demonstrated, UN-sponsored forces have found it very difficult to take the sort of decisive action that is typically required for effective and durable conflict resolution.

Adjusting to a changing environment: Britain's postwar foreign policy responses

Two main factors have underpinned Britain's response to the postwar changes in its external environment: the relative decline in its economic

and political position; and the way in which the British foreign policy elite
has defined British interests.

Britain's relative decline

The extent and origins of Britain's relative decline as a global power have
been extensively debated by both practitioners and academic observers.
Although a complex set of causes has certainly been at work, two stand
out as being of particular importance – economic problems and an
overextension of foreign policy.

At the root of the decline has undoubtedly been the declining international
competitiveness of British industry, a process which some observers date
from the last quarter of the nineteenth century and which has led to the
marked fall in Britain's share of global trade that was highlighted earlier.
This loss of competitiveness has variously been traced to: the propensity
of British businesses to export capital abroad, thereby reducing the amount
of capital available for investment at home; the tendency of British consumers
to devote a disproportionately high percentage of current income to consumption rather than to savings, which again reduces the funds available
for domestic investment; the existence of 'protected' markets in the Empire,
which insulated British industry from the invigorating effects of foreign
competition; and the long-term tendency for British governments to pursue
policies that have overvalued sterling and thereby made manufactured
exports more expensive than they would otherwise have needed to be.

Whatever the causes of Britain's industrial decline might have been,
however, it is clear that the decline itself deprived Britain of the material
capability that was required to perform the sort of great power role in global
politics and economics that had been pursued before 1939. After 1945, the
problems associated with declining capability were compounded by the
'overextension' of Britain's foreign policy. Put simply, Britain's postwar
foreign policy makers tried to do too much given the resource base available
to them. The wartime government had mortgaged most of the country's
income-earning overseas assets to pay for the war effort. The long-term
relative decline of British industry meant that, in comparison with competitor
states, fewer resources were available for foreign policy adventures. Yet, until
the late 1960s, and in some cases until much later, British military forces
were stationed at a large number of strategic sites throughout the world.
The Empire in the Caribbean, Africa and the Far East had to be garrisoned
and defended. The Indian Ocean, the Persian Gulf and the Suez Canal (until
1956) had to be patrolled to protect British (and western) shipping. Over
50,000 British troops had to be kept in West Germany – initially to protect
the Germans against themselves and subsequently to protect them against
the Soviets.

All this activity, of course, was partly aimed at sustaining and nurturing
exclusively British interests. But it was also Britain's historical misfortune

to be the only other major capitalist power that was in a position to assist the USA in its efforts to protect and develop the interests of the west more generally. It was believed in Washington and London (probably correctly) that the Soviet Union and its communist allies constituted a profound long-term threat to the very survival of capitalism and liberal democracy. The non-communist world therefore had a collective interest in ensuring that defections of countries to the communist camp were kept to an absolute minimum. Instead of free-riding on American largesse, as the rest of the western world did, British policy makers chose to maintain their place at the 'top table' of world diplomacy by playing a support role to the USA in its efforts to defend western interests globally. In so doing, they almost certainly overestimated Britain's capacity to undertake such a role effectively. And they failed to recognise that the very effort of playing the support role would divert resources away from the sort of civilian investment that might, in time, have removed the most important source of Britain's postwar problems – its long-term relative economic decline.

The problem of defining British interests

To criticise British policy makers for having overestimated Britain's global importance and capabilities, however, makes unfair use of the advantage of hindsight. It is never an easy task to determine exactly where the interests of a particular state (or states) lie. Real policy makers are obliged to analyse problems and to take decisions in positions of imperfect information and extreme uncertainty. Postwar British foreign policy makers appear to have defined British interests as:

1 the need to protect the territorial integrity and social and political stability of Britain itself;
2 the need to maintain and, as far as possible, to raise the living standards of British citizens;
3 the need to maintain overseas governments in power that are either sympathetic to Britain or which share the British government's liberal, pro-private enterprise/mixed economy world view;
4 the need to sustain a stable world economy that continues to demand the sorts of goods and services that British industry and finance produce, and to ensure that British enterprises maintain sufficient overseas market share to pay for the imported goods and services that are required at home;
5 the need to maintain a stable international political order that pre-empts the need for Britain to participate in international conflicts;
6 the need to ensure the continuing success of those international regimes to which Britain subscribes and which produce tangible net benefits for it.

Simply defining interests in this way, however, gives little direct guidance as to how, in practice, interests are to be maximised. Real policy makers are almost invariably confronted with conflicting advice as to which specific strategies are most likely to achieve the desired goals. And they are frequently obliged either to make trade-offs between competing interests or to sacrifice one set of interests in the short term for some greater long-term good. In these circumstances, foreign policy management is extraordinarily difficult. Although British governments may not have excelled in protecting British interests over the last fifty years, there can be no doubt that the furtherance of those interests was at the forefront of their calculations.

The remainder of this chapter considers the precise ways in which successive governments sought to maximise British interests in order to cope with the changing exigencies of the postwar world. For presentational convenience, the changes in British strategy are described in terms of developments in each of Churchill's three 'circles' – in the Empire, in terms of the 'special relationship' and, finally, in Europe.

The retreat from the Empire, 1947–71

The British government began its first wave of decolonisations in India in the late 1940s. Throughout the interwar years, the British had sought to head off demands for self-government in India by making a series of constitutional concessions which, though they granted limited autonomy to the indigenous population, left executive control of Indian affairs in the hands of the India Office. By 1946, however, partly as a result of the inter-communal tensions between Muslims and Hindus and partly because of the determination of the leaderships of both communities to be rid of their colonial masters, India had become ungovernable. Unable to control a deteriorating security situation and unable to effect a political compromise between the rival religious traditions, in February 1947 Attlee's government announced its intention of ending British rule some 15 months later. Remarkably, the announcement resulted in a compromise between the Muslim League and the Hindu Congress Party in which a post-independence partition of India was agreed, with the predominantly Muslim regions in the north-west and north-east securing independence as the bifurcated state of Pakistan. Such was the success of the compromise that the date for independence was brought forward to August 1947.

Yet, even though Britain had been obliged to withdraw from the 'jewel in the crown' of the Empire, the British government could reasonably argue that it had done so on terms that were still favourable to British interests. Both India and Pakistan became members of the Commonwealth, thus retaining some of the old political ties with the former imperial country. At a time when western fears about the encroachment of communism were intensifying, it was a considerable comfort to London's strategic planners that both countries retained (for the most part) a commitment to liberal democracy and a tolerance of private enterprise capitalism. And although India flirted with the USSR in the 1960s and 1970s, its broad stance on the major strategic issues of the Cold War was always more inclined to be pro-western than pro-Soviet.

In May 1948, Britain was also obliged to withdraw from Palestine – and for reasons similar to those which had obtained in India: the British were no longer in de facto military control. Although Palestine had not been part of Britain's formal Empire, it had been mandated to Britain, first by the League of Nations in 1923, and subsequently by the UN in 1945. With the British withdrawal, part of Palestine was incorporated into Jordan; the remainder became the new state of Israel.

As far as the British government was concerned, however, the close sequencing of the Indian and Palestinian withdrawals risked sending a dangerous signal to other parts of the Empire that might feel restive. The Attlee government was convinced that the remainder of the Empire had to be retained – partly because of the protected export markets that it held for British manufacturers and partly because further British withdrawals might create the sort of political vacuum that the Soviets would be all too ready to fill. Accordingly, after 1948, the British embarked on a strategy of imperial 'retrenchment'. This strategy sought to ensure that indigenous pressures for change in Britain's remaining colonies were prevented from developing sufficiently to threaten the continuation of British rule. The chosen combination of military action (as in Malaya 1948–57 and Kenya 1954–59) and diversionary constitutional concessions (as in most of the African and Caribbean colonies in the 1950s) proved remarkably effective. For eight years after the Palestinian evacuation, Britain grimly clung on to its colonial possessions, continuing to overstretch its military capability but resisting any possible extension of communist influence inside its imperial territories.

The diplomatic disaster of the 1956 Suez Crisis, however, changed everything. Having colluded with the French and the Israelis in a vain attempt to remove the vigorously nationalist Nasser government from power in Egypt, Britain was ignominiously forced to withdraw its 'protective' military force from the Suez Canal Zone. Although the immediate (and critical) pressure for a British withdrawal was applied by the Americans, the crisis enabled Nasser to present himself to third world opinion as the leader of a recently liberated state that had been the innocent victim of a neo-imperial power bent on furthering its own selfish interests. Here was a lesson for would-be nationalists throughout the Empire. With the correct political strategy, British imperial power could be effectively challenged.

The British response was swift. Once the dust of the Suez affair had settled, the new prime minister, Harold Macmillan, eagerly embraced the 'wind of change' – a rising tide of demands for independence – that was 'sweeping through the Empire'. By the late 1950s, Britain was decolonising with some vigour. By 1966, all but the smallest dependencies (together with the peculiar case of Rhodesia, which in 1965 had made its own unilateral declaration of independence) had been granted independence. The British government's calculation in this process was simple. Britain no longer possessed the military capability to retain control of the colonies for very long. If the colonies were to be 'lost' anyway, it was better to minimise the resentment that a protracted armed struggle for independence might engender; better to seek to install in power those groups and individuals who might be sympathetic to British values and interests than to risk the sort of radicalisation of the indigenous population that could result from an extended conflict. The fact that so few of Britain's ex-colonies subsequently defected to the Soviet sphere of influence suggests that the rapid decolonis-ation strategy adopted after 1956 achieved a moderate degree of success.

Even in face of the 'second wave' decolonisations, however, the British government decided to retain a significant military presence 'east of Suez'. This presence focused on the Indian Ocean and mainly involved the retention of 'strategic' bases in Aden, the Persian Gulf and Singapore – which had originally been acquired in order to defend the sea routes to India. It was considered that, by maintaining control of these sites, Britain could continue to play a world role and thereby assist the USA in its efforts to resist Soviet encroachment in the third world. It rapidly became clear in the late 1960s, however, that Britain simply could not afford the costs of this continued presence given competing resource demands at home. In 1968, Harold Wilson's Labour government announced that, for financial reasons, Britain would withdraw from east of Suez by 1972. The policy was continued by Edward Heath's Conservative administration after 1970, and the withdrawal was duly completed by the end of 1971.

With the withdrawal from east of Suez, the most damaging feature of Britain's overextended foreign policy had been removed. Britain could now concentrate its defence efforts on the European theatre, where they were most needed. It would leave its friends in the Indian Ocean region to fend for themselves – though they might be able to secure some help from the USA. As events turned out, this strategy did not result in serious long-term damage to western interests in the Indian Ocean. Although Aden (as part of South Yemen) was rapidly transformed into a Soviet base, Moscow proved unable to use it effectively as a platform for extending its influence in the region. By the late 1980s, the Yemenis had required Moscow to withdraw its forces from Aden altogether.

The main factors underpinning Britain's withdrawal from the Empire, then, were almost prosaic in their simplicity. Indigenous nationalist pressure for self-determination built up such a momentum in the 1950s that (quite apart from the moral imperative of allowing colonial peoples to rule themselves) it became pointless for a rational British government which sought to maximise the country's own interests to delay decolonisation any further. The withdrawal from east of Suez, on the other hand, was forced on the British government primarily by financial considerations. In order to bring its level of defence spending more into line with that of its industrial competitors, Britain had to make large-scale defence cuts somewhere. Rather than impose cuts across the board, the government chose to focus its defence efforts where British interests were most directly affected – in Europe.

The Empire circle after 1971

Having dispensed with the Empire, Britain sought to preserve a residual amount of British influence in its former colonies through the Commonwealth. Its efforts in this regard, however, did not prove particularly successful. In the political sphere, much of the 'new' Commonwealth joined the Non-Aligned Movement during the 1960s – signalling their intention to distance themselves from the Cold War conflict that preoccupied Britain's foreign policy makers. In the economic sphere, Britain found itself progressively losing market share in most of its ex-colonies to its European and Far Eastern competitors. In many respects, the Commonwealth rapidly became little more than a talking shop which 'new' Commonwealth members used primarily as a vehicle for extracting aid concessions from their richer 'partners'.

In the 1980s, Britain's involvement in the Empire and the question of its world role underwent something of a revival. This was partly because of developments outside Britain's control. The negotiations in London in 1979 which preceded Zimbabwean independence involved Britain discharging an imperial responsibility that had been suspended in 1965 because of the illegal actions of Rhodesia's white settler regime. The 1982 campaign to reclaim the Falkland Islands was a responsibility that had been imposed on Britain by an Argentine military government desperate for some sort of foreign triumph to secure its position at home. Britain's subsequent interest in out-of-area operations, however, owed much more to Britain's renewed interest in the 'special relationship' and to Margaret Thatcher's desire to see Britain reasserting its former world role in order to challenge the malign global influence of the Soviet Union. It is the character of this 'special relationship' that we now examine.

The changing 'special relationship', 1945–95

There can be no doubt that the relationship between Britain and the USA during the Second World War was extremely close. It is equally clear that, after 1945, the relationship was always more 'special' for the British than for the Americans – as Washington demonstrated as early as 1946 when it unilaterally opted to end Anglo-American collaboration in nuclear research. This said, despite periods of cooling, relations between Washington and London were close throughout the Cold War. As noted above, the ubiquitous threat of communism was a continuing stimulus to the major western powers to cooperate with one another: it was believed that the only beneficiary of any division within the western camp would be the Soviet Union.

In 1948, following the Soviet blockade of Berlin and the extension of Soviet-style communist regimes to the whole of eastern Europe, the Americans and the British led a series of efforts aimed at creating a west European/North American defensive alliance. The result, in April 1949, was the formation of NATO, a mutual assistance pact with a permanent military command structure headed by the USA. Although it is difficult to determine the extent to which the Soviet-led Warsaw Pact constituted a real and immediate threat to western Europe's security, the sense of security that NATO provided to its members states' populations was considerable. The confidence that, if necessary, the USA would be involved in Europe's defence from the outset of any east–west conflict was always enormously important.

The quid pro quo for Washington's promise to protect Europe, however, was that Britain was obliged, as noted above, to support US efforts to keep the world safe for capitalism. Washington's first call on British assistance was during the Korean crisis, which flared up in 1950. In June, communist North Korea, with suspected Chinese and Soviet backing, invaded the non-communist South. With the Soviets for other reasons boycotting the UN Security Council, the USA and Britain sponsored a Council resolution which authorised the use of force against the invading North Korean army. Although the bulk of the UN-backed force was American, Britain played its part by assembling the 'Commonwealth Brigade', which was deployed alongside the US contingent. The military role played by British forces, however, was far less important than their political significance. Crucially, by participating in the joint military operations, Britain provided international legitimacy to Washington's actions: the UN force was a multinational one, not one that sought solely to advance the interests of the USA.

In the aftermath of the 1956 Suez Crisis, Anglo-American relations went into temporary reverse. Washington had been affronted by London's resort to gunboat diplomacy and had applied pressure to effect a British withdrawal accordingly. The British, for their part, felt that the Americans had unjustifiably ambushed them in their hour of need – and that, as a result, the western cause in the third world had been dealt an unnecessary blow. The logic of the Cold War, however, soon produced a mending of fences. Within eighteen months of the Suez fiasco, Washington and London were jointly sending troops to Jordan and to the Lebanon where pro-western governments faced insurgencies that, it was feared, were sponsored by, if not directed from, Moscow.

By 1960, Britain and the USA had resumed collaboration in nuclear weapons research. Significantly, the US government also agreed to sell nuclear weapons (the Skybolt air-launched missile system) to Britain. Such a sale implied a remarkably high degree of intergovernmental trust between London and Washington. (Indeed, the fact that the Americans have consistently been prepared to sell nuclear weapons to the British – and only to the British – is taken by some observers as compelling evidence that the relationship was, and remains, 'special'.) The cancellation of the Skybolt project in 1962, however, on the grounds that the system was technically flawed, produced a curious hiatus in Anglo-American relations. Britain was at the time negotiating with the six member states of the European Economic Community (EEC) with a view to joining. The French hoped that Skybolt's cancellation, coming in the middle of these negotiations, would propel London into nuclear collaboration with Paris – thereby cementing Britain's commitment to 'Europe' and weakening its Atlantic links. In the event, however, Prime Minister Macmillan reached agreement with President Kennedy that the Americans would supply the Polaris (submarine-launched) nuclear missile system to Britain on very favourable financial terms. The Polaris deal firmly locked Britain's military capabilities into a security strategy that was distinctly Atlantic in orientation. The French, believing that the British were not sufficiently committed to the idea of 'Europe' to merit membership of the EEC, promptly vetoed the British application for membership.

Yet, just as the Polaris agreement had appeared to set the scene for even closer Anglo-American collaboration in defence of the west's global interests, relations between London and Washington began to weaken. In 1964, the escalating war in Vietnam, in which the pro-western South Vietnamese government was increasingly under guerrilla attack from the communist North, provided one major source of irritation. As in the Korean crisis, Washington wished to legitimise its own military intervention by presenting it as multinational. In this instance, however, the new Labour government under Harold Wilson refused to send even a token military presence in Washington's support. The Americans were furious. As former secretary of state Dean Acheson put it, 'All we needed was one regiment. Don't expect us to save you again' (cited in Baylis 1984: 155).

In the 1960s and 1970s, as Britain completed its decolonisations and then withdrew its forces from east of Suez, London simply became less valuable to Washington as a Cold War ally. With its military presence in the third world massively diminished, Britain was no longer in a position to dispatch forces to remote trouble spots where western interests might be subject to either challenge or attack. Moreover, once Britain joined the European Community in 1973, the European focus of its foreign policy was bound to increase. To make matters worse, during the 1970s Britain seemed to be sinking into ever greater ungovernability and economic decline. In these circumstances, it was perhaps not surprising that Washington and London should have drifted apart both economically and diplomatically.

The character of Anglo-American relations changed yet again with the election of Margaret Thatcher in May 1979 and of Ronald Reagan in November 1980. Thatcher and Reagan shared the same world view. First, they were economic liberals: they both believed that the health of western economies lay in 'rolling back the state' and in giving market forces free reign. Second, they were strategic realists – believers in the importance of realpolitik – who felt that anti-western forces throughout the world had for too long been allowed to make progress at the west's expense, and that what was needed now was a resolute strategy of confrontation with the 'evil empire' of the Soviet Union and its agents.

The early 1980s accordingly witnessed an intensification of the Cold War, in which Britain once again began to play a supporting role behind the USA, underpinning and legitimising US efforts to defend the west's global interests. From 1980 onwards, both the USA and Britain increased their defence spending – with the clear aim of compelling the Soviets to join a renewed arms race that would put further pressure on their already overstretched economy. In 1982, a small British contingent joined the predominantly US multinational force that Washington sent to Lebanon in order to cover the withdrawal of Israeli forces from Beirut. In 1983, London lent its full diplomatic support to a US force which invaded the Caribbean island of Grenada in order to remove its Marxist government. In 1986, Britain provided vital logistical support for a US bombing raid on the Libyan capital Tripoli, undertaken in reprisal for Libya's sponsorship of terrorist attacks on US targets around the world. In 1987, British naval forces were dispatched to the Gulf in support of US efforts to protect neutral shipping that was increasingly being threatened by the conflict between Iran and Iraq.

By the late 1980s, even though the renewed Cold War which had reinvigorated Anglo-American relations was clearly coming to a close, it became fashionable in Foreign Office circles to speak of Britain as 'punching above its weight' – as being able to exercise greater international influence than was merited purely on the basis of its economic and military strength. The departure from office of both Reagan (in 1988) and Thatcher (in 1990) brought little change. With the end of the Cold War in 1990, Britain continued to commit itself to actions that defended western interests but that continued to overstretch its resource base. When Saddam Hussein invaded Kuwait in August 1990, thereby threatening the stability of Middle Eastern oil supplies, it was Britain that provided the second largest contingent (behind the USA) to the force that removed him in April 1991. When UN-sponsored peace keepers were needed in the former Yugoslavia in 1992–95, Britain supplied a major component of the force. And when NATO took over responsibility for enforcing the Dayton agreement on Bosnia-Herzegovina in December 1995, British troops again represented the second largest contingent.

In one sense, of course, all this post-Cold-War activity merely represented Britain living up to its obligations as one of the five permanent members of the Security Council. To critical observers, however, such ambitious and profligate military action – when Britain's long-term economic performance still lagged far behind that of its major industrial competitors – looked decidedly inappropriate. They recognised that Britain might well be 'punching above its weight'. They remained curious, however, as to what benefit Britain derived from this activity. Playing a support role behind the US efforts to maximise western interests was all very well. The important question was whether Britain could afford to play such a role and what it gained (and lost) as a result of so doing. To critical observers, the British government would be well advised to recognise that Britain no longer possessed the wherewithal to pursue a world role; that its attachment to supporting US global strategy yielded little tangible benefit to Britain; and that Britain's primary interests lay in strengthening its ties with the rest of the EU.

The shift towards Europe, 1945–95

In 1945, Britain was the dominant power in Europe. (Nicholas Henderson – British ambassador in Bonn, Paris and Washington – later remarked that 'We could have stamped Europe as we wished' (Henderson 1979: 34).) In the late 1940s, however, Britain's foreign policy makers were sufficiently absorbed by imperial commitments that their attention to the European theatre rarely extended beyond the need to ensure that western Europe remained safe from Soviet infiltration or attack. Accordingly, when France, West Germany, Italy and the Benelux countries decided to create the European Coal and Steel Community (ECSC) in 1952, the British opted to remain outside it. The key feature of the ECSC was that it embodied the principle of supranational decision making. In joining the ECSC, member states ceded their policy-making rights in the areas of coal and steel production to a 'High Authority', whose task was to devise policies that would optimise production across the Community as a whole. As far as London was concerned, the loss of national sovereignty engendered by this ceding of decision-making autonomy to a supranational body was too high a price to pay for any possible (and, in 1952, uncertain) benefit that might derive from a single, Community-wide market for coal and steel. Such was the practical success of the ECSC, however, that at Messina, in 1955, the six member states decided to extend the 'functional cooperation' that they had begun in coal and steel to cover virtually all areas of economic activity. The creation of the EEC in 1957 duly reflected this 'spillover' effect. Throughout the 1950s, British economists watched the developing EEC with great interest. For one thing, EEC growth rates clearly outstripped those of Britain. For another, it became evident from the late 1950s that a shift was taking place in the character of Britain's overseas trade. Between 1955 and 1965, the proportion of exports sold to Overseas Sterling Area countries (pre-dominantly the Empire and Commonwealth) fell from roughly one-half to one-third. Increasingly after 1955 – and well before Britain joined the EEC in 1973 – western Europe took over as the main market for the goods and services that Britain produced. (By the mid-1990s, over 60 per cent of British exports went to EU destinations.) In these circum-stances, British policy makers recognised that there might be much to be gained if Britain were formally to join the economic club that the 'Six' had so successfully constructed. Not only would British producers benefit from the greater market opportunities that EEC membership would confer, but Britain would be able to join with other European states in order to articulate a more powerful, European voice in future international trade and global economic strategy negotiations.

Britain's first two attempts to join the EEC (in 1961–63 and in 1967–68) were unsuccessful. By the early 1970s, however, the British government had made enough of a commitment to the supranational principles of EEC policy making to persuade the Six that it was worthy of membership – and Britain (along with Ireland and Denmark) duly joined the renamed European Community on 1 January 1973. Yet, even as a member state, Britain retained its reputation as the reluctant European. In 1974, Harold Wilson's government sought to renegotiate the terms of Britain's entry. In 1975, Britain held a retrospective referendum on whether the country should remain within the Community. In the early 1980s Margaret Thatcher's government engaged in a long and acrimonious series of negotiations (which eventually produced the Fontainebleu compromise in 1984) about the size of Britain's contribution to the budget of the European Community (EC).

The 1985 Single European Act (SEA) appeared to resolve some of the difficulties that had beset the Community since Britain's accession. Britain agreed to the introduction of qualified majority voting (and the accompanying loss of its veto) in certain areas of Community policy – thus demonstrating its commitment to the principle of supranational decision making favoured by European federalists. For its part, the EC as a whole undertook to complete the creation of the single market in goods, services, capital and labour (which the 1957 Rome Treaty had originally stipulated) by the end of 1992.

The SEA, however, also envisaged that renewed efforts aimed at the monetary and political integration of the EC would be made. The subsequent negotiations over the 1991 Maastricht Treaty established the EU and provided a timetable for the creation of an EU-wide monetary union. The negotiations also laid bare the two fundamentally different views of the way in which the Community should develop that had been at the root of Britain's European reluctance since the 1950s. The primary objective for most of Britain's 'federalist' European partners at Maastricht was to devise ways of developing the EU as a union of peoples in which supranational decision making gradually extends to encompass all major policy areas including the monetary and security spheres. Britain's primary Maastricht objective, on the other hand, was to promote the development of the EU as an association of sovereign states which would cooperate extensively with one another for mutual protection and benefit.

The Maastricht agreement failed to resolve these fundamental differences of vision. The timetable for monetary union, aimed at achieving a common EU currency by 1999, was very much in line with the long-term designs of the European federalists, who saw monetary union as the necessary precursor to political union. The opt-out concessions secured by Britain and Denmark, however, left open the possibility that, in a 'two-track' EU, certain countries outside the inner core would be able to retain national sovereignty in significant policy areas. In early 1997, these differences remained unresolved. The British government, in its continuing attempts to maximise British interests, was confronted by two competing sets of arguments: one that claimed that a further strengthening and deepening of the EU was very much 'in Britain's long-term interests'; and one that claimed the reverse. The core arguments advanced in both contexts are summarised in the appendix to this chapter. The real problem was that it was impossible to assemble the necessary empirical evidence that would enable the adequacy of either set of arguments to be properly assessed. The ambivalence of the empirical evidence, moreover, was reflected in the divisions both inside the governing Conservative Party and among the British public. It was small wonder in these circumstances that the government should seek as far as possible to keep its European policy options open. It accordingly remained uncommitted to the establishment of a common currency by 1999 without ruling out the possibility that Britain would seek to participate fully in the project when conditions were propitious. Only time would tell if Britain's hesitancy was justified or not.

Summary and conclusions

Throughout the postwar period, in the face of considerable changes in global politics and economics, British policy makers sought to maintain British interests in all three of Churchill's 'circles'. From the 1960s onwards, and especially after 1972, Britain's external strategy became much more focused on Europe – as Britain's grip on the Empire steadily weakened and trade with Europe became much more important to British exporters. Even after decolonisation, however, Britain never altogether relinquished its aspirations to perform a global, post-imperial role. During the Cold War, the Americans frequently needed both military and diplomatic support in their efforts to prevent communism from damaging the global strategic interests of the west. In order (*inter alia*) to keep Washington committed to Europe's defence, Britain was generally (though not invariably) prepared to play the sort of supporting role that the USA required. Such a role, however, could not be effected without cost. The cost to Britain was that, throughout the Cold War years, it devoted a higher proportion of its GDP to defence expenditure than almost all its major industrial competitors. It might have been better if these resources had been diverted to the reconstruction of the industrial base, thereby alleviating some of the difficulties created by Britain's long-term relative economic decline.

Even after the end of the Cold War, however, Britain's foreign policy makers still strove to ensure that Britain continued to play a world role. They reasoned that Britain's long diplomatic experience in global politics, arising partly out of its former imperial responsibilities, should be put to good use. There were certainly merits in this argument but it carried a major difficulty with it. Britain's continuing pretensions to global influence might act as a brake on its ability fully to commit itself to Europe. Dean Acheson had remarked in 1963 that Britain had 'lost an empire but not yet found a role'. In the late 1990s, this remark was still remarkably appropriate. Britain was a member of the EU but its vision of the way that the Union should develop was far more restrictive than that of most of its partners. The British foreign policy elite recognised that Britain's international role must be a primarily European one. The difficulty was how to fashion the sort of 'Europe of nation states' that the Conservative Party appeared to favour at a time when other powerful voices inside the EU favoured a federal Europe comparable to the federal USA. Britain had in effect been hovering at a strategic crossroads since it lost its empire and joined the EC in 1973. In 1996, it looked set to carry on hovering for several more years.

Appendix. Arguments for and against the further strengthening and deepening of the EU

The case for strengthening and deepening the EU

The intra-European political-strategic argument
The EEC transformed Franco-German relations but Germany – especially a united Germany – is still the dominant economic power in Europe. Any possible future German ambition to convert its economic dominance into other, less desirable, forms of dominance is best thwarted or pre-empted by locking Germany into a closer political union with the rest of Europe.

The extra-European political-strategic argument
The collapse of the Soviet Union and the increased uncertainties of the post-Cold-War era mean that Europe needs to be increasingly unified –

especially in foreign policy terms – in order to meet any new threats or challenges that might emerge from Asia, the Middle East or even Africa. Europe accordingly needs to move towards a common foreign and defence policy – which can only be achieved by strengthening the central institutions of the Union.

The extra-European economic argument
Changes in technology and the growing economic power of the countries of the Pacific rim are creating an increasingly competitive global economic system which threatens both the internal and the external markets of industrial and agricultural producers inside the Union. Deepening the Union in economic and financial terms – for example, by introducing a common currency – will enable the Union's producers to compete more effectively in the internal Union market and strengthen the Union's bargaining position in world markets more generally. Deepening the Union in terms of education, social welfare and employment standards provision will protect Union workers from being forced to accept lower and lower wage rates as they compete with workers in low-wage economies to attract inward investment.

The democratic deficit argument
In the EU decision making and policy implementation are at present subject to very limited popular control. The Council of Ministers is not answerable to the European Parliament and the unelected and largely unaccountable Commission has far greater decision-making autonomy than any national civil service. Greater democratic accountability within the EU's institutions is accordingly necessary. Any increase in Union-level accountability and democracy will necessarily involve strengthening the relative bargaining position of Union institutions vis-à-vis national institutions. In short, the EU's institutions have to be made more democratic; making them more democratic will strengthen and deepen the Union itself.

The momentum argument/the bicycle analogy
Unless the Union keeps moving forward – towards ever closer integration – then it will atrophy. (This argument is frequently stated but never demonstrated.)

*The case for Britain resisting or not participating in the
strengthening and deepening of the EU*
The following arguments assume that a British withdrawal from the EU is not a serious possibility since 60 per cent of British exports go to EU destinations. They are essentially arguments in support of the idea of a two-speed or even a multi-speed Europe.

*The dangers of a common currency when 'real' economic
convergence has not occurred*

The Maastricht convergence criteria (inflation, interest rates, debt/GDP ratios) are inappropriate. The important criteria are employment rates, economic activity and growth rates. Any geographical area that has a common currency needs a central government that possesses the redistribution capacity (through transfer payments and regional aid) to even out regional imbalances in economic activity. The US federal government, for example, controls some 20 per cent of US GDP; the equivalent British figure is over 40 per cent. This compares with an EU figure of under 1.5 per cent. The EU 'structural adjustment fund' and EU regional policy do not possess anything approaching the resources needed to make the kind of regional transfer payments that will almost certainly be necessary if low economic activity rates persistently afflict a sizeable number of EU regions. The key danger of a common currency is that low-activity economic areas will remain so because they will be unable to devalue themselves into activity and the EU will not possess sufficient central funds to stimulate economic activity in them. A common currency could be a recipe for continuing recession/depression in certain regions.

Insufficient support of electorates in the member states

At present there is a disjunction between the views of the European political class and public opinion in most member states. There is always a role for 'leadership' in any novel social or political venture but leaders must be capable of carrying followers with them. There is little evidence that this is happening at the moment. It may also be the case that 'real democracy' is impossible in such a large and diverse community: there may always be a perceived democratic deficit.

The dangers of judicial legislation

Judicial legislation (judges in effect creating new law by interpreting established legal principles or commitments in the light of new situations) is a permanent feature of all systems of law. In an embryonic political union, however, judicial legislation is very dangerous because the decisions of the judiciary are by definition not susceptible to political control – and are therefore not accountable to electors. The prominent role accorded to the European Court of Justice accordingly carries with it considerable political risks. European law risks being brought into disrepute because decisions taken may be completely out step with public opinion in certain member states – and perhaps in all of them. Further moves towards union, if they are to proceed at all, must accordingly be accompanied by the imposition of much greater constraint on the ability of the EU-level judiciary to enact judicial legislation.

The uneven operation of rule-implementation agencies in different member states
Injustices in the operation of EU law and rules will increase in the future and will produce a concomitant increase in popular resentment aimed at EU institutions.

The objective of a common EU foreign and defence policy is
a recipe for inaction and impotence
The indecisiveness of the EU over the collapse of Yugoslavia foreshadows the likely dithering that will characterise EU foreign and defence policy in the future as diverse interests and diverse perceptions compete with one another for supremacy in policy determination. Effective foreign policy – and above all effective defence policy – requires a singularity of vision (a degree of blinkering almost) that will never be possible in the EU.

The common market element of the EU will operate to the long-term
detriment of producers
The real market of the future is the global market. An insulated EU market, strengthened by the introduction of a common currency – economic fortress Europe – will produce atrophy in the same way that the system of imperial preference gradually reduced the global competitiveness of British industry after 1932, by insulating it from the invigorating winds of genuine competition.

British interests are best served by retaining maximum strategic flexibility
Circumstances constantly change. The EU will necessarily be too unwieldy in the future to respond effectively to new economic, political, ecological and military challenges.

References

Baylis, J. (1984), *Anglo-American Defence Relations, 1939–1984* (2nd edn), London, Macmillan.

Henderson, N. (1979), Britain's economic decline: its causes and consequences, *The Economist*, 2 July.

Porter, B. (1988), *The Lion's Share: A Short History of British Imperialism*, London, Longman.

Sanders, D. (1990), *Losing an Empire, Finding a Role: British Foreign Policy Since 1945*, London, Macmillan.

Sanders, D. and Edwards, G. (1994), Consensus and diversity in elite opinion: the views of the British foreign policy elite in the early 1990s, *Political Studies*, 42, 413–40.

Stein, A. (1993), Coordination and collaboration: regimes in an anarchic world, in D. A. Baldwin (ed.), *Neorealism and Neoliberalism: The Contemporary Debate*, New York, Columbia University Press.

2

From provider to enabler: the changing role of the state

Martin Burch and Bruce Wood

This chapter is about change in the role and operation of the state. It traces the shift from a provider, welfare state to an enabling and regulatory one. This shift is in no sense complete and is still being carried out, though the potential lines for development are in place. The change has been in both the definition of the state and in views about what it should do. The chapter is also about when and why this change took place. We argue that changes in the state reflect changes in elite thinking, which in turn are shaped by a mix of economic, social and political factors.

How to understand the changing state

Elite attitudes are central to understanding how change takes place. Changes in the complexion and operation of the state result from alterations in the views of policy makers, their advisers and other key opinion formers. These, in turn, are shaped by the elite's understandings of changes taking place in the wider economic, social and political environments in which the state is located. Thus, as circumstances change so elite views alter, but these views of how the world is changing and how these changes are to be understood take time to shift. It takes time both for the significance of events to register and for old understandings to be cast aside. This is because elite perceptions tend to cohere into established viewpoints based on a set of values and assumptions which provide a particular way of appreciating and understanding the world. These constitute what might be termed the current orthodoxy. Such orthodoxies dominate elite thinking for a period until perceptions of real world events require that the assumptions and beliefs on which they are based are reordered (Vickers 1965: 67–70). The move from a provider to an enabling state reflects just such a change from one orthodoxy to another. It follows from our understanding of change that there can be no one right view of what the state is or what it should do. Such notions change as perceptions change and as circumstances underlying them alter.

In analysing these changes we distinguish:

- changes in principles and assumptions about the operation of the state;
- changes in organisation;
- changes in practice.

It is important to note that while changes may have taken place in principles and even organisation they may not necessarily be fully reflected in practice. In the remainder of the chapter we outline the nature of the old orthodoxy and its underlying assumptions. We look at why, how and when this old orthodoxy was undermined. And we conclude by examining the ideas underlying and the practices involved in the emergent orthodoxy of the enabling state.

The old orthodoxy and the postwar provider state

The 'provider' state which became fully established in the immediate postwar period was one that directly provided a full range of public services and had a substantial part to play in the management of the economy. A number of principles guided what the state should and could be expected to do. These principles derived from particular theories about the role of the state in relation to the economy and society. They formed the basis of the postwar settlement or broad agreement across the political spectrum about the role of the state and the era of so-called 'consensus' politics which it established. These principles remained paramount as guides to action until the 1970s, when they began to be increasingly questioned.

In the economic sphere the key principles were derived from an interpretation, and simplification, of the work of contemporary economists, especially that of Maynard Keynes. Keynesianism, as this simplified interpretation came to be called, held that the state could and should intervene in the economy to ensure sustained economic growth and full employment. In particular, the state's role was to boost the economy during any downturn in economic activity and to reduce demand when economic growth seemed unduly rapid. In this way the state 'smoothed out' the disturbances created by market forces. The state had three main instruments to stimulate or curb activity at the level of the economy as a whole (so-called 'macro-economic activity'): changes in taxation; spending on public works and services; and reducing or raising the cost of borrowing through manipulating interest rates. Of these three instruments the first two were the most extensively used. Beyond 'macro-economic' controls, some held that it was justified for the state to intervene at the micro level of particular industries by special schemes to encourage innovation and investment, or even through direct control or ownership. It was this area of micro, rather than macro, management that produced the major differences between the political parties on economic matters from the Second World War until the 1970s.

In particular there was much debate about 'nationalising' (taking into public ownership) industries such as steel and road haulage.

The central aim of economic policy under the postwar settlement was to encourage economic growth so as to sustain full employment. This objective was a direct product of contemporary experience, notably a desire to avoid the destabilising and dreadful effects of joblessness experienced in the 1930s. This aim was enshrined in the 1944 white paper *Employment Policy*, which was supported by all parties in the wartime coalition (Hennessy 1993: 186–7). It was the first clear, official statement about the policy assumptions that were to be developed from 1945 onwards. The emphasis on growth leading to full employment as the primary objective of economic policy meant that other objectives, notably controlling inflation, were relegated (Donaldson 1973: 48–59; Keegan 1984: 17–18). This, as we shall see, was a fatal flaw in the conventional wisdom that dominated economic thinking in the immediate postwar period.

These perceptions of the state's role in relation to the economy were complemented by assumptions about the role of the state in the wider society. Here the central principle was state provision 'from the cradle to the grave'. It was inspired by the 1942 Beveridge report, *Report on Social Insurance and Allied Services* (cmnd 6404), which argued in favour of a concerted attack on the 'five giants' of want, disease, idleness, ignorance and squalor (see chapter 3). These were to be tackled through policy initiatives which, in addition to measures for full employment, covered social insurance and cash benefits (notably family allowances), health care, education and housing (Hill 1993: 15). Two notions were central to this view of the social role of the state: that citizens have social as well as political and legal rights (Marquand 1988: 29); and that state benefits, whether in cash or kind, should be available to all sections of the community (Walsh 1995: 4–6). This emphasis on welfare rights and universalism is an important aspect of the post-1945 conception of the social function of the state.

On these social welfare matters there was also a high degree of consensus between the parties. Indeed, the welfare state that emerged after the war was in large part a consolidation of measures already enacted or accepted in principle (Marquand 1988: 28–31; Hill 1993). But another important idea was more contentious: that the state, mainly through alterations to the tax and benefit systems, should endeavour to redistribute income and create a more equal society. This view was mainly held on the left in politics, by social democrats. Its most influential advocate claimed that increases in the income of the poor could be achieved by distributing to them some of the extra resources gained from a growing economy (see Crosland 1956). Clearly, if economic growth was not achieved or its fruits could not be redistributed, then this social democratic perception of the role of the state was likely to prove problematic.

Thus, conventional thinking in both the economic and social spheres envisaged a more substantial role for the state than had previously been considered acceptable. This new vision of the state drew on well established traditions in British political life. From the right it drew on the Tory, benevolent, strand in Conservatism which emphasised the elite's responsibility for the welfare of the people and an important role for the state in its achievement (Glickman 1961; Greenleaf 1973). From the left it drew on the Fabian tradition, which emphasised wide-scale public provision and effective public administration. Apart from these traditions, the immediate factor shaping the elite's perceptions was the impact of unemployment and poverty between the wars. The policy perceptions of the elite in 1945 reflected a reaction against the failures of the interwar years. The experience of running a closely controlled economy and society during the 1939–45 war also meant that the public and policy makers had become used to an extended and active state.

The type of state which emerged after the war was not just a provider state: it was also large and interventionist. It had four key features. First, it had a role not only in managing the economy, but also in providing some of the basic services on which the economy depended. These services included public transport and energy supply (coal, gas and electricity). Such activities were largely brought within the public sector through nationalis- ation. This development plus the growing size of the public sector in general meant that state institutions were key players in what was termed the mixed economy, with a well developed public as well as private sphere. Second, the state provided a comprehensive range of welfare benefits and public services. Third, these were supplied direct to the public through three types of state organisation: central government departments; local government; and a variety of appointed boards and quasi-autonomous non-governmental organisations (quangos). Finally, this large, comprehensive, directly providing state was subject to a system of accountability based on traditional mechanisms, most notably through the accountability to parliament and county, borough and district councils of ministers and council committee chairpersons for the work of the departments and agencies for which they were responsible. In effect a new kind of state had been created, but new mechanisms of control and accountability had not been fully developed to match these institutional changes.

In keeping with this new state form there developed a style of policy making which can be best described as consultative. It involved careful consideration of the views of the relevant and accepted interests in each policy area. These were ascertained through contacts with and the involve- ment of key interest groups. The contacts were usually through civil servants in relevant central government departments, either through direct personal links or through formalised structures such as advisory committees on which the various interests and experts were represented. For example, twenty advisory committees were advising the Ministry of Housing and Local Government on housing, local government and public health in 1964 (Ministry of Housing and Local Government 1965: 62–7). This figure can be multiplied for each of the major policy and service-provision ministries.

By the early 1960s these links had become more formalised as the state became involved in national economic planning. Some characterised this style of policy making as corporatist: that is, a system of policy making in which key interest groups are formally and closely involved in the formulation of policy, and in turn fulfil a role in its implementation. This form, at the national level, reached its most developed expression in the series of attempts to create an effective prices and incomes policy which spanned the period from 1961 to 1978. At the centre of these initiatives was a tripartite relationship between the state and the interest groups representing business and the trade unions (Craven and Lee 1982: 62–8). This consultative form of policy making tended to lead to policy outcomes that reflected the consensus of opinion between the principal players involved. Thus, a consensus-seeking style of policy making complemented the broad consensus between policy-making elites about the economic and social role of the state. Both developments led some to characterise the postwar period as one of consensus politics (Marquand 1988, 2–3; Kavanagh and Morris 1994: 1–23).

The postwar consensus began to weaken in the late 1960s and early 1970s. The factors contributing to this involved a reordering of the elite's perceptions and the emergence of a new set of assumptions about economic, social and political matters. A new agenda was emerging which the liberal wing of Conservatism was able to benefit from in the latter part of the 1970s and to develop further in the 1980s and early 1990s. Change took place both in world conditions and in the perceptions of the elite. The change was gradual, but persistent. The new thinking that emerged involved a questioning of the old orthodoxy and its replacement with an alternative vision of the role and nature of the state.

Why and when was the old orthodoxy questioned?

A major cause of the decline of the old orthodoxy was its failure to produce the predicted results. The assumptions on which it was based seemed less and less applicable. This was especially evident in the economic sphere, where there was a growing disenchantment with the performance of the British economy. Although the economy had expanded during the 1950s and 1960s, it had not developed at the same pace as competitor economies. They were speeding ahead of Britain in terms of both their share of world trade and their rate of growth (Coates 1994: 5–7). This relative decline was seen as chronic (Gamble 1981: 17–23), reflecting a deep lack of competitiveness on the part of British industry on grounds of both quality and price.

The orthodox techniques of economic management seemed unable to reverse this trend. At the level of macro-economic management there was increasing awareness of the need to address the problem of inflation, especially wage inflation. At the micro level there was increasing concern about the performance of particular industries and even individual firms. The initial response to these problems was to develop and refine certain aspects of the orthodox approach. Attempts were made to reduce inflationary pressures throughout the economy by successive versions of prices and incomes policies, usually involving both sides of industry on either a voluntary (1961–66 and 1974–78) or a statutory (1967–69 and 1972–74) basis. Periodic attempts were also made to boost the economy through expansionary budgets, and through devaluations of the currency designed to encourage export-led growth. The result of these initiatives was to create instability in the economy. This was often summed up in the phrase 'stop–go': a period of expansion would lead to an overheating of the economy and a rise in inflation; this would then be followed by a state-engineered slowdown. Thus one of the main claims of Keynesian economic management – that state intervention could 'smooth out' the disturbances of a market economy – seemed to be falsified by the practice of Keynesianism in Britain. At the micro level, attempts were made to increase the competitiveness of industry by more direct intervention in industrial matters by the state (Marquand 1988: 45–7, 49–52).

None of these approaches was judged to be wholly successful. Indeed, by the mid-1970s policy analysts had begun to identify a new problem, that of stagflation, that is low growth coupled with rising unemployment and rising inflation. This ran contrary to conventional Keynesian expectation that there would be a 'trade-off' between unemployment and inflation so that the former would tend to redress the latter (Smith 1987: 30). Not only were orthodox versions of economic management failing to deliver economic growth but the basic assumptions at the centre of policy no longer seemed to apply. In keeping with all these changes, by the mid-1970s the central aim of economic policy had shifted from achieving full employment to dealing with the problem of stagflation.

Underlying this shift in policy concerns was the need to adjust to the changing nature of the world economy. The emergence of a more open global currency market and the collapse of the postwar system of semi-fixed exchange rates, emanating from the Bretton Woods conference of 1944, meant there was less stability in international markets and consequently less control over what happened within them (Smith 1992: 85–7). As a reserve currency, sterling was especially vulnerable. To this increasingly unstable international financial environment was added in 1973 a rapid increase in energy costs for developed economies. This was a result of the formation of an oil producers' cartel – the Organization of Petroleum-Exporting Countries (OPEC) – which, flexing their collective muscles, in late

1973 increased the price of oil fourfold. Changes in international financial markets already meant that the domestic economic policy of all developed nations was increasingly sensitive to international economic forces. The sudden rise in energy prices meant that developed economies needed to retrench quickly in order to achieve cuts in domestic costs as the world economy moved into recession. British policy makers were slow to react to both developments. Spending budgets, far from being cut back, actually over-ran planned totals in 1973 and 1974 (Wright 1977). The results were: a run on sterling; the need to borrow, ultimately in 1976 from the International Monetary Fund (IMF), in order to support the falling currency; and, partly as a condition of the deal, the introduction of tighter controls on public spending and the availability of money in the domestic economy (Burk and Cairncross 1992).

Thus, by the late 1970s the old orthodoxy in the economic sphere was being undermined by world events and, partly as a consequence of this, was increasingly questioned by policy makers. The signs were many. In 1975, the Wilson government accorded priority to defeating inflation as a primary goal of economic policy. Over the following year, the Labour government began to introduce new controls over public spending and money supply. In practical terms this marked the beginning of the acceptance by state personnel of a redefined role for the state in economic matters. It was these changes which were later built on by the Conservatives after 1979. It is important to note that Labour maintained a balance between the old orthodoxy and new thinking. Indeed, by the time of the 1979 election really two options for further development were on the table: either a tight policy on wages and public spending plus industrial policy initiatives made through consensus politics and further tripartite initiatives; or abandonment of the consultative style of policy making and the introduction of more market-led solutions.

The old orthodoxy was also breaking down in the social and political spheres. It became increasingly clear that the welfare state had achieved only limited success over Beveridge's 'five giants'. Studies in the 1960s and 1970s showed that despite considerable public expenditure, poverty still existed (Abel-Smith and Townsend 1965). This rediscovery of poverty was coupled with its redefinition. The problem was seen as one of relative as opposed to absolute deprivation. Moreover, tendencies were identified for family poverty to persist across generations, and for poverty to be concentrated in particular locations, notably inner-city areas (Banting 1979: 68–77; McGregor 1981: 137–41). Consequently, attention began to be focused on ways in which the cycle of deprivation could be broken and the persisting pockets of poverty more effectively targeted through special help directed at the most needy and at areas of severe urban decline (Alcock 1993: 243–6).

There was also a growing questioning of the general equalising effects of welfare-state activity. Many of the findings which emerged over the

1960s and 1970s were summed up in an influential study by Le Grand. This showed that in health, education, housing and public transport, 'welfare' spending often benefited middle- and higher-income groups more than the poorest sections of the population (Le Grand 1982: 3, 129). These findings, coupled with the evident failure to eradicate poverty, seemed to imply that the welfare state was failing to fulfil its objectives. This in turn led to a questioning of both its operation and the principles on which it was based.

These doubts about the impact and effectiveness of the welfare state were coupled with a growing concern about its rising costs. Public expenditure on benefits and health care, in particular, was greatly increased from the late 1960s on by two demographic developments: an ageing population and the growth of unemployment. Indeed, it was spending on welfare benefits and payments that was the main contributor to the public-spending crisis of the mid-1970s. Thus, in relation to both performance and costs, the welfare state came increasingly under attack (see chapter 3).

At the political level there were two growing strands of criticism that found fault with the extensive nature of the state and the consultative and consensus-seeking style of policy making associated with it. Both emphasised the significant part played by influential pressure groups. One argued that the state was becoming overloaded in terms of the activities it was engaged in and the pressures it was subject to (King 1976: 25–7). A central theme of this thesis was that the state was severely constrained by the demands made of it and was incapable of breaking free and striking out to pursue the kind of bold and unpopular policies that many began to see as essential. The second strand argued that the process of appealing to different interests and bidding for votes in order to gather support led to an inevitable extension of the activities of the state and an inexorable rise in public spending (Brittan 1977: 255–6).

Thus, the questioning of the old orthodoxy was both intense and comprehensive. As criticism mounted, a new and radically different vision of the role of the state began to emerge. The shift was, in the 1970s, tentative, piecemeal and spasmodic. By no means all policy makers subscribed to it. However, the outlines of a new agenda can be discerned. It centred on four key propositions:

- reinvigorating the private sector;
- limiting the state's direct economic role;
- defeating inflation;
- improving the costs and sharpening the focus of public provision.

These propositions were, initially, most strongly supported and articulated on the right in politics and a particular interpretation of them informed the activities of the post-1979 Conservative governments. Later they became the conventional wisdom across a large part of the political spectrum.

The first proposition held that the private sector should provide the primary means of achieving economic growth. The idea of a balanced, mixed economy was questioned and the public sector, especially its non-productive elements, was increasingly seen as a constraint on the productive forces in the economy (Bacon and Eltis 1976: 110–12). In particular, the state was seen as imposing unnecessary burdens on business. These were considered to be most pressing in two areas. First, high levels of taxation on both companies and individuals were seen as a major disincentive to potential entrepreneurs. The latter were increasingly characterised as the 'wealth creators', whose activities needed to be encouraged rather than restricted by state action. Second, businesses were seen as being over-regulated by the state. Major aims, therefore, were to lift the burden of the state by curbing the state's interventionist role in business and to shift the incidence of taxation from income and profits to spending.

Clearly, such an analysis of the importance of the private sector and the need for its regeneration directly touched upon the second proposition: a more limited economic role for the state. On the right, the implication of liberating the private sector was a much reduced state. According to this view the state should not only do less, but should also be smaller. On the new left, the acceptance of the primary role of the private sector implied a secondary and supportive role for the state in facilitating and assisting beneficial private-sector activities.

The third proposition meant the replacement of full employment by low inflation as the primary goal of economic policy. This also had implications for the activities of the state in the field of economic management. Initially, it implied a greater emphasis on restricting economic activity through raising interest rates. In the 1970s, however, especially on the right in politics, there was increasing emphasis on the need to control the amount of money in the economy as the primary means of lowering inflation. This so-called monetarist approach was based on the assumption that an oversupply of money in the economy was the most important cause of inflation, and prices and wages would directly respond to manipulations in the supply of money (Gilmour 1992: 15–16). Monetarism chimed very well with the idea of limiting the state: it suggested that one kind of intervention alone – controlling the money supply – was the heart of the state's responsibilities.

The fourth proposition that emerged in the 1970s was concerned with achieving a leaner and more effective public sector. The desire to constrain costs was a direct reflection of the rising levels of public spending. The emphasis on sharpening the focus of public provision also followed on from this, and from the recognition of the failure of the welfare state adequately to deal with the problems of poverty and inequality. As a consequence, some felt that a more targeted approach was needed, thus bringing into question the universalist principles upon which the welfare state had been founded.

Others argued not only that services should be reformed to ensure they achieved their goals, but that attention should be given to the efficiency with which they did so. On the right, the provision of income support through the payment of benefits was further queried on the grounds that it produced a state of welfare dependency on the part of recipients, thus undermining personal initiative and individual responsibility.

Underlying all four of these propositions was a philosophy that gave greater attention than previously to the role of the individual and the utility of market forces. It implied a questioning and rejection of the more collective emphasis of the old orthodoxy and the belief that where markets fail the state can succeed. In the 1970s there was a shift in the views of the policy elite about the nature of the problems they were confronting and the available solutions. Notably, the driving force behind this reassessment had been problems thrown up by world events, especially in the economic sphere. The old orthodoxy no longer seemed appropriate as a means of either understanding or responding to the new situation. This transformation of elite values remained partial both in the number who subscribed to it and in the extent to which it represented a cohesive and systematic stance. But the thinking was there and it emerged both in response to changes in the context of policy making and before the election of the Conservative government in 1979. The Thatcher and Major governments built on, clarified and extended the new agenda. They carried it through, but they did not originate it. Arguably, given the importance of contextual factors, a non-Conservative government might have ended up carrying through a broadly similar agenda (as has indeed been the case in other countries) though possibly using a different, and more consensual (old orthodox) style of policy making.

The new orthodoxy: the enabling state

The new structure of the state and the new thinking underlying it emerged gradually over the period of the Thatcher governments. At the core of this rethinking has been the notion of an 'enabling' state, one that oversees the activities of other agencies that act on its behalf rather than itself being the direct provider of services (Wilson and Game 1994: 15, 341–2). In terms of detailed and integrated policy initiatives this new state form began to emerge only from about 1987, in the last few years of the Thatcher governments. And it was really only under the Major governments, from 1990 onwards, that the full package of measures that constitute this new form of state began to be implemented. However, it should be noted that, while the new state form can be discerned in outline and in terms of certain policy initiatives, its actual impact on the structure of the state has so far been patchy. The principles and practices of the new state form are well established in such areas as the organisation of the civil service, the National Health Service, public housing and some local authority services. In other areas less change is evident. As in the case of the old orthodoxy, the new one is based on certain broad perceptions about important economic and social issues and the required form of state organisation. In similar vein there are a number of central features of state operation coupled with a particular style of policy making.

In the economic and social spheres, the key principles are refinements and extensions of the new thinking that had emerged in the 1970s, especially the stress on the importance of market-led solutions and the primacy of the private sector in achieving economic change and development. This has involved a redefinition of the economic purpose of the state; less stress is placed on management and direct involvement and more on facilitating market and private-sector endeavours. The notion of markets is central to this new thinking, though precisely what is meant by the term is a matter of some dispute and differing conceptions of markets have produced quite distinct policy solutions and ideas about the economic role of the state.

On the political right, the view has tended to be that markets, operating within a proper framework of law, are self-regulating (Letwin 1992: 348–50). Hence, the smaller the state is and the less state involvement there is, the better. On the centre right, the centre and the centre left, markets have increasingly been viewed not only in economic but also in political terms. They have been seen as institutions in which tendencies towards self-regulation are from time to time perverted by the patterns of interest and power that inevitably arise within them. Consequently, while no market can ever be said to work perfectly, some do work to such a beneficial extent that they are best left to their own devices. Less effective markets, however, require assistance to ensure they are more effective and that they operate, in the long run, to the general benefit of the community. This implies a role for the state in redressing market failure and in encouraging the development of successful markets that goes beyond solely relying on legal intervention.

In addition to the role of markets in the economy, the idea of applying market disciplines to the internal operations of the state has also gained currency. The argument is that market disciplines can in some cases be important means of ensuring more effective and efficient public services. This increasing emphasis on the metaphor of the market has been coupled with an alteration in the chief goals of economic policy, with a move away from defeating inflation as the primary aim towards seeking a balance between low inflation, on the one hand, and sustained growth, on the other. Again, this implies a role for the state in assisting the private sector to lead regeneration, through, for instance, policies to encourage investment, training, better communications and improved transport links.

The elite's perceptions of the nature of society, social problems and welfare provision have also been transformed. The predominant picture of society that has emerged since the 1970s is of one that is both more divided and less stable. This is reflected in a number of developments. The distribution of income and wealth has become less equal. Those households that fall within the bottom 10 per cent of income levels have seen a decline in their share of total overall income in real terms, while the top 10 per cent have seen a significant increase (Department of Social Security 1992; Johnson and Webb 1993: 434; Goodman and Webb 1995: 52–3, 76). Moreover, the effects of declining incomes on the poorest households, coupled with long-term unemployment, have led some to suggest that an underclass has emerged who have little opportunity to move into the conventional, stable society based on work and home ownership. In addition, new social identities have arisen based on race, region and gender that criss-cross and to some extent undermine traditional class patterns. And, within these broader structures, household units have altered, with the dramatic increase in one-person households and single-parent families. Growing awareness of a more diverse, complex and fragile society has been coupled with concern about changes in the dominant values within society, especially the move which some have detected towards more materialism and individualism.

These alterations in the elite's perceptions of the nature of society have affected thinking about what the social and welfare roles of the state should be. In addition to questions of social need, greater emphasis has been placed upon matters concerning potential and actual social instability. As a consequence, greater attention has been given to policies designed to target resources, provide a safety net for the least fortunate, ensure greater equality of opportunity, and maintain social order. These concerns imply less emphasis on the universalism and income equality which underlay the old orthodoxy.

It is these changes in the elite's perceptions of the nature of the economy and society that have underlain the shift from the old orthodox model of the state as a provider to the new one of the state as enabler. The move towards this model of the state is only in its infancy, though it is already possible to discern five central features of the new form of state organisation.

First, the enabling state is a disaggregated state in which state activities are distributed out to a series of subsidiary agencies within the state or, beyond that, are hived off, farmed out or even handed over to semi-independent or private agencies (Walsh 1995: 164–5). In part this distribution has been based on drawing out the distinction between the functions of developing policy and providing policy advice, on the one hand, and the delivery of services, on the other. These have been seen as tasks that require different forms of organisation and, in the case of service delivery, to which techniques of management derived from private-sector operations can most effectively be applied. This separation of the policy-making and service-delivery functions of the state was most clearly developed in the *Next Steps* report, which launched the programme of executive agencies (Efficiency Unit 1988). These agencies are detached from the relevant government department which, having set the broad policy and resource framework, leaves the agency, under its chief executive, to organise and manage its own work. By January 1996 more than 68 per cent of civil servants were employed in 110 such agencies, ranging in size from the Social Security Benefits Agency with more than 66,000 staff to the National Weights and Measures Laboratory with forty-five staff. This principle of disaggregation has been applied widely within the state and it has raised problems about accountability and control. The growth in the power of unelected quangos, for example, is a feature of the late 1980s and early 1990s (Weir and Hall 1994), although it should be recalled that under the old orthodoxy there was also a serious accountability deficit.

Second, the enabling state is a significant purchaser as well as provider of services. Its purchasing, however, is done by contracting and tendering. Thus, an important feature of the enabling state is its role as contractor. The agencies that bid for contracts may be located in the public or the private sector. The purchase of services by these means on a substantial scale was introduced in local government and the National Health Service and was later extended to central government departments and the agencies connected to them. It involves a completely new set of tasks for central state personnel or, to put it more meaningfully, for those within the state who act as principals overseeing the agents who carry out the contracted services. These principal state personnel are engaged in setting the terms, allocating, monitoring the application and evaluating the outcome of contracts (Greer 1994: 79–80; Walsh 1995: 40–3, 112–18, 126–31). Not only does this imply a new set of tasks for state personnel and a new set of relationships, it also requires new ways of thinking about the boundaries of the state as the line between the public and private is softened.

Third, the enabling state is also a regulatory state. In fulfilling this function it has become a key task of top state personnel to provide a framework of rules and guidelines within which public and private organisations are expected to work. Such a framework can involve not only formal, legal rules, but also less evident incentives to compliance, such as special favours and tax concessions or impositions. The regulatory state also requires some machinery for judging the application and ensuring the enforcement of rules. Hence an essential feature of the regulatory state is the creation of substantial and effective regulatory bodies. The most evident of these are those that apply to the privatised utilities, such as the Office for Water Services (OFWAT), which oversees the water industry, and the Office of Gas Supply (OFGAS), which monitors the activities of British Gas PLC, the privatised near-monopoly gas supplier.

Fourth, the enabling state is a monitoring and evaluating state. Because it is disaggregated, purchases through contract and regulates the activities of others, the new state form is obliged to monitor and evaluate the activities of subsidiary and connected agencies. In part this is done by regulatory bodies and central or principal personnel, but this task is also fulfilled by specialist, semi-independent organisations, such as the Audit Commission, which is responsible for auditing the accounts of local authorities, the National Health Service and other public bodies and helping them to ensure that they provide good value for money. In order to fulfil this monitoring and evaluative function state personnel have begun to develop a range of techniques such as performance indicators and measures that allow comparisons to be made between the performance of units providing similar types of service (Carter *et al.* 1992).

Finally, the enabling state is also characterised by competitive, entrepreneurial funding: that is to say, an increasing range of its activities are funded through grants which are distributed on a competitive basis as a result of agencies and service providers putting forward schemes, usually in partnership with other public or private agencies, and with the grant-awarding body choosing the best or most eligible proposal. This bidding for funding applies to a whole range of grants and awards but has been especially applied in the areas of urban regeneration and job creation. Notable funding regimes subject to bidding criteria include the Single Regeneration Budget, City Pride, City and Regional Challenges, national lottery distributions and, from outside Britain, European Union structural funds (Stoker and Young 1993: 153–5, 185–9; Atkinson and Moon 1994: 120–38). This new competitive grants economy requires the development of new skills, contacts and relationships on the part of resource-seeking agencies. They need to have personnel who know what is available, how and when to bid for it, and whom to draw into partnership. Like other aspects of the enabling state, competitive funding also blurs the boundary between the public and private sectors.

Alongside the development of this enabling state a new style of policy making has begun to emerge. At high policy level it has involved a less consultative approach than was characteristic of the old orthodoxy. More central direction, standards and broad objectives are being laid down from above (Jessop 1992: 31–4; Walsh 1995: 203–5). Gone are the days of close consultation with major interests, especially the trade unions, on high policy questions. Although consultation has continued in more narrow and specialised areas of policy making, it is more often at the detailed stage of policy development rather than at the point of initiation. At the low policy level, however, where the task is to carry out policy, a variety of styles have emerged in keeping with the various manifestations of the new state form. Change in the structure of the state has produced intricate and complicated relationships. These range from the more directive, and often interventionist, approach of principal or core personnel when engaged in setting and monitoring contracts or regulating subsidiary agents or activities, to the more consensual, even corporatist, styles of public–private-sector partnerships that are often involved in the delivery of policy at the local level.

This enabling state is gradually emerging in the 1990s. It entails a new set of tasks for state personnel and a new set of relationships. It also requires new ways of thinking about the dimensions and the boundaries of the state. As we have noted, the divide between the public and private sectors has become increasingly fluid. This new state form implies a decrease in the activities of the state as a direct provider of services, but it does not necessarily mean a less interventionist state. Rather it implies an alteration in the nature of state intervention, with the core of the state assuming a more directive and regulatory role in relation to a variety of subsidiary bodies in both the public and the private sectors. This is why the enabling state can be regarded as a kind of second-removed state, one that may provide less, but does not necessarily do less. To some extent it does different things, but, more importantly, it carries out its activities in a different way.

This shift from provider to enabler has raised two broad sets of issues on the political agenda. The first centres on questions to do with the efficiency and effectiveness of the new form and the second on questions about accountability and control. These are likely to be central issues of debate over the next few years. It remains a moot point, however, as to what aspects of the enabling state will become more fully embedded in the years ahead. We would expect the principles to be maintained, though the exact pattern of development is hard to predict. This conclusion follows from our way of understanding change as a consequence of changes in the elite's perceptions, which in turn reflect their interpretations of world events, especially in the economic and social spheres. The new state form has emerged out of policy makers' changing perceptions of the economic and social realities with which they have to deal. Moreover, the patterns of economic and social change and the elite's responses to them are not peculiar to Britain. Similar developments with similar effects can be seen elsewhere. Indeed, key aspects of the enabling model have emerged in nearly all other western countries, though the precise manifestation of this phenomenon has varied with local circumstances. This suggests that the new type of state is, in part, a response to deep-seated, universal factors and is not fundamentally the product of this or that national administration or even party platform. Thus, even a change in government will not mean a full reversion to the provider state but rather a change in the emphasis given to the various attributes of the new form. A Labour government is likely to highlight the role of the state as regulator and correspondingly to downgrade the role of contractor. But the basic structure of the new form is unlikely to be cast aside until the elite's perceptions of world changes render it redundant.

Acknowledgements

The authors would like to thank their colleagues Michael Moran and Ian Holliday for their very useful comments on an earlier draft of this chapter.

References

Abel-Smith, B. and Townsend, P. (1965), *The Poor and the Poorest*, Occasional Papers on Social Administration, no. 17, London, Bell.

Alcock, P. (1993), *Understanding Poverty*, London, Macmillan.

Atkinson, R. and Moon, G. (1994), *Urban Policy in Britain*, London, Macmillan.

Bacon, R. and Eltis, W. (1976), *Britain's Economic Problem: Too Few Producers*, London, Macmillan.

Banting, K. C. (1979), *Poverty, Politics and Poverty*, London, Macmillan.

Brittan, S. (1977), *The Economic Consequences of Democracy*, London, Temple Smith.

Burk, K. and Cairncross, A. (1992), *Goodbye Great Britain: The 1976 IMF Crisis*, London, Yale University Press.

Carter, N., Klein, R. and Day, P. (1992), *How Organisations Measure Success*, London, Routledge.

Coates, D. (1994), *The Question of UK Decline*, London, Harvester Wheatsheaf.

Craven, B. and Lee, P. (1982), Corporatism and tripartism, in H. Elcock (ed.), *What Sort of Society?*, Oxford, Martin Robertson.

Crosland, A. (1956), *The Future of Socialism*, London, Jonathan Cape.

Department of Social Security (1992), *Households Below Average Income 1988/89*, London, HMSO.

Donaldson, P. (1973), *Economics of the Real World*, Harmondsworth, Penguin.

Efficiency Unit (1988), *Improving Management in Government: The Next Steps*, London, HMSO.

Gamble, A. (1981), *Britain in Decline*, London, Macmillan.

Gilmour, I. (1992), *Dancing with Dogma: Britain Under Thatcherism*, London, Simon and Schuster.

Glickman, H. (1961), The Toryness of English Conservatism, *Journal of British Studies*, 1, 1.

Goodman, A. and Webb, S. (1995), The distribution of UK household expenditure: 1979–92, *Fiscal Studies*, 16:3, 55–80.

Greenleaf, W. H. (1973), The character of modern British Conservatism, in R. Benewick and B. Parekh (eds), *Knowledge and Belief in Politics: The Problem of Ideology*, London, Allen and Unwin.

Greer, P. (1994), *Transforming Central Government: The Next Steps Initiative*, Buckingham, Open University Press.

Hennessy, P. (1993), *Never Again: Britain 1945–51*, London, Vintage.

Hill, M. (1993), *The Welfare State in Britain: A Political History Since 1945*, Aldershot, Edward Elgar.

Jessop, B. (1992), From social democracy to Thatcherism: twenty five years of British politics, in N. Abercrombie and A. Warde (eds), *Social Change in Contemporary Britain*, Cambridge, Polity.

Johnson, P. and Webb, S. (1993), Explaining the growth in UK income inequality: 1979–1988, *Economic Journal*, 103, 429–35.

Kavanagh, D. and Morris, P. (1994), *Consensus Politics: From Attlee to Major* (2nd edn), Oxford, Blackwell.

Keegan, W. (1984), *Mrs Thatcher's Economic Experiment*, London, Allen Lane.

King, A. (ed.) (1976), *Why is Britain Becoming Harder to Govern?*, London, BBC.

Le Grand, J. (1982), *The Strategy of Equality*, London, George Allen and Unwin.

Letwin, S. (1992), *The Anatomy of Thatcherism*, London, Fontana.

McGregor, S. (1981), *The Politics of Poverty*, London, Longman.

Marquand, D. (1988), *The Unprincipled Society: New Demands and Old Politics*, London, Fontana.

Ministry of Housing and Local Government (1965), *Annual Report*, cmnd 2668, London, HMSO.

Smith, D. (1987), *The Rise and Fall of Monetarism*, London, Penguin.

Smith, D. (1992), *From Boom to Bust: Trial and Error in British Economic Policy*, London, Penguin.

Stoker, G. and Young, S. (1993), *Cities in the 1990s*, London, Longman.

Vickers, G. (1965), *The Art of Judgement: Policy Making as a Mental Skill*, London, Chapman and Hall.

Walsh, K. (1995), *Public Services and Market Mechanisms*, London, Macmillan.

Weir, S. and Hall, W. (eds) (1994), *Ego Trip: Extra-governmental Organisations in the United Kingdom and their Accountability*, London, Charter 88 Trust.

Wilson, D. and Game, C. (1994), *Local Government in the United Kingdom*, London, Macmillan.

Wright, M. (1977), Public expenditure in Britain: the crisis of control, *Public Administration*, 55, 143–69.

3

The welfare state:
changes and challenges

Paul Wilding

To make a clear judgement about the success or failure of fifty years of the so-called British welfare state is extremely difficult. To do so it would be necessary first to establish agreed aims and then to work out methods of measuring success in achieving them. With every service having multiple aims, and with plenty of scope for disagreement as to whether particular outcomes constitute success or failure, the chances of agreement are poor. There is also the problem of disentangling the contribution to particular outcomes of welfare-state policies, economic growth (or its absence), cultural change and so on.

An even more fundamental problem is that there is really no such thing as 'the British welfare state' – Rudolf Klein speaks of it as a 'useful shorthand, but a dangerous abstraction' (1993: 14). There are various policies, programmes and services dealing with issues such as health, education, income maintenance and social care but to dignify them with the title of 'the welfare state' is to suggest a greater unity of philosophy or purpose than actually exists. The welfare state is no more than a shorthand for a group of policies used for different purposes with different degrees of enthusiasm and conviction by different governments – an agglomeration of the rather ad hoc.

The most obvious way of tackling the task of making a judgement would be to take the five giants that Beveridge depicted as guarding the road to reconstruction – want, disease, ignorance, squalor and idleness – and see how the war against them has proceeded. Nicholas Deakin, however, has described such an approach as 'the most primitive verdict of all' (1993: 17). He goes on to look at alternative approaches and criteria, but none is altogether satisfactory. The fundamental problem is that there is no escaping value judgements. When the figures have been analysed to the last decimal point, there will still be disagreement about whether they constitute success or failure. By the nature of things, those with the highest hopes of what we call the welfare state tend to be its harshest judges.

46

The approach here is to try to come to a verdict by evaluating the welfare state on three criteria. First, I say something very briefly about the welfare state's success in tackling Beveridge's five giants. It may be a primitive approach but it does give a useful perspective. Second, I draw out what, in my judgement, are the main changes in the welfare state since 1945. Ideally, those changes would be evaluated against a set of aims and objectives but, in the space available, that is just too complex. What I do is to analyse the changes and make some passing reflections about them. Third, I set out what I see as the major challenges that have faced the welfare state and say something about how effectively, in my view, it has responded to them.

The struggle against the giants

The nature of want has changed significantly since 1945, but that giant is still very much alive. Some 9 million people in 1992 lived in families that depended on income support, which is generally taken as being an unofficial poverty line. Nearly 5 million people lived in families that were not on income support but had incomes that were less than income support. Nearly 14 million people were, therefore, living on poverty incomes (House of Commons Social Security Committee 1995). Of course, income support is worth much more in real terms than was national assistance in 1948 – probably about twice as much – but all the evidence we have is that it fails to provide an acceptable standard of living (Bradshaw 1993).

In relation to disease, there has been enormous progress on some key health indices. In 1951, for example, the infant mortality rate was 31 per 1,000 live births. By 1993, it had dropped to 7 (Central Statistical Office 1995). This reflects a range of medical and social improvements. There have also been significant improvements in the expectation of life – of more than seven years for men and of around eight years for women. Most of the great killer diseases of childhood have been virtually eliminated – to be replaced by the very different chronic illnesses that afflict an ageing population.

There has been significant progress on a range of indices of educational achievement – though 40 per cent of twenty-one-year-olds in 1992 reported difficulties in writing and spelling (Central Statistical Office 1995: 58). There has been an expansion of the percentage of children under the age of five in school, with 55 per cent of all three- and four-year-olds in school in 1992/93 compared with only 20 per cent in 1970/71. At the other end of the educational race, there has been a sharp decline in the percentage of young people leaving school with no passes in GCSE examinations or equivalent, from 20 per cent of boys and 18 per cent of girls in the mid-1970s to 7 per cent of boys and 6 per cent of girls in 1991/92. Over the same period the percentage of boys leaving school with one A level pass or better has risen from 18 per cent to 28 per cent and for girls from 16 per cent to 31 per cent. In 1946 there were less than 70,000 students in universities. In the last twenty years the number of undergraduate enrolments in universities and other establishments of higher education has risen from around 240,000 to 416,000 in 1992/93. In 1946, university education was the preserve of an elite. We now have mass higher education, with 18 per cent of eighteen- to twenty-one-year-olds in higher education (Central Statistical Office 1995: ch. 7).

In the battle against squalor there are also impressive achievements. In 1951 some 38 per cent of households lacked a bath or shower. In 1991 the figure was an almost irreducible 0.3 per cent. In 1952, one in three households lacked a flush toilet. Virtually all now have that amenity. Among households lacking basic amenities we now list those who lack central heating – an amenity which would have been seen as pure luxury in 1945. On the other hand, homelessness increased sharply in the 1980s and 1990s.

It is in relation to idleness – unemployment – that, along with want, the record of the welfare state is perhaps most depressing. For thirty years after the Second World War, full employment was a central goal – and it was achieved. In the mid-1970s unemployment rates began to rise and since the early 1980s have hovered around 10 per cent. That is the official rate. Experts would put the true figure much higher. Alongside unemployment rates we need to put economic activity rates. What we see here from the mid-1970s is a decline in economic activity rates for men over the age of forty-five. In 1971, for example, 93 per cent of men aged between fifty-five and fifty-nine were economically active. In 1993 the figure had dropped to 75 per cent. For the age group sixty to sixty-four years, the figures were 83 per cent and 52 per cent, respectively. The economy is simply not providing work for all those who want and need it (Central Statistical Office 1995: ch. 10).

Data of this kind are obviously crude. Every statistic needs exposition and clarification. All the statistics can provide is a very crude picture of seeming successes and failures. The reality is much more complex. Definitions and expectations change. There may, for example, have been victories in the battle against squalor but many people still live in conditions that the mass of their fellow citizens would find unacceptable. But the figures, crude as they are, do provide some useful context and background. But it is to open rather than to close a debate.

The major changes

For thirty years after 1945 the welfare state changed relatively little. Of course, there were changes – the move towards earnings-related social security benefits, the creation of social services departments, for example, but the *basic* approaches and structures established in 1945 were still largely in place. It was in the 1980s that major changes began, reaching a climax in the legislation of the years 1988–90. These changes are, however, only part of a broader pattern of change. I pick out ten changes which I see as the key ones.

There is much debate as to the degree of consensus between the political parties about the proper role of the state in economic and social policy in the years between 1945 and 1975 (Glennerster 1995: 9–10). What *is* plain is that there was consensus about the commitment to full employment (Lowe 1993: 85; Gladstone 1995: 10). That has clearly changed. As Glynn puts it, 'Since the mid 1970's Britain has moved from a political consensus in which welfarism and full employment were regarded as fundamental, to an uncertain political climate in which these considerations take second place' (1994: 87). Maintenance of full employment has been defined as secondary to conquering inflation – and in Norman Lamont's judgement, 'That price is well worth paying' (quoted in Glynn 1994: 82). Abandoning full employment as a goal was a policy change of immense importance, at a stroke rendering the attainment of other welfare goals impossible because of the financial costs it imposed on the Treasury and because of its other social costs.

A second major change was the growth of doubts about the effectiveness and efficiency of the classic instruments of the welfare state – government, bureaucracy and professionals. Taylor Gooby says that 'The central theme running through the contemporary sociology of welfare is distrust of the state' (1991: 140). Le Grand and Bartlett speak of 'a major offensive against bureaucratic structures' (1993: 2) as characterising developments in social policy in the 1980s. Certainly, there was a loss of confidence in state capacity, in the state's power to implement the policies required to achieve desirable goals. There was a parallel loss of confidence in professionals. They were to be managed more explicitly (e.g. hospital doctors), they were to have their hours of work specified and a national curriculum imposed upon them (e.g. teachers); they were to have the quality of their research and teaching evaluated (e.g. university lecturers); they were to be given tight practice guidelines rather than left to follow their own professional judgement (e.g. social workers).

A third change, which is sufficiently important to merit separate treatment but is, in a sense, an example of the previous point, is the stripping of key roles and responsibilities from the local authority. Local authorities were forced to sell large numbers of their most desirable properties. They virtually ceased to be builders of houses for general needs and in 1988 were put under strong pressure to transfer their stock to housing associations or groups of tenants. Schools were encouraged to opt out of local education authority control in favour of grant-maintained status. Local education authorities' control of resources was weakened by the introduction of decentralised budgets and local management. Education authorities also

49

lost control of polytechnics and further education. The National Health Service and Community Care Act 1990 aimed to end the role of the local authority as a major provider of social care services. Its future was as an enabler – a funder but not a provider, a maker of contracts with private and voluntary bodies to deliver the services that the local authority felt were required.

Through the 1980s the Conservative government passed a series of measures designed to deprive local authorities of the right to fix local levels of taxation at a rate they deemed appropriate. It was a long drawn out struggle but by the end of the decade local authorities had lost this key element of their independence. They could raise only that amount of revenue deemed appropriate by central government.

The loss of powers and functions was a major change. The local authority's historic role as a major planner and provider of social services seemed to be either bypassed or sidelined by conflicting movements towards both centralisation and decentralisation. If these reforms, said Le Grand, describing the changes of the late 1980s, 'are carried through to their logical conclusion, the welfare state in the 1990's will be one where local authorities will not own and operate schools, houses and residential homes' (1990: 351) – all central and historic local government responsibilities.

A fourth change, again a reaction to the supposed failings of public administration, was the development of internal markets. Le Grand regards this as the most important break from the traditional pattern of social policy provision (quoted in George and Miller 1994b: 29). The idea is a simple one – that market relationships are the only route to efficiency. To secure maximum efficiency in, for example, the National Health Service, the service needs to be broken down into a series of independent units which buy and sell to and from each other. Hospitals will offer services to a range of purchasers – general practitioners designated as fundholding practices, and district health authorities.

The local authority is bidden in the 1990 Act to develop a market in social care by signing contracts with the independent sector – private or not-for-profit agencies. The idea is the same – that contracts and competition will secure a better and cheaper service than could ever be secured by the blunt and flabby instruments of public provision.

It is too early as yet to come to a judgement. Certainly, enormous amounts of time, energy and money have been expended to bring the new system into being. Some lethargic departments have been spurred into new life and increased productivity. Some inequities have been exposed. The most obvious casualty is the idea of standards to which all citizens have access irrespective of where they live. Much now depends on local deals between purchasers and providers. It is much less clear than in the past who, if anyone, is ultimately responsible for ensuring necessary services are provided.

A fifth important change in approach and philosophy is the emphasis on welfare as a mixed economy. The idea has exerted a powerful influence on developments in the welfare state from the late 1970s. The idea represents an undeniable fact – welfare *is* a mixed economy, a mix of private, public, voluntary and family provision. It also represents an ideology – that the state provision of welfare should be only one element in a broader pattern of provision and not necessarily the most important one. But it was an idea which legitimated and encouraged the active promotion of private and voluntary welfare provision and the idea of partnership between the state and the independent sector. It legitimated a bigger role for the private pension industry, the granting of tax relief on private medical insurance contributions to elderly people, the massive social security payments in the 1980s that fuelled a huge expansion in private residential care. Most important of all, perhaps, it was the idea that welfare is a mixed economy which underlay the thinking embodied in the 1990 National Health Service and Community Care Act. That legislation sought to offer private and voluntary providers a major role in the provision of social care services. The state would finance but other bodies would provide.

Another strand in the 'mixed economy of welfare' argument was the reassertion of family responsibility. It was argued as morally right that families *should* take responsibility for their members, as socially desirable because mutual responsibility binds people together, as economically desirable because it would ease the pressures on public expenditure, with all the liberation of primeval economic energies that would mean. The assertion of family responsibility, for example, for community care or for the financial support of young people or students – the average parental contribution to student grants nearly doubled in real terms between 1980/81 and 1986/87 – legitimated cuts in benefits or other services. It was an ideology that took scant account of reality – the more prolonged and more expert care required by elderly people than in the past, elderly people's growing sense that they had a right to publicly provided services, young people's reluctance to be dependent on parents once they had left secondary education. What it actually meant was not so much a reactivation of family responsibility as an abdication of public responsibility.

The sixth major change we need to explore is the retreat from universal-ism. If one word represented the hopes and visions of 1945 it was *universalism* – the idea that services should be available for everyone as a right of citizenship, free at the point of need. That principle has suffered massive erosion. It has been portrayed as anachronistic, as belonging to a world we have left behind, as relevant only to a world of austerity and poverty but not to a world of affluence, as reflecting a restrictive collectivism rather than a dynamic individualism, as being just too expensive to be affordable at the standards that people have come very reasonably to expect, as wasteful in that it provides services – for example child benefit – to those who have no conceivable need of public help.

The attack on universalism has had three strands. First, there has been much emphasis on the virtues of targeting – of concentrating benefits and services on those with the greatest needs. What it has meant in social security, for example, is the ever-increasing importance of means-tested benefits. Means-tested benefits, Lister (1989: 17) concluded, 'are now explicitly presented as the fulcrum of the system'. A second strand in the move against universalism is the shifting of responsibilities from the state as universal provider to individuals or other bodies. The sale of local authority housing and the virtual ending of local authority general-needs building marks an assertion of private, individual responsibility for housing. Changes in pension provision place the responsibility for securing an adequate income in old age on individuals rather than on the state. The third strand, the proliferation of charges for services, represents a retreat from the principle of universal provision for all according to need.

A seventh change is the way the welfare state has become increasingly concerned about economics over the last twenty years. Partly, of course, that is a direct product of the difficulties the British economy has faced since 1973. But it is also the product of a change of philosophy and priorities.

This concern also has a number of strands. First, there is the public burden model of welfare, which has come to dominate thinking – the idea that public expenditure is a burden on the economy. Second, there is the idea, fostered by Conservative governments since 1979, that economic growth rather than further development in the welfare state is the best way to enhance individual and social wellbeing. A third strand is the new paradigm of 'the affordable welfare state' (George and Miller 1994a: 17). That paradigm has two central elements – first, that the volume of public expenditure should be determined by rates of economic growth and the supposed needs of the economy not by notions of social need, and, second, that rates of direct taxation should be kept as low as possible. Low rates of personal taxation, say George and Miller (1994c: 217) 'are now an established public expectation' – an expectation that has been carefully fostered by government. Fourth, there is much less argument about the value of welfare expenditure – to the economy, to the individual, to society. All the emphasis is on the cost of such provision because of beliefs and assumptions about the implications of such expenditure for the economy. Finally, there is the new concern about competitiveness that has developed as a particular element in the 'public burden' critique. The concern is partly the product of a sense of an economy under threat from more dynamic and efficient economies that have lower rates of welfare expenditure. Partly, it is simply a new ideological stick with which to beat welfare expenditure.

Another important change – the eighth – in the welfare state since 1979 is a change of ethos. The dominant values of the classic welfare state in the years between 1945 and 1975 were a mix of equity, egalitarianism, and collective responsibility for economic and social casualties. That has changed. In education policy since 1976, say Glennerster and Low, 'Equity goals have receded almost to vanishing point' (1990: 55–6). Kenneth Baker, then Secretary of State for Education, was able to reassure the 1987 Conservative Party conference that 'the pursuit of egalitarianism in education is over' (Johnson 1990: 126). In their analysis of social security policy in the years between the mid-1970s and the late 1980s, Barr and Coulter see as one of the central themes the change of stated goals from a concern for equity and the reduction of inequality to a new emphasis on labour market efficiency and incentives (1990: 274).

The two final charges – nine and ten – are closely connected and cannot easily be treated separately: the new emphasis on management and the new stress on evaluation.

The stress on management was the product of a concern about the supposed inefficiency of the public sector, a belief in the inherent superiority of private-sector approaches and a lack of confidence in professionals' traditional self-management. There was the introduction of a new cadre of managers into the National Health Service in the early 1980s. There was the attempt to persuade all kinds of people – professors, doctors, head teachers, social work team leaders – that they were really managers – and should behave as such.

There were all kinds of implications. There was the break-up of some government departments – for example Social Security – into separate agencies with clear contractual responsibilities for running elements of the system, described by Ling as 'the most radical break in the history of the civil service since the Northcote-Trevelyan report of the 1850s' (1994: 38). A welcome implication of the new emphasis on management was a concern with quality of service.

A concern for management meant that those in responsible positions must be driven by a number of key questions – what are the aims and objectives of the services? What is it costing? What are the outputs and outcomes? New bodies were created as elements in the new 'evaluative state', as Henkel (1991) called it. The Audit Commission became the central element in the government's emphasis on economy, efficiency, effectiveness and evaluation, asking sharp questions and exposing some dark corners in local authority policy and practice.

The change, essentially, was to a new, more critical, questioning climate. Aims and objectives needed to be clearly specified. Outcomes needed to be measurable. Above all, what was being done needed to be justified. There was much that was positive in this new emphasis. There were dangers too. It is always easier to measure costs than benefits. Costs are clear. Benefits are much less clear; they may be long term, they may be intangible – even if real.

Emphasis on management also has its dangers. As Clarke *et al.* (1994: 231) argue, managerialism in social policy has helped to shift the public discourse about social policy away from traditional concerns with inputs and outputs towards an overarching concern with efficiency and the organisation of service delivery. Management is about means rather than ends. In the classic welfare state there was, perhaps, too little concern about means, but it is dangerous when means became the dominant concern.

Another strand in the management–evaluation change is the government's adoption of consumerism. Partly this was a product of Conservative governments' faith in market-type relationships as the ideal model – relationships in which the consumer reigned. Partly, it was adopted by the government as a useful weapon to use against bureaucracy and professional dominance.

The attempt – reflected in the range of charters for citizens, patients and parents – to infuse the welfare state with a new concern for the user – redefined as the customer – was in part a public relations and political exercise, but it did mark the coming of age of the service user and gave users certain formal rights that they had not had before. At the same time, through restriction on expenditure, government made it more difficult for many organisations to respond to user demands.

Responding to new challenges

One of the reasons why welfare-state policies develop is the perception that markets are not meeting individual or social needs, new needs generated by economic and social changes or needs newly recognised and defined as requiring social action. So it is appropriate to take the welfare state's success in responding to new needs and challenges as a crucial element in the making of an overall judgement. In this section we assess the welfare state's success in responding to key challenges that developed after 1945.

The ageing population

One of the major changes of the years since 1945 has been the ageing of the population. In 1951 there were some 6 million people over the age of sixty-five – 11.5 per cent of the population. Over the next forty years the number of people aged over sixty-five increased to 9.1 million – nearly 16 per cent of the population. From the 1970s it became plain that the trend was not merely one of increasing numbers of elderly people but also an ageing of the elderly population: in the past twenty years the number of people aged between seventy-five and eighty-four has risen by 44 per cent, while the number of those over eighty-five has increased by 70 per cent.

How successfully has the welfare state met the challenge of an ageing population? Increasing affluence in the 1950s and 1960s made the funding of increasing numbers of pensions relatively unproblematic but as a society we never agreed about the extent and nature of public responsibility for providing income in old age. There were various attempts in the 1960s and 1970s to redefine public responsibility and to seek to move towards a state earnings-related pensions scheme for those who were not members of occupational schemes. Those rather unconvincing experiments ended in 1988 when the government decided that a state earnings-related pension would become intolerably expensive in the next century and the scheme had better be cut back. People were urged to see financial provision beyond the barest minimum as a private responsibility through the use of sweeteners from public funds.

The other dramatic attempt to respond to the ageing population was the decision in the early 1970s that pensions, along with other long-term benefits, should be up-rated every year in line with increases in earnings or prices, whichever was the greater. The decision marked a commitment to guarantee pensioners a share of the fruits of economic growth. In 1982, the commitment was abandoned. Pensions were to be increased only in line with increases in prices. Within ten years a pensioner couple was £20–25 per week worse off than under the earlier up-rating scheme. In 1992, 28 per cent of pensioners had incomes at or below the level of income support.

What about the health and caring needs of elderly people? The changes there are massive. In 1950, 20 per cent of National Health Service expenditure was devoted to elderly people. By the early 1990s it was almost 50 per cent. Certainly, there has been a massive expansion of caring services. The crucial question is whether that expansion has matched the massive expansion of need. Successive governments have accepted a need to expand caring services simply to maintain effective levels of provision, but the Department of Health's figure of 2 per cent growth per year as what is required is widely regarded as much too low – and as possibly only half what is actually needed. Evandrou *et al.* (1990: 233), in their detailed review of developments from the mid-1970s to the late 1980s, concluded that 'What is evident from these statistics is that both residential and domiciliary services have failed to keep pace with increases in the level of potential demand'. They have not kept pace because of concern about cost and because of the belief that public caring services were, in the words of Patrick Jenkin, Secretary of State for Health and Social Security 1979–81, 'a long stop for the very special needs going beyond the range of voluntary service' (quoted in Baldock 1994: 173). There were also the beliefs about family responsibility mentioned above.

The challenge of the ageing of the population is one facing developed and developing countries alike. It is one which goes to the heart of the welfare state's ideals because it is about the nature and extent of collective responsibility and provision. The British state has defined the challenge as too hard and too heavy. It has not been prepared to accept that the nature and scale of old-age dependency must force a review of the spheres of private and public responsibility.

The two-thirds society

Another major challenge to the welfare state, to which changes in benefits and services also contributed, has been the emergence of the 'two-thirds society': a society in which two-thirds of the population are affluent and secure but one-third are poor, insecure and excluded. From around 1980, it became increasingly plain that economic and social trends were having particularly serious effects on certain vulnerable groups. They were being increasingly excluded, not only from the fruits of economic growth, but also from the standard of living customary in their society.

As the 1980s proceeded, the figures showed that ever-larger numbers of people were living at, or below, basic levels of social security – 13.7 million people by 1992 – 2.4 million more than in 1989 and 5.5 million more than in 1979; and an ever-increasing number of people were dependent on social security – nearly 9 million in 1992 compared with just over 7 million in 1989. Over the years 1979–91 the value of supplementary benefit/income support fell sharply in relation to earnings – from 26 per cent to 19 per cent of full-time male earnings for a married couple and from 16 per cent to 12 per cent for a single person (Commission on Social Justice 1993: 23).

In the 1980s the poor actually – if almost incredibly – became poorer. Between 1979 and 1991 government data show that the real incomes of the poorest 10 per cent of the population fell by 14 per cent after housing costs. Incomes of the population as a whole went up by 36 per cent and for the richest 10 per cent by 62 per cent (Oppenheim 1994: 4). In 1979 the bottom half of the population received a third of total income. By 1991 this had dropped to a quarter (Commission on Social Justice 1993: 44). Piachaud's estimate is that the proportion of people in poverty by equivalent relative definitions has roughly doubled in the past thirty years (quoted in Dean 1994: 89).

The two-thirds society, however, meant more than a simple increase in poverty. It was about a new kind of society, in which a substantial proportion of the population – up to one-third – was marginalised, trapped, excluded. It was about changes in the labour market and about increased polarisation in the world of work. The proportion of men, for example, whose wages fell below the Council of Europe's 'decency threshold' doubled from 14.6 per cent to 28.1 per cent in the 1980s (George and Miller 1994b: 41). The two-thirds society was also about increased homelessness. In the 1980s in Britain over 1 million people became homeless and in the early 1990s there were over 400,000 officially registered homeless people – a figure which was a gross under-representation of the problem because it excluded all the single homeless.

There was much debate in academic circles as to whether these trends amounted to the emergence of a new underclass (e.g. Field 1989; Dean and Taylor Gooby 1992). Much of the debate was to do with theories and explanations and was about the rather esoteric question of whether those trapped at the bottom of society can properly be described as 'a class'. But when the debating stops, what is all too plain is that a very large number of people are living in genuine poverty and deprivation, excluded from the way of life which most of their fellow citizens take for granted.

Children and families

Concern for children and the family has always been a central theme in social policy. In the last half of the fifty years after 1945, the family changed radically. There was a sharp increase in family break-ups and a steadily rising proportion of children living, at any one time, in single-parent families. There was also a rise in the number of step-families. In the 1980s, in particular, there was a steady increase in cohabitation both as a prelude to marriage and as an alternative to it. By the end of the decade around one-third of all births were outside marriage and in some urban areas the figure was close to 50 per cent.

Partly as a result of some of these trends, and partly as the result of increasing unemployment and more low pay, there was a sharp increase through the 1980s in the number of children living in poverty. By 1992, of people living in families with children, the proportion in poverty had reached 26.4 per cent – up from 21.1 per cent in 1989 – an increase of nearly 1.5 million people. Eighty per cent of those living in families with only one parent were living in poverty (House of Commons Social Security Committee 1995). In 1979 one in ten children lived in households with less than half average income. By 1991, the figure had risen to three in ten (Hewitt and Leach 1993: 28). Families with children were the fastest-growing group in poverty in Britain in the 1980s. Children in single-parent families – one in five of children at the end of the decade – were at the highest risk of poverty.

Deacon, in a survey of how children fared between 1946 and 1979, concludes that 'One of the most striking features of this period was the decline in the value of the support provided to families with children by the tax and social security systems'. He calculates that in 1946 the total child support for a family with three children was equivalent to 27 per cent of average male manual earnings. By the end of the 1970s the proportion had dropped to 11 per cent (Deacon 1995: 80).

What government signally failed to do was to develop anything approaching a family policy. Stress on the importance of the family as a social unit, on its key role in rearing the next generation and on its key role in caring for dependent, particularly elderly, people was not accompanied by any supporting policies. The driving forces in the non-development of policy were twofold – the ever-present concern about public expenditure and a concern that support for families would act as a perverse incentive to families to retreat from their responsibilities or would actually increase the problems that it was attempting to ameliorate – for example the number of single-parent families. Other countries developed much more active family policies uninhibited by obsessions about public expenditure or nostalgic models. Norman Lamont, then Chancellor of the Exchequer, may have been right when he spoke in the House of Commons in March 1991 about the 'widespread view in the House and in the country that more should be done to help families with children' (Board for Social Responsibility 1995: 159). But that view stopped well short of action.

Affluence

The greatest single economic and social change of the years 1945 to 1995 was the growth of affluence. Real incomes rose steadily for most people. The possession of many hitherto luxury consumer goods became widespread or virtually universal. People's expectations rose and they consumed increasing quantities of social goods such as health and education.

What were the challenges posed by affluence? Essentially they were twofold – what was provided and how it was provided. Affluence raised expectations. People expected more and better services. They came to expect more than a basic minimum. As private households became more affluent and better equipped they came to expect similar improvements in the public sector. There were indeed massive improvements in the latter, on a whole range of indices. But there remains a key question as to whether Britain's welfare services really developed in line with economic growth and rising standards.

Hills (1993: 10) points out that the relative scale of Britain's welfare state is smaller than that of most industrialised countries – in this respect Britain is seventeenth out of the twenty-one countries listed in a report for 1989 from the Organization for Economic Cooperation and Development (OECD). Contrary to popular views, we are a low-tax country. In the view of some commentators – for example Will Hutton – we simply do not pay enough tax to secure adequate public services.

What successive British governments have been slow and unwilling to grasp is that an affluent society demands higher levels of spending and services than a poorer society. People expect higher standards of provision in schools, health centres, hospitals and elderly persons' homes. Increased dissatisfaction with the National Health Service in recent years (Bosanquet 1992), for example, reflects a service failing to meet those higher expectations.

Affluence also affects how people expect services to be provided. It generates a new, more educated, critical consumerism. People expect a say in what is provided and how. They demand more and better information. They expect to be taken seriously as parents and patients and users by service providers. They expect there to be accessible and easily activated complaints systems. People are also concerned about choice. Their lives as consumers are enriched by choice. They expect more of it in the public sphere.

An affluent society requires a new concept of public service, a new public service orientation in services (Clarke and Stewart 1987). John Major showed that he grasped some aspects of this important truth in his launching of the Citizen's Charter and charters for patients, parents and other users. This move is to be welcomed. Users do have rights and it is useful to spell them out, but a focus on user rights that ignores service needs is doomed. Clearer rights require better-funded services and a new approach to the role of public services in an affluent society. Neither the Conservative Party or the Labour Party shows an adequate awareness of that vital fact.

The welfare state has tended to remain at a level of a Webbian welfare minimalism, still smelling of the world of austerity in which it had come of age after 1945. It has failed adequately to reflect the higher aspirations and expectations that were the inevitable accompaniment of a more affluent lifestyle.

New issues

Another aspect of this failure to respond to new challenges was the way the British welfare state remained pivoted on the initial five main areas of service provision – health, housing, education, social security and social care. Of course, those areas are central to the life of a good society. But times change and individual and social needs change with them. The British welfare state changed remarkably little in the fifty years since 1945 in the range of social needs which it sought to address. It failed, for example, adequately to respond to new knowledge about the determinants of health. The whole thrust of British health policy remains firmly curative. That is important, but we know – and have known for a quarter of a century – that, at the moment, a curative health policy has a relatively marginal effect on the great killer diseases of the late twentieth century. To set out to construct a genuine health policy requires a vigorous, imaginative leap but such a policy is a logical development from curative medicine – and is surely no more imaginative than the creation of a health service free at the point of use to all citizens, which was the vision in 1945.

Equally, the British welfare state has signally failed to accept transport as a basic human need. Pinker (1971: 150) argued that transport had every claim to be regarded as a social service – but the proliferation of individual methods of transport concealed the social nature of the issue. What we now know is that a good subsidised transport system can be of enormous benefit to individual wellbeing and to economic development. But we continue to see transport as a private rather than a public issue. And we are all the losers.

Another failure of imagination and development is leisure services. There is little sense of provision for leisure as a basic, essential service which the good society will provide. In a crowded urban environment, however, provision for people's leisure needs is central to welfare and wellbeing. If it is left to private entrepreneurs, those with the greatest needs will be least likely to secure access. With more and more people with more and more leisure time – those who are unemployed, in part-time work, retired and early retired – we need public provision.

A further example of a challenge to which the welfare state has failed to rise is that of the environment. Certainly, there have been important achievements – for example the Clean Air Act 1956 – but we have failed to assert the centrality of the environment to our quality of life. We have failed adequately to develop policies to protect and preserve. We have allowed the environment to be defined as the sum of various private goods rather than as the most public of all public goods.

In relation to policies to combat unemployment Leadbeater and Mulgan comment on Britain's failure to develop an adequate careers service. It has always been a low-status sector that has never really been professionalised. With high rates of unemployment and more job changing, developments in the service could clearly be a very good investment. Leadbeater and Mulgan's view is that 'A career or job advisory service should be one of the highest status institutions in the land' (1994: 9).

A final example of failure to respond creatively and effectively to new issues is in relation to the needs of women. From the 1970s, feminist analysis has made us increasingly aware of the many ways in which the welfare state discriminates against women and fails to meet their particular needs. Certainly, there has been legislation to try to promote equality of opportunity but its approach has been narrow and tentative and its impact has been limited. Particular services still fail to take account of women's needs.

Community care

One of the major challenges of the postwar years has been to develop community care. It is a challenge where the welfare state's record has been uninspired and uninspiring. It was in the 1950s that attention was first drawn to the quality of life in the great caring institutions of the welfare state – mental hospitals, geriatric hospitals, elderly people's homes, long-stay hospitals for those with physical disabilities. What was revealed was a grim picture of unsatisfactory buildings, poorly trained staff, neglect and maltreatment.

At the end of the 1950s, community care became government policy – but what exactly the term meant was left and remains unclear. In his 1988 review, Sir Roy Griffiths spoke of community care as 'everybody's poor relation but no one's baby' (Griffiths 1988: 5). The policy remained little more than an aspiration backed by periodic flurries of activity.

In the 1980s, the closure of institutions accelerated. The term community care was replaced by the rather more accurate concept of 'deinstitutionalisation'. But as a society, we signally failed to provide community or care. Of course, there were pockets where genuine community care came into being – as the Audit Commission found (1986) – but generalising from such successful experiments proved very difficult.

In essence, society failed to respond to the needs of large numbers of very dependent people. It settled for a slogan rather than a policy. As a result, many very vulnerable people suffered greatly diminished lives. It also meant that the task of caring was firmly pushed back from community to family, to women as the main carers. Many studies (e.g. Ungerson 1987) have shown just how heavy were the burdens of unshared care and how they affected the lives of carers.

One of the central characteristics of 1945–95 was the growth of dependency. Caring became a much more significant social activity. The welfare state failed – or refused – to recognise the fundamental changes in the nature of caring that took place – that care of the elderly had changed massively from the past when the period of dependency of elderly people was generally much shorter. There was inadequate recognition of the scale or nature of the changes, and no proper review of what such changes meant for the wellbeing of cared-for or carer.

Social order

One of the differences between Britain in 1995 and Britain in 1945 was the way in which it had become a much less orderly society. There is now much less deference to authority – which is not necessarily a bad thing. There is much more property crime. There is much more violence. There is much more vandalism. There is much more fear of crime, which greatly diminishes people's welfare. There is also, more intangibly, less sense of a society bound together by common aims and values. 'In advanced western societies,' says Boswell, 'our consciousness of community has become threadbare' (1990: 1).

The welfare state has never really come to terms with the issue of social order. The Labour Party, until the 1990s, was reluctant to emphasise the issue. The Conservative Party gave law and order a great deal of attention but its response was in the direction of tough policies towards lawbreakers and deviance rather than positive or preventive policies.

There is no sign that any government in these years grasped that the systems and processes that traditionally maintain order – family and neighbourhood ties, shared belief systems, respect for authority – were weakening and that the moral legacy of a pre-industrial, pre-urban, religious society might be almost exhausted. There was little sense that government might have to widen its responsibility from dealing with disorder to maintaining order.

What has became increasingly plain in recent decades is that we can no longer assume order as the norm. In a rapidly changing, more fragmented, more divided, more plural, more secular society, the maintenance of order must become a central task of government. Responding vigorously to disorder contributes little to the maintenance of order when the basic bonds and order-maintaining beliefs and systems are fraying badly.

Just how order is to be maintained in the world that is emerging is an unresolved issue – but ignorance is no justification for inaction. There are obvious lines open to experiment. For example, the youth service in Britain remains a Cinderella service. We invest tiny sums in facilities for young people while bewailing their alienation. We do not know what kind of youth service we need. What we need is experiment and a codifying of successful experience as a basis for informed policy making.

Equally, we have failed to provide an adequate network of preschool facilities. We have known for years the value of such investment to both young children and parents as a way of securing a good start in education. We know the value of such investment for children who start formal schooling with educational disadvantages and then become alienated young people ten years later. One American study showed how disadvantaged children who had preschool education were five times less likely to have been in trouble with the law by the age of twenty-nine than children who had not enjoyed such education (Commission on Social Justice 1994: 125).

The weakening of the natural order-maintaining mechanisms of society is a social change of major importance. In some societies, order is natural. There are shared norms and values and people are bonded by the ties of custom, kinship and neighbourhood. In other societies – late-twentieth-century urban industrial societies – those natural order-maintaining ties have weakened. Order has to be deliberately sustained and developed – not an enforced conformity, but an order of shared basic values and norms and patterns of behaviour. Such an order in such societies has to be made and supported.

Employment and unemployment

For twenty-five years after 1945, unemployment, the great scourge of the interwar years, seemed to have been vanquished. Then it returned. Between 1977 and 1991 the male unemployment rate in Britain rose from 5.1 per cent to 9.4 per cent of the active labour force. At the same time the percentage of working-age men without work – the non-employment rate – rose from 9 per cent to 18 per cent (Balls 1993: 7). For most of the 1980s the official rate of unemployment was over 2.5 million. Britain topped the Group of Seven unemployment table in the 1980s with a standardised rate of 10 per cent (George and Miller 1994b: 25). Whiteside's judgement (1995: 61–2) was that 'Unemployment is now higher and more persistent than it has ever been at any point in British history, including the 1930s'. For some groups – young people, young black men in particular, unskilled workers over the age of fifty-five – and for some areas, for example the inner city, the situation was much worse than that suggested by the national figures.

What has been happening since the 1950s is massive changes in the job market. Five million jobs, Leadbeater and Mulgan calculate, have gone from manufacturing industry since 1950. Eight million new jobs have been created in service industries but they have not been taken by those, mostly men, displaced by the collapse of manufacturing. In the years after 1979, the pace of these changes accelerated. A third of all surviving jobs in manufacturing disappeared between 1979 and the early 1990s. The result of the changes was the collapse of unskilled work for men. About a third of unskilled men are now without a job (Leadbeater and Mulgan 1994: 6–7).

Many such men will have great difficulty in securing employment in the future, because 'skills and knowledge have become the currency of the modern economy' (Leadbeater and Mulgan 1994: 8). Without such skills, securing employment becomes increasingly problematic. Britain's labour force stands out for its poor qualifications and lack of training. An OECD report on Britain in 1991 referred to 'chronic skill shortages and inadequate training of the labour force' (quoted in Taylor Gooby 1991: 114). Two-thirds of British workers have no vocational or professional qualifications, compared with only one-quarter of the German workforce (Commission on Social Justice 1993: 34).

Full employment was, perhaps, the greatest achievement of the postwar welfare state. It did more to abolish poverty than the Labour government's social security provisions. It arguably did more for people's quality of life and sense of wellbeing than the other innovations in social welfare policy. High rates of unemployment make the attainment of other welfare-state goals unattainable because of the cost of unemployment and the way it creates and exacerbates other problems. It also has broader social implications. 'To tolerate high unemployment while maintaining social stability,' say Leadbeater and Mulgan, 'means accepting authoritarian measures to police a society divided against itself' (1994: 4).

What has been the government response? After some activity in the early 1970s, the government response after 1979 was that there was little government could do. It was all a question of market adjustment. Essentially, government in the 1980s did three things. First, it almost continuously reconstructed the unemployment statistics, allegedly in search of greater statistical accuracy. Second, government worked hard to reduce the value of the social security benefits available to the unemployed and to tighten the conditions of eligibility. The aim was simple – and, the government argued, constructive – to encourage the unemployed back into low-paid employment. Third, the government promoted a succession of training schemes. Such schemes did, at the least, keep some of the unemployed off the streets and did something to maintain work habits.

In the 1992 general election, no political party, says Glynn, 'offered a convincing programme for what was confidently expected to be a long term problem' (1994: 84). In fact, no party offered any real strategy, let alone a strategy that might be described as convincing. Simply pursuing economic growth is clearly no answer. Jobless growth is now clearly a fact of life – and if total unemployment does fall a little that can still be accompanied by increases in long-term unemployment. There was no attempt to develop a full-blooded employment service. There were no broad initiatives to improve education or develop high-quality training. There was no attempt, either, at public-sector job creation, which experts (e.g. Layard 1986) showed could be achieved at very low cost with considerable economic and social benefits.

The return of mass unemployment was by far the biggest challenge which confronted the welfare state in the period 1945–95. Governments in the 1980s and early 1990s failed the test – not because of action but because of inaction.

To a proactive stance

The conception of the welfare state that was dominant in 1945, and that dominated the next fifty years, was a reactive one. The welfare state was about reacting to perceived problems – want, disease, ignorance, squalor and idleness – to use Beveridge's categorisation. The welfare state has remained trapped in this reactive mode – responding to problems rather than seeking to prevent problems, promote welfare or extend opportunities.

The Labour Party's Commission on Social Justice argues very vigorously for a new, positive concept of the welfare state. 'To be an effective Commission on Social Justice,' the Commission argued, 'we must equally be a Commission on Economic Opportunity' (Commission on Social Justice 1994: 1). The Commission went on to argue that public policy must shift its focus from Beveridge's five great evils to the 'five great opportunities' that the Commission saw as the basis of social cohesion and economic security in the future – lifelong learning, work, good health, a safe environment and financial independence (Commission on Social Justice 1993: 50).

The welfare state has failed to move from a reactive to a promotional mode, to a redefinition of the role of social policy. We know much more about the significance of the five great opportunities for a productive, contented society at peace with itself. We know something about how to pursue them but we need a much more positive approach to the potential of public and social policy to promote the good society. To see the welfare state as being simply about responding to acknowledged problems is inadequate. We need to move to see it as a mechanism for extending opportunities.

Race and gender

Since 1945 the position of women in society has changed dramatically and Britain has become a multiracial society. How successfully has the welfare state responded to those challenges?

The crucial change in women's position has been in relation to paid employment. Seventy per cent of women are in paid employment in the 1990s and women constitute almost half the workforce. The economy needs them – indeed, depends upon them.

To what extent has social policy responded to the changed employment position of women, to the challenge of supporting them in their new economic role? The brief answer is that it has failed to respond. There has been little expansion of day care for young children, and little attempt actively to support women in caring for elderly people, which are still seen primarily as women's responsibilities. A clear illustration of the failure of social policy is that motherhood is still a major handicap in the labour market. Joshi (1991) attempted to calculate the loss of earnings that a woman suffers as a result of moving from marriage to motherhood. It remains enormous.

The increased proportion of women in paid employment is both a cause and a result of changing views of the position of women in society – their role and rights. We have become much more aware of the discrimination women suffer in employment, of the fact that women's earnings average about 70 per cent of male earnings, of male biases in the education system, of the National Health Service's failure adequately to respond to women's particular health needs, of what has come to be known, not altogether accurately, as the feminisation of poverty.

Just as feminist analysis has highlighted a range of issues where the welfare state has responded poorly to facts and insights about women's position, so has analysis of the position of ethnic minorities. Such analysis has pointed out how the education system has failed to adapt to the special needs of ethnic minority children, how the Health Service has been slow to recognise their particular health needs, how there is discrimination at work, earnings are lower, unemployment is higher, housing conditions are worse than those of the native population – and so on.

The welfare state *has* responded. There has been legislation outlawing discrimination on grounds of race or gender. There has been legislation seeking to guarantee equal pay. There have been attempts to make schools and health services more responsive to the needs of ethnic minorities and women. But there are very clear failures. Women's opportunities are clearly *not* equal. There has been no major development of day care for young children or elderly dependent people. Members of ethnic minorities still suffer a range of disadvantages.

The crucial weakness of welfare-state policies in relation to women is society's continued failure to define the personal as political. Until society can accept the clear finding of research that it is demands on women in the home that determine their opportunities outside the home, in the public sphere, there can be little progress. Equally, until society accepts the correction of the disadvantages of race as an important issue for public policy there will be little progress on that front.

Conclusion

How successfully has this collection of policies, programmes and institutions that we call the welfare state responded to the changes and challenges of the last fifty years? It is a question both about an approach to managing economic and social affairs and about actual government policies. A balanced judgement would be that though there have been important achievements, these have been limited and there has been a failure to respond creatively to new challenges. Supporters of the welfare state have failed to grasp the need for continuous creative review. Governments have lost confidence in welfare-state policies – for a variety of reasons but partly, at least, because of their seeming inability to respond to new challenges.

The conclusion to be drawn is not that the state has no useful role in welfare but that we need to think hard and creatively about what that role is and how best – in the light of fifty years of experience – we can as a society respond to the challenges to the quality of our social life that we have so far failed properly to face.

Acknowledgement

I am much indebted to Marion Crowley for help with the statistics for this chapter and for her comments on an earlier draft.

References

Audit Commission (1986), *Making A Reality of Community Care*, London, HMSO.
Baldock, J. (1994), The personal social services: the politics of care, in V. George and S. Miller (eds), *Social Policy: Towards 2000*, London, Routledge.
Balls, E. (1993), *Danger: Men Not at Work*, London, IPPR.
Barr, N. and Coulter, F. (1990), Social security, in J. Hills (ed.), *The State of Welfare*, Oxford, Clarendon Press.
Board for Social Responsibility (1995), *Something To Celebrate*, London, Church House Publishing.
Bosanquet, N. (1992), Interim report: the NHS, in R. Jowell *et al.*, *British Social Attitudes: 9th Report*, Aldershot, Dartmouth Publishing.
Boswell, J. (1990), *Community and the Economy*, London, Routledge.
Bradshaw, J. (1993), *Household Budgets and Living Standards*, York, Joseph Rowntree Foundation.
Central Statistical Office (1995), *Social Trends 25*, London, HMSO.
Clarke, J., *et al.* (1994), The impact of managerialism, in J. Clark *et al.* (eds), *Managing Social Policy*, London, Sage.

Clarke, M. and Stewart, J. (1987), The public service orientation and the citizen, *Local Government Policy Making*, 14:1, 34–40.

Commission on Social Justice (1993), *The Justice Gap*, London, IPPR.

Commission on Social Justice (1994), *Social Justice*, London, Vintage.

Deacon, A. (1995), Spending more to achieve less? Social security since 1945, in D. Gladstone (ed.), *British Social Welfare*, London, UCL Press.

Deakin, N. (1993), A future for collectivism, in R. Page and J. Baldock (eds), *Social Policy Review 5*, Canterbury, Social Policy Association.

Dean, H. (1994), Social security. The cost of persistent poverty, in V. George and S. Miller (eds), *Social Policy Towards 2000*, London, Routledge.

Dean, H. and Taylor Gooby, P. (1992), *Dependency Culture: The Explosion of a Myth*, Hemel Hempstead, Harvester Wheatsheaf.

Evandrou, M., *et al.* (1990), The personal social services, in J. Hills (ed.), *The State of Welfare*, Oxford, Clarendon Press.

Field, F. (1989), *Losing Out*, Oxford, Blackwell.

George, V. and Miller, S. (1994a), Squaring the welfare circle, in V. George and S. Miller (eds), *Social Policy Towards 2000*, London, Routledge.

George, V. and Miller, S. (1994b), The Thatcherite attempt to square the circle, in V. George and S. Miller (eds), *Social Policy Towards 2000*, London, Routledge.

George, V. and Miller, S. (1994c), 2000 and beyond, in V. George and S. Miller (eds), *Social Policy Towards 2000*, London, Routledge.

Gladstone, D. (1995), Introduction: change, continuity and welfare, in D. Gladstone (ed.), *British Social Welfare*, London, UCL Press.

Glennerster, H. (1995), *British Social Policy Since 1945*, Oxford, Blackwell.

Glennerster, H. and Low, W. (1990), Education and the welfare state: does it add up?, in J. Hills (ed.), *The State of Welfare*, Oxford, Clarendon Press.

Glynn, S. (1994), Employment: welfare, work and politics, in V. George and S. Miller (eds), *Social Policy Towards 2000*, London, Routledge.

Griffiths, R. (1988), *Community Care: Agenda for Action*, London, HMSO.

Henkel, M. (1991), The new 'evaluative' state, *Public Administration*, 69, 121–36.

Hewitt, P. and Leach, P. (1993), *Social Justice, Children and Families*, London, IPPR.

Hills, J. (1993), *The Future of Welfare*, York, Joseph Rowntree Foundation.

House of Commons Social Security Committee (1995), *First Report. Low Income Statistics: Low Income Families, 1989–1922*, London, HMSO.

Johnson, N. (1990), *Reconstructing the Welfare State*, Hemel Hempstead, Harvester Wheatsheaf.

Joshi, H. (1991), Sex and motherhood as handicaps in the labour market, in M. Maclean and D. Groves (eds), *Women's Issues in Social Policy*, London, Routledge.

Klein, R. (1993), O'Goffe's tale, in C. Jones (ed.), *New Perspectives on the Welfare State in Europe*, London, Routledge.

Layard, R. (1986), *How to Beat Unemployment*, Oxford, Oxford University Press.

Leadbeater, C. and Mulgan, G. (1994), The end of unemployment: bringing work to life, *Demos*, 2.

Le Grand, J. (1990), The state of welfare, in J. Hills (ed.), *The State of Welfare*, Oxford, Clarendon Press.

Le Grand, J. and Bartlett, W. (eds) (1993), *Quasi-Markets and Social Policy*, London, Macmillan.

Ling, T. (1994), The new managerialism and social security, in J. Clarke, *et al.* (eds), *Managing Social Policy*, London, Sage.

Lister, R. (1989), Social security, in M. McCarthy (ed.), *The New Politics of Welfare*, London, Macmillan.

Lowe, R. (1993), *The Welfare State in Britain Since 1945*, London, Macmillan.

Oppenheim, C. (1994), *The Welfare State: Putting the Record Straight*, London, CPAG.

Pinker, R. (1971), *Social Theory and Social Policy*, London, Heinemann.

Taylor Gooby, P. (1991), *Social Change, Social Welfare and Social Science*, Hemel Hempstead, Harvester Wheatsheaf.

Ungerson, C. (1987), *Policy is Personal: Sex, Gender and Informal Care*, London, Tavistock.

Whiteside, N. (1995), Employment policy: a chronicle of decline?, in D. Gladstone (ed.), *British Social Welfare*, London, UCL Press.

4

Political leadership

Philip Norton

The prime minister and cabinet form the apex of British government. They exercise no legal powers. Their capacity to determine public policy is based on convention and political reality. Parliamentary elections determine which party will dominate in the House of Commons. The leader of that party is invited to form the government and then appoints a cabinet composed of other leading members of that party. The ministers so appointed are responsible, individually and collectively, to parliament. The cabinet agrees the measures to be laid before parliament and the party majority in the House of Commons is usually sufficient to ensure that those measures are then passed.

So described, leadership in British government is both coherent and responsible. It is a description that has come under increasing criticism in recent years. Ministers have been variously criticised for failing to abide by the conventions of individual and collective ministerial responsibility, and for failing to resign when mistakes are made by them or in their name. Collective decision making has been displaced by personal rule by the prime minister. The claim that Britain had a form of prime ministerial government was variously debated in the 1960s and 1970s. In his 1976 Dimbleby lecture, Lord Hailsham warned of the potential for an 'elective dictatorship' in Britain (Hailsham 1976). For many commentators, that potential was realised during the premiership of Margaret Thatcher. She led a government composed of ministers determined to ensure that her ideological agenda was implemented. The impact of Thatcherism on the political, economic and social system of Britain could be taken as giving credence to this perception of leadership in government.

However, this critique is misleading. It suggests major changes in practice when none has taken place. It emphasises an accretion of power to the premiership when longer-term pressures are at work that are limiting, rather than enhancing, the capacity of ministers to affect outcomes. Recent years may have seen a greater desire by ministers to achieve a particular programme of measures, but their capacity to achieve those outcomes has been increasingly limited. This is not to suggest that the Thatcher premiership was not powerful in affecting the political agenda, nor in achieving particular outcomes, but it is to suggest that it was unique in British politics.

This chapter advances three basic propositions about the nature of leadership in British government. First, there has been no paradigmatic change in the practice of ministers in exercising responsibility, individually and collectively. Ministers are no less likely to resign now than they were in previous decades for mistakes made by them or under them.

Second, the capacity of the prime minister to determine policy outcomes derives from the combination of several variables, notably the purpose of the individual in seeking office, the political skills of the individual, and the circumstances faced by the individual in office. Given that purpose and skill differ from individual to individual, prime ministerial power varies from premiership to premiership. Given that circumstances change, prime ministerial power is variable during the course of a premiership.

Third, pressures on the prime minister and other ministers are increasing, with responsibilities growing but the capacity to affect outcomes decreasing. These pressures are particularly marked in the case of departmental ministers, limiting the roles that they can perform. Though Margaret Thatcher's leadership over eleven and a half years may stand out as a feature of political leadership in postwar decades, the most important feature may prove to be the increasing demands made on those occupying the apex of government. Though Margaret Thatcher has departed, the pressures on ministers have not.

Ministerial responsibility

The relationship of government to parliament is governed by two conventions of the constitution, those of individual and collective ministerial responsibility. The former stipulates that ministers are responsible to parliament for their own actions and those of their officials. The latter stipulates that ministers as a collective body are responsible to the House of Commons for the decisions of government. Once decisions are taken by cabinet, ministers are expected loyally to support them. They stand united before the House and the country. If the cabinet fails to maintain the confidence of the House of Commons, it is expected to tender its resignation or seek a dissolution of parliament.

There are a number of problems with these conventions. One is the relationship between the two. Even if individual ministers make mistakes, the cloak of collective responsibility may be invoked to protect them. If their colleagues in government stand by them, then the party majority in the House may be used to ward off critical motions. Another problem is that of definition. What precisely is meant by 'responsibility'? As Marshall and Moodie (1967: 58) noted, the word has a range of nuances. It may attribute action to the author, indicate a relationship or division of function, or designate blame or praise. In practice, each definition has been applied to the convention. The one that has attracted most critical attention has been that attributing blame. If serious mistakes are made, be it by the minister or a civil servant acting in the minister's name, then the presumption is that the minister should resign.

The presumption in recent years appears to be that the doctrine has been largely rendered untenable by the refusal of ministers to resign following mistakes by them or their officials. This presumption embodies two myths. One is that the convention has little relevance today. Even were the basis for this presumption (that ministers are less willing to resign than used to be the case) to be true, the presumption derived from it (that the convention is no longer relevant) is not. However, the basis for the presumption is unfounded. Ministers may be unwilling to leave office if they make mistakes, but in that there is no deviation from past practice.

The convention of individual ministerial responsibility remains important, and it does so for legal and parliamentary reasons. There are four points that can be made about the convention that establish its continuing importance and the extent to which there has been no significant shift in the practice of ministers.

First, the convention remains important in legal terms because it stipulates that statutory powers are vested in individual ministers. No statutory powers are vested in the prime minister or cabinet. As Nevil Johnson (1980: 84) has noted, 'the enduring effect of the doctrine of ministerial responsibility has been over the past century or so that powers have been vested in ministers and on a relentlessly increasing scale'. The past fifty years have seen a substantial increase in the volume of legislation (Hansard Society 1993: 10–13). That legislation has conferred important powers on ministers. One of the most substantial acts passed in the 1980s, for example, was the Education Reform Act. It is replete with sections beginning: 'This section applies where the Secretary of State proposes to make...', 'The Secretary of State may make regulations requiring...', 'The Secretary of State may by order direct that the provisions of sections 5 and 6(1)(b) of this Act shall have effect as if...', 'The Secretary of State may by order amend...'. Expressed purely in legal terms, the doctrine dictates a form not of prime ministerial or cabinet government but of ministerial government.

Second, the convention remains important in parliamentary terms because it dictates that ministers appear in parliament to speak for their departments. Ministers speak and answer questions at the dispatch box. They alone can do so. Their officials are confined to a box at the back of the chamber and can take no formal part in the proceedings. Civil servants may appear before a parliamentary select (but not standing) committee, but they answer for their ministers, not for their departments (with the exception of permanent secretaries, who appear before the Public Accounts Committee in their own right as accounting officers for their departments). It is the minister in practice who decides which officials, if any, will appear. What civil servants may say is circumscribed, the restrictions being detailed in the Osmotherly memorandum (*Memorandum of Guidance for Officials Appearing before Select Committees*), first issued in 1972 and variously updated and modified since. The doctrine may be seen as both useful and a limitation from the perspective of parliament. It is useful in dictating that ministers are answerable to parliament – thus providing a clear focus for parliamentary questions and attention – but a limitation in that it restricts what may be obtained directly from civil servants. Regardless of the normative aspect, the convention shapes parliamentary practices.

Third, it remains important in stipulating that ministers are culpable for mistakes that they themselves make. It does not necessarily follow that culpability should lead to resignation and ministers have not necessarily made it a practice to resign when criticised for poor decisions or errors of judgement. Nonetheless, the doctrine ensures that ministers are the focus of criticism, and that criticism can lead to resignation. There has been no change of practice in recent years (see, for example Finer 1956; Marshall 1984; Pyper 1994). Ministers are just as likely – indeed, more likely – now to resign as in the past for errors on their part. In the thirty-four years from 1945 to 1979, thirteen ministers resigned because of mistakes of one sort or another on their part. In the sixteen years between 1979 and 1995, the number was sixteen. The increase since 1979 is accounted for, in part, by ministers resigning as a consequence of scandal or criticism surrounding their personal lives, but the number resigning for policy failures or errors of political judgement is even more significant (almost twice the number that resigned between 1945 and 1979). The former category (personal scandals) comprises cabinet ministers Cecil Parkinson and David Mellor, and junior ministers Michael Mates, Neil Hamilton, Tim Smith, Patrick Nicholls, Tim Yeo, Michael Brown and the Earl of Caithness. The latter category comprises cabinet ministers Lord Carrington, Humphrey Atkins, Leon Brittan, and Nicholas Ridley, and junior ministers Richard Luce, Nicholas Fairbairn and Edwina Currie.

Fourth, the doctrine stipulates that ministers are answerable for the actions of their civil servants. This has been taken to encompass culpability for mistakes made by civil servants. A mistake by officials is assumed by some commentators to justify the minister's resignation. Ministers have been criticised in recent years for not resigning following mistakes made by their departments. However, there has again been no change in practice. There is no pattern of ministers resigning because of errors made by their departments. The resignation of Agriculture Minister Sir Thomas Dugdale in 1954, in the Crichel Down affair,[1] is cited as an exemplar of a resignation resulting from a minister complying with the doctrine (Chester 1954: 389). More recent research suggests that Dugdale did not resign because he felt responsible for his officials but rather because he had lost the support of his backbenchers (Griffith 1987) – exactly the same reason given for resigning by Leon Brittan over the Westland affair in January 1986.[2] In practice, ministers distinguish between policy, for which they take the blame if things go wrong, and policy implementation by officials; if there is a failing in the latter, of which the minister could not realistically have cognisance, then the minister takes corrective action to ensure that the mistake is not repeated and that action is taken against the officials who made the mistake. This distinction was central, for example, in the decision of William Whitelaw not to resign following a breach of security at Buckingham Palace in 1982. He was told by the prime minister that 'the Home Secretary could not be regarded as directly responsible for the operational action of members in the organisations for which he had overall responsibility'. He noted that similar arguments had been made by his ministers and officials at the Home Office (Whitelaw 1990: 277). The doctrine remains important in stipulating that the minister is the one who answers to parliament for what has happened and takes such action as necessary to prevent a repetition.

The doctrine thus remains important and it is as important now as it was fifty years ago. It may not be as important as some commentators believe it to be, but there has been no dramatic change in the doctrine and in compliance with it during that period. It has seen some changes. Civil servants are now more visible, given the increase in appearances before select committees, there has been some naming of civil servants in reports on maladministration and policy failures (Norton 1982: 58–60), and parliamentary written questions about *Next Steps* agencies are answered by the head of the agency rather than directly by the minister (Pyper 1994),

---

1 In 1937 the Air Ministry acquired by compulsory purchase land in Dorset known as Crichel Down. After the war the land passed into the hands of the Ministry of Agriculture. Promises to local landowners that they could bid for the tenancy were not kept. A local landowner who had previously owned part of the land was not able to buy it back. Protests from the local MP and others led to an official inquiry and criticism in the resulting report of named officials. After initially playing down the impact of the report, the Minister (Dugdale) announced to the House of Commons that he was resigning.

2 At the end of 1985 a dispute between two cabinet ministers – Defence Secretary Michael Heseltine and Trade and Industry Secretary Leon Brittan – over whether Britain's last helicopter manufacturer (the Westland Helicopter Company) should enter into a partnership with an American company or a European consortium became public. In January 1986, extracts from a confidential letter from the Solicitor General to Mr Heseltine, warning of certain inaccuracies in a letter he had written were leaked to the press. A subsequent inquiry traced the leak to Brittan's office. The day after he had faced a highly critical meeting of Conservative MPs at the party's 1922 Committee, Brittan resigned. Heseltine himself had earlier resigned in protest at the way the issue had been dealt with in cabinet by the prime minister.

but the overall picture remains one not greatly dissimilar to that of fifty years ago.

A similar generalisation can be drawn about collective ministerial responsibility. There has certainly been an erosion of some aspects of the convention. The most notable erosion has taken place in terms of the confidentiality accorded cabinet deliberations and the unity of ministers once a decision has been made by cabinet. The secrecy of cabinet meetings was undermined significantly by the publication of the Crossman diaries and later by the diaries of other cabinet ministers such as Tony Benn and Barbara Castle. Ministers now frequently brief journalists on an unattributable basis about what went on in cabinet. The Labour governments of Harold Wilson and James Callaghan, and the Conservative governments of Margaret Thatcher and John Major, have been marked by semi-public and sometimes public disagreements among cabinet ministers, spectacularly so in the case of the Westland affair (Linklater and Leigh 1986). Some have had difficulty supporting government decisions on the public platform and even on occasion in the division lobbies. The convention was formally suspended by the prime minister in 1975 in order to allow ministers to campaign on both sides in the referendum debate on continued membership of the European Community and again in 1977 in order to allow ministers to vote in either lobby on the second reading of the European Assembly Elections Bill. The convention, it can be argued, is clearly not what it was.

Yet the convention of collective responsibility continues to have a powerful effect on government practices and ministerial behaviour. Cabinet minutes remain secret for thirty years. It is these minutes, rather than a particular interpretation given by a minister to a journalist, that guides official action. Even extensive unofficial reports, such as those provided by Crossman, appear well after the event. The suspension of the convention in 1975 followed a precedent set in 1932 and did not extend to allowing ministers to speak in the House against the government's recommendation. (One junior minister, Eric Heffer, did so and was dismissed.) Ministers unable to accept government decisions resign. In the fifty years from 1945 to 1995, thirty-one ministers resigned because they could not support government decisions. Of these resignations, nineteen took place in the thirty years from 1945 to 1975 and twelve took place in the twenty years after 1975.

The convention not only ensures unity in voting behaviour by ministers but has been used in recent years to ensure voting loyalty on the part of parliamentary private secretaries (PPSs), the ministers' unpaid backbench helpers. The convention developed in the nineteenth century. The position of junior ministers was ambiguous but ceased to be so in the twentieth century. In recent decades, PPSs have become sporadically subject to the convention. Some prime ministers have required ministers to dismiss their PPSs for voting against the government. The prospect of dismissal has a powerful effect on PPSs contemplating dissension and so the effect is to extend the government's 'payroll vote' in the House, and to do so at a time when the number of PPSs has grown significantly.

The convention also remains important in determining the stance of the government in response to a defeat in the House of Commons. If defeated on a vote of confidence, the government is expected to resign or to seek a dissolution. In postwar years, the view developed that most, if not all, votes in the House were effectively votes of confidence and that a serious defeat, or even any defeat, would be sufficient to trigger the government's resignation (see the sources cited by Norton 1978a). The continuance of the government in office in the 1970s after several defeats was viewed by some commentators as a change in practice (Schwarz 1980). There was no change in practice (Norton 1978a). Successive governments responded in accordance with precedent. The convention stipulates that the government resigns or requests a dissolution if defeated on an explicitly worded vote of confidence or one declared by the government to constitute a vote of confidence. A defeat on an issue central to government policy, but not one declared a vote of confidence, allows the government the option of seeking a vote of confidence or deciding to resign or request a dissolution. A defeat on any other issue has no constitutional import and the decision facing government is whether to accept the defeat or seek its reversal de facto at a later stage. This delineation has been clear throughout the twentieth century and was enunciated by Prime Minister Stanley Baldwin in 1936 (*House of Commons Debates*, vol. 310, col. 2445; see Norton 1978a: 362). Governments in postwar years have acted in line with precedent.

The convention remains important politically in that it helps maximise party voting in the House of Commons. The government may resort to making a vote one of confidence in order to get its way. John Major resorted to it in May 1993 in order to ensure the House came to a resolution on the European social chapter – necessary in order for the Maastricht Treaty to be ratified – and again in November 1994 to ensure passage of the European Communities (Finance) Bill. The use of the confidence vote may ensure that the government gets its way but it may be a high-risk strategy. If defeated, the prime minister goes to the Palace to tender the government's resignation or (more usually, as in March 1979) to ask for a dissolution. Some Conservative MPs have proved willing to vote against a Conservative government on a vote of confidence – in 1972 on the second reading of the European Communities Bill – or to abstain, as on the second reading of the European Communities (Finance) Bill, but not to do so in sufficient numbers to deny the government a majority.

The conventions of individual and collective ministerial responsibility have seen some changes over the years, but the most notable characteristic of both is the extent to which they remain important in shaping political behaviour and practices. Some commentators bemoan the effects of one or both conventions (e.g. Sedgemore 1980: 74–8), but their comments serve to reinforce the significance of those conventions. As Colin Turpin (1985: 79) has noted of the convention of collective responsibility: 'despite quite frequent minor breaches, occasional major defiance, and different degrees of observance between one administration and another, the principle does express in a general way the actual practice of government'. It continues to do so.

Prime ministerial leadership

If the conventions of the constitution have not changed significantly over the past fifty years, prime ministerial leadership certainly has. Some argue that the change has taken the form of a constant accretion of power to the premiership (Norton 1988: 108). Those who argue this have a problem in explaining why Margaret Thatcher failed to get the trade union reforms she wanted, why she failed to impose her will during the Westland crisis, and why she failed to achieve the results she wanted in the European Community. Some contend that there has been no such accretion of power, arguing instead that collective decision making by the cabinet remains central to British government. They have a problem in explaining why Margaret Thatcher managed to achieve the implementation of key components of her Thatcherite agenda even though she never managed to craft a wholly Thatcherite cabinet or parliamentary party (Norton 1993a; Whiteley *et al.* 1994). There is a third approach, which argues that prime ministerial power is not a constant but rather varies depending on the incumbent and the situation faced by that individual. This approach helps resolve the problems faced by the other approaches.

In an analysis of presidential power in the USA, James Barber (1972) has contended that the president's capacity to affect outcomes is determined by the interaction of three variables: the president's personality, the power situation and the climate of expectations. Personality he dissected into three components: character, world view and style. He then proceeded to offer a study of selected presidents. That study has been subject to various critiques (e.g. George 1974). Particularly pertinent for our purposes, it has been criticised for concentrating on character to the detriment of world view (that is, ideology) and for neglecting the impact of the external environment, even though the significance of that environment was acknowledged in the introduction to the book.

Elsewhere, I have sought to apply an analysis of the individuals occupying the premiership in Britain, but utilising a model that avoids the pitfalls encountered by Barber (Norton 1987). The analysis focuses on the purpose of seeking the premiership. Why does an individual seek to occupy No. 10 Downing Street? The focus is one that allows ideology (wanting to achieve a particular policy goal or agenda) or character (seeking power for personal satisfaction) to emerge as the principal influence, or for both to emerge as important influences. Based on an analysis of purpose, I have generated a typology of premiers. There are four types.

Innovators. These are power-seeking individuals who gain office in order to achieve some future goal, a goal that they themselves have set. The principal example is Margaret Thatcher; she sought office in order to carry out a neo-liberal agenda, later subsumed under the nomenclature of Thatcherism.

Reformers. These are power-seeking individuals who gain office in order to achieve some future goal, but a goal that has been set for them rather than one that is of their own creation. The prime example here among premiers of the past fifty years is Clement Attlee, who led a reforming Labour government in implementing the 1945 Labour manifesto, *Let Us Face the Future.*

Egoists. These are individuals who seek power in order to have power. Being in power is not seen as a means to an end but rather an end in itself. They are concerned with the here and now of politics and doing whatever is necessary to get and to retain power. The most recent example is Harold Wilson, willing to take action to maintain his position and frequently worrying (according to the Crossman diaries) about plots to oust him. According to Crossman, 'He cares about being PM, about politics, about power. He has become de-partied to a great extent, an occupant of Downing Street who adores running things well' (Crossman 1973: 180). Another postwar premier falling in this category is Sir Anthony Eden.

Balancers. These are individuals who are concerned to ensure balance in society. They put present harmony in society ahead of future goals. There are *power-seeking balancers*, who gain office in order to ensure balance, and there are *conscripts*, who do not overtly seek the premiership but who come to the office as compromise candidates for party leadership. Power-seeking balancers include Harold Macmillan on the Conservative side and James Callaghan on the Labour side. Callaghan's political career was 'largely anchored to the ideals of party unity and support for the leader of the day'. He 'applied rigorously Harold Laski's injunctions to secure consent, and to perform the role of broker of ideas' (Kellner and Hitchens 1976: 173, 176). The only postwar conscript is Sir Alec Douglas-Home.

The four categories are not mutually exclusive. Some prime ministers have exhibited the characteristics of more than one type. Edward Heath, for example, was both an innovator and an egoist. One politician who worked closely with him noted that the egoism came first and that he acquired the ideological baggage along the way (Norton 1988: 110).

An analysis of purpose is important in a study of the premiership because it helps explain why occupants of the premiership seek to use the powers of the office. As the examples cited clearly reveal, the purpose has differed significantly among prime ministers over the past fifty years. It does not help explain how or with what effect the powers are used. For the former we have to look at skill; for the latter we have to consider the circumstances.

Skill embodies the way in which prime ministers attempt to achieve their goals. At a general level, a prime minister has to look the part and to have a feel for the job. At a more specific level, a prime minister needs to be able to select, to lead, to anticipate and to react. In leading and in reacting, a prime minister may seek to command, to persuade, to manipulate, or to hide. Knowing which of these approaches to employ constitutes a feel for the office. Its use constitutes a specific skill (Norton 1987: 334).

Some occupants of Number 10 are good at knowing how to use particular skills to achieve their ends. Attlee showed some skill in his appointment of ministers; Heath appointed a personally loyal cabinet – not one minister resigned on policy grounds during his tenure of office. Thatcher was good at times in using her power of command (as during the Falklands War in 1982) but more often than is perhaps realised had to resort to persuasive techniques. Churchill and Macmillan were gifted with an ability to persuade, both of them through a particular rhetorical style. Wilson and Thatcher, especially the former, variously deployed manipulative skills. Few have been good at hiding: that is, leaving others to get on with jobs that attract political flak. Attlee left ministers to get on with their jobs, as did Douglas-Home. Thatcher had a track record of deploying these various techniques as seemed appropriate to achieving her ends.

Some premiers have not demonstrated a surfeit of these skills. Sir Anthony Eden is a good example of someone with remarkably poor skills as a political leader. He was forever interfering in the departmental affairs of his ministers and had difficulty making up his mind. According to one MP, 'his performance prior to Suez had been feeble. He forever temporised and chopped and changed his mind' (Bevins 1965: 37). 'It began to be said of Sir Anthony,' recalled Randolph Churchill (1959: 306), 'that he was a fidget, a fusspot who could not leave well alone'. Heath used command at the expense of persuasion (Norton 1978b). John Major has adopted a reactive style that has been criticised by some within his own party, though he has proved skilful in extricating himself from difficult situations.

A clear purpose and effective political skills may be necessary for a prime minister to achieve what he or she wants, but they are not sufficient. Circumstance is all important. This has various components. What Barber (1972) has defined as the power situation is crucial. A prime minister may be constrained by a divided or critical cabinet, by a small or non-existent parliamentary majority, by an activist House of Commons, an active judiciary, and by the institutions of the European Union. James Callaghan, for example, had to contend with a House of Commons in which his party was outnumbered by the opposition parties. Margaret Thatcher had to contend with a split cabinet during the Westland crisis. The climate of expectation is also important. Citizens may be looking to government to provide results that run counter to what the prime minister wants to achieve. A negative climate (a 'feel bad' factor) among the public or key economic and political actors is also an important constraint. The Major premiership has been marked by a significant and enduring 'feel bad' factor – citizens not expecting the economic situation to improve. A positive climate is an important political resource. A third component of circumstance, not covered by Barber, is objective external conditions. Some of these may be within Britain and potentially within the purview of the prime minister, such as a national strike. Others may be external to British shores and beyond the capacity of the prime minister to influence. If there is a worldwide recession, or climatic changes that affect agricultural production, or regional conflicts that affect international confidence or alliances, then these can limit the capacity for action by the prime minister. In 1974, for example, Heath had to contend with a strike by the National Union of Mineworkers at home and an energy crisis resulting from events in the Middle East.

We thus have five variables that have to come together in order to produce the condition identified by critics as a form of prime ministerial government:

- a goal-oriented prime minister;
- a prime minister with notable political skills;
- a favourable power situation;
- a climate of expectation consonant with the prime minister's goals;
- favourable objective external conditions.

What emerges from this analysis is the recognition that Margaret Thatcher was able to achieve what she did because of a unique combination of variables. There was the combination of a clear future goal (an innovator), with (for most but not all her period of office) political skill, a relatively favourable power situation (large parliamentary majorities, fairly quiescent cabinet, but an increasingly disputatious 'Europe' and judiciary), a relatively favourable climate of expectation (demand for change in 1979 and for economic wealth in the 1980s), and mostly favourable external conditions (economic boom). These were not all present throughout her premiership – hence the variations in her capacity to achieve desired outcomes – and were notably reduced in the late 1980s, creating a situation in which she was politically vulnerable.

That particular combination necessary for a form of prime ministerial government was not present throughout the tenure of her predecessors and successor. The strongest prime minister after Thatcher is Attlee (future oriented, skilful, favourable domestic power situation and – for most of his tenure of office – climate of expectation). But the rest are as notable for the variables that limited their capacity to achieve desired results as for those that facilitated their attempts to get the outcomes they wanted. Churchill, Eden, Macmillan, Douglas-Home, Wilson and Callaghan lacked any clear future goal. Churchill, Eden and Douglas-Home were not skilful political operators. Heath was a forceful premier but his prime ministerial style created difficulties in his relationship with backbenchers. Wilson and Callaghan had to contend with a badly divided party and Callaghan with a non-existent parliamentary majority. Changes in the climate of expectation affected adversely the premierships of Macmillan (after 1960), Douglas-Home and Callaghan. External conditions adversely affected Macmillan, Heath, Wilson and Callaghan.

As for Margaret Thatcher's successor, he is a balancer rather than an innovator, who, after 1992, has had to contend with a small – and decreasing – parliamentary majority, a divided party (and, on occasion, cabinet), an activist judiciary, a 'feel bad' factor, a recession and an increasingly powerful 'Europe', especially following ratification of the Maastricht Treaty in 1993. By 1995, claims of prime ministerial government appeared rather hollow.

The combination of variables changes over time, producing shifts in the capacity of the prime minister to achieve desired results. These variables have rarely come together in a way that allows the prime minister to be the dominant force and to achieve a particular political agenda. Nonetheless, given the experience of the Thatcher premiership, it is legitimate to ask whether there is the possibility of another Margaret Thatcher emerging? The answer is that it is increasingly unlikely. Margaret Thatcher exploited a combination unique to a short period. There has been a change in some of the components that enabled her to achieve near dominance in policy making. Those changes were already becoming apparent during her tenure of office and will serve to constrain any future occupant of the office from achieving what she did. Prime ministerial government is giving way to prime ministerial frustration. There are clear underlying trends limiting the capacity of the prime minister and other ministers to determine outcomes.

The pressures of office

Though a forceful individual such as Margaret Thatcher may be able to influence government decisions, the capacity of the prime minister to determine outcomes is limited and increasingly limited. The demands on the office of prime minister, and of other ministers, are such as to create a situation in which more responsibilities are assumed but in which the power to decide action is declining.

The changes that have served to limit political leadership can be subsumed under two heads: increased responsibilities and power fragmentation.

Increased responsibilities

The responsibilities of government have grown enormously in the latter half of the century. The public sector increased dramatically in the late 1940s with the creation of the welfare state. Growth in the public sector has pushed government to the fore as a provider and, on the face of it, strengthened government as a political actor. Yet the growth of government has had the effect also of placing burdens on individual ministers. A growth in the sectors covered by government has not been matched by a dramatic increase in the number of ministers. Consequently, the departmental burdens on ministers have become greater. As the public sector has grown, so more and more groups have lobbied government to achieve particular policies or policy adjustments. The time for ministers to reflect and impose their own agenda has decreased as more and more time has been taken up having to act as brokers between competing demands.

The formal responsibilities have become greater since 1973 as a consequence of membership of the European Community, now the European Union (EU). More issues have to be discussed with EU partners and more time is absorbed travelling to Brussels and to national capitals. Those responsibilities have grown as the sectors covered by the EU treaties have increased in number.

The burden of responsibilities is not confined to formal ministerial duties in the department. Most ministers are drawn from the House of Commons. They have responsibilities to the House in terms of answering questions, taking part in debates and seeing legislation through. They are also required to take part in votes. The changes in these burdens have not been great over the half century. What has changed significantly has been the demands made of them by other MPs and by their constituents. There has been a dramatic increase in the demands made of MPs by constituents and by pressure groups (Norton 1993b: chs 9, 10). MPs pursue the matters raised by constituents and groups with the appropriate minister. This is done through correspondence and through meetings, formal and informal. A relatively small volume of correspondence flowed between MPs and ministers in the 1950s, a much greater volume in succeeding decades. By 1990, ministers were sending out in total about 250,000 letters a year, mostly to MPs (Elms and Terry 1990). Though the letters were drafted by officials, many ministers read each draft and some spent time revising and rewriting them. MPs have also taken the opportunity to arrange meetings with ministers – leading delegations of constituents or representatives of local authorities or particular organisations – and to corner ministers in the division lobbies to pursue an issue. The use of the division lobbies as a means of raising issues personally with ministers is an often overlooked feature of parliamentary voting practices. And ministers themselves have responsibilities as constituency MPs. They have to deal with constituency issues, raising them with the appropriate fellow minister, and are expected to be visible in the constituency. Ministers hold constituency surgeries. Time is taken up dealing with constituency correspondence. 'Ministers who have constituencies to look after don't stop and can't hand over the work to someone else: it just has to be fitted in somehow' (Currie 1989: 233).

On top of all this, ministers have party duties (addressing conferences and meetings at national, regional and local level), public duties (meeting representatives of different bodies, addressing conferences of bodies affected by the department's activities) and media tasks (giving interviews, issuing statements and press releases). The result is that they have little time for personal relaxation and little time, individually and collectively, to think strategically about policy. 'It is hard enough work to govern,' wrote one former cabinet minister, 'to think anew while governing is desperately difficult' (Patten 1995: 2). When, exceptionally, in September 1995 the cabinet gathered at Chequers for a forward look in policy terms, the gathering lasted less than a day – ministers had departed by early evening – and no papers had been prepared for circulation in advance.

By the end of the period under review, the lives of individual ministers were largely dictated by their diary secretaries and dominated by their red boxes, packed each evening with papers that required attention by the following day: departmental submissions, cabinet papers, letters for signature, parliamentary questions, constituency mail, briefings for speeches, and various requests to attend meetings, be interviewed, or write something (Currie 1989: 231–3). In 1992, one junior minister so organised his work that he refused to 'do' boxes. He was very much the exception that proved the rule.

The effect of the increased responsibilities appears to have bred a culture of desk dependence, ministers getting on with departmental duties and neglecting both strategic thinking and collective deliberation. One cabinet minister in the period 1992–94 did not always endear himself to colleagues by daring to comment on other ministers' proposals. The fact that he should stray into territory other than that of his own department was deemed unusual. During the Conservative leadership contest in 1995, one minister was asked in a television interview if the contest was not taking ministers away from their duties. 'No,' replied the minister, 'I have been at my desk in the Treasury today'. The premise that ministers should be working at their desks – rather than going away and thinking about the direction their party and their leader should be taking – was accepted uncritically.

The more responsibilities ministers individually have acquired, the less time they have, individually and collectively, to adopt a proactive role in policy making. The Thatcher government achieved it briefly, but the broad direction was shaped largely by thinking before entering office. The emergence and direction of Thatcherism during the period of office was in large part fortuitous. Ministers increasingly got bogged down in detail and in reacting to events.

Power fragmentation
The period also witnessed a significant fragmentation of power. A great deal of policy-making power moved beyond the domestic arena. Within the

British polity, there was greater pluralism, manifested in a notable proliferation of pressure groups. The divide between domestic and international issues was eroded as more 'intermestic' issues came to the fore. The capacity to affect economic outcomes moved increasingly beyond the control of national institutions and, indeed, international institutions.

In terms of policy-making power flowing formally to institutions beyond the British polity, the most significant change was wrought by membership of the European Community. The Single European Act (1987) and the Treaty on European Union (1993) effected further shifts in the power relationship between the institutions of the nation state and the institutions of the European Community. Nugent (1994: 75–6) aptly summarised the effects of the Treaty on European Union: 'more policy competencies are passed from the member states to the European level, the powers of the institutions at the European level are strengthened, and supranationalism is given a further boost'. National governments, and their political heads, are consequently limited, and increasingly limited, by decisions of those institutions. When Margaret Thatcher returned from the Rome summit in October 1990 and declared 'no, no, no' at the dispatch box in commenting on Jacques Delors' vision of Europe (Norton 1993a: 52), she was expressing her frustration at a situation that was increasingly beyond her control; she had been outvoted by eleven votes to one in Rome on the timetable for implementing stage 2 of the Delors report.

Ministers fly to Brussels for lengthy negotiations. In those negotiations, the British minister is one of fifteen. If the treaties indicate that the issue is to be determined by qualified majority voting, then the decision can be taken and enforced even though the minister has opposed it. Furthermore, most of the preparation for meetings of the Council of Ministers is undertaken not by ministers but by officials, both in the departments and in the Committee of Permanent Representatives. Sometimes ministers do not get a chance to study the papers in any detail until they are on the flight to Brussels.

Some power has therefore passed in effect to officials. But there has been a much more pervasive fragmentation of power within the polity. Since the mid-1960s, there has been a greater activism on the part of the judiciary (Norton 1994: 500–2). In 1993, a ruling of the House of Lords meant that ministers could no longer rely on the doctrine of crown immunity to ignore orders of a court. The power of the courts has also been enhanced by membership of the EU, as European law takes precedence over British law. In 1990, in the *Factortame* case, the European Court of Justice held that the courts had the power to suspend the application of an act of parliament that on the face of it appeared to breach European Community law. Parliament is also a less predictable body than it was. Government since 1970 has been more vulnerable to pressure from backbenchers than it was in the quarter century after 1945 (Norton 1996). It is also subject to greater parliamentary scrutiny than before, through the medium of departmental select committees (Drewry 1989). These parliamentary changes may not have made a dramatic difference. Their importance is as one element of several which, in combination, serve to constrain ministers. And organised interests have grown substantially in number and been prepared to enter the political arena. The years since 1960 have witnessed a dramatic increase in the number of pressure groups, especially cause groups determined to influence public policy (of interest groups listed by Shipley 1979, more than 40 per cent had come into existence since 1960). Organised interests are better able than unorganised interests both to lobby and to resist government. Some interests are especially well entrenched and prepared to fight their corner. When the Thatcher government moved against organised interests, its successes were against essentially 'soft' targets, enjoying relatively little public support, such as trade unions and universities.

The fragmentation of power has taken place against a backdrop of economic change that renders national governments and international organisations even less able than before to affect outcomes. Many problems – environmental as well as economic – do not recognise national borders. International bodies are set up to address these problems but even they cannot cope with them. The institutions of the EU cannot cope with economic developments that transcend EU borders. 'There will certainly not be a Europe that can control international flows of money and information' (Waldegrave 1995: 175). However dynamic and forceful national leaders may be, they are individually unable to affect these developments. These developments offer the potential for conflict between popular expectations and the capacity of governments to meet those expectations. Where that conflict occurs, the likelihood is a mood of popular dissatisfaction with government.

Conclusion

The conventions of collective and ministerial responsibility help shape ministerial behaviour in Britain. Changes in adherence to those conventions over the past fifty years have not been substantial. Debate about adherence to the conventions tends to miss the more significant developments that have reduced the capacity of ministers to affect outcomes. The consequence of a fragmentation of political power and greater global economic interdependence is that the responsibilities of ministers have increased while their capacity to affect outcomes has decreased.

The opportunities for the prime minister and ministers to determine outcomes are thus increasingly limited. Political leadership has become more demanding. Underlying pressures suggest that it will be even more difficult to achieve in future years. The Thatcher premiership should therefore be recognised as a specific and limited phenomenon, as prime ministerial hegemony was confined to a period shorter than the length of the premiership, and is not something from which generalisations about 'prime ministerial government' can be drawn. Some leadership in British government is possible, but those exercising it effectively have to choose the particular goals they wish to achieve and overcome substantial hurdles in order to achieve them. In short, the capacity for political leadership is not what it was. The top of Disraeli's 'greasy pole' has splintered.

References

Barber, J. D. (1972), *The Presidential Character* (4th edn 1992), Englewood Cliffs, Prentice-Hall.

Bevins, R. (1965), *The Greasy Pole*, London, Hodder and Stoughton.

Butler, A. (1995), Unpopular leaders: the British case, *Political Studies*, 43:1, 48–65.

Chester, D. N. (1954), The Crichel Down case, *Public Administration*, 32, 389–401.

Churchill, R. (1959), *The Rise and Fall of Sir Anthony Eden*, London, MacGibbon and Kee.

Crossman, R. (1973), *Diaries of a Cabinet Minister*, vol. 3, London, Hamish Hamilton/ Jonathan Cape.

Currie, E. (1989), *Lifelines*, London, Sidgwick and Jackson.

Drewry, G. (ed.) (1989), *The New Select Committees* (revised edn), Oxford, Oxford University Press.

Elms, T. and Terry, T. (1990), *Scrutiny of Ministerial Correspondence*, London, Cabinet Office Efficiency Unit.

Finer, S. E. (1956), The individual responsibility of ministers, *Public Administration*, 34, 277–96.

George, A. (1974), Assessing presidential character, *World Politics*, 26, 234–82.

Griffith, J. (1987), Crichel Down, *Contemporary Record*, 1:1, 35–40.

Hailsham, Lord (1976), *Elective Dictatorship*, London, BBC.

Hansard Society (1993), *Making the Law: The Report of the Hansard Society Commission on the Legislative Process*, London, Hansard Society.

Johnson, N. (1980), *In Search of the Constitution*, London, Methuen.

Kellner, P. and Hitchens, C. (1976), *Callaghan: The Road to No. 10*, London, Cassell.

Linklater, M. and Leigh, D. (1986), *Not With Honour*, London, Sphere Books.

Marshall, G. (1984), *Constitutional Conventions*, Oxford, Oxford University Press.

Marshall, G. and Moodie, G. (1967), *Some Problems of the Constitution*, London, Hutchinson.

Norton, P. (1978a), Government defeats in the House of Commons: myth and reality, *Public Law*, 360–1.

Norton, P. (1978b), *Conservative Dissidents*, London, Temple Smith.

Norton, P. (1982), *The Constitution in Flux*, Oxford, Blackwell.

Norton, P. (1987), Prime ministerial power: a framework for analysis, *Teaching Politics*, 16:3, 325–45.

Norton, P. (1988), Prime ministerial power, *Social Studies Review*, 3:3, 108–15.

Norton, P. (1989a), Collective ministerial responsibility, *Social Studies Review*, 5:1, 33–6.

Norton, P. (1989b), The constitutional position of parliamentary private secretaries, *Public Law*, 232–6.

Norton, P. (1993a), The Conservative Party from Thatcher to Major, in A. King (ed.), *Britain at the Polls 1992*, Chatham, Chatham House.

Norton, P. (1993b), *Does Parliament Matter?*, Hemel Hempstead, Harvester Wheatsheaf.

Norton, P. (1994), The judiciary, in B. Jones *et al.* (eds), *Politics UK* (2nd edn), Hemel Hempstead, Harvester Wheatsheaf.

Norton, P. (1996), Parliamentary behaviour since 1945, *Talking Politics*, 8:2, 107–14.

Nugent, N. (1994), *The Government and Politics of the European Union* (3rd edn), London, Macmillan.

Patten, J. (1995), *Things to Come: The Tories in the 21st Century*, London, Sinclair-Stevenson.

Pyper, R. (1994), Individual ministerial responsibility: dissecting the doctrine, *Politics Review*, 4:1, 12–16.

Schwarz, J. (1980), Exploring a new role in policy making: the British House of Commons in the 1970s, *American Political Science Review*, 74:1, 33–4.

Sedgemore, B. (1980), *The Secret Constitution*, London, Hodder and Stoughton.

Shipley, P. (1979), *Directory of Pressure Groups and Representative Institutions* (2nd edn), Sevenoaks, Bowker.

Turpin, C. (1985), Ministerial responsibility: myth or reality?, in J. Jowell and D. Oliver (eds), *The Changing Constitution*, Oxford, Oxford University Press.

Waldegrave, W. (1995), The future of parliamentary government, *Journal of Legislative Studies*, 1:2, 175–7.

Whitelaw, W. (1990), *The Whitelaw Memoirs*, London, Headline.

Whiteley, P., Seyd, P. and Richardson, J. (1994), *True Blues*, Oxford, Oxford University Press.

5

British political parties in the last fifty years

Stephen Ingle

Vote, vote, vote for Mr Attlee,
Punch old Churchill on the jaw.
If it wasn't for the King
We would do the blighter in.
Then he wouldn't go a-voting anymore.
(Anon.)

A somewhat less decorous version of this doggerel was chanted by working-class children during the 1950 general election. The inconceivability of such a thing happening in the 1990s tells us a great deal about the way the perception of political parties has changed and indeed about the way the world which political parties inhabit has changed over the last half century. I propose to explore the nature of those changes.

The party system: consensus years, 1945–62

There was great uncertainty concerning the outcome of the general election of 1945. Consider for a moment: the Second World War had been won under a coalition government headed by the Conservative Winston Churchill. His popularity as a war leader had been enormous and he had come to symbolise Britain's refusal to succumb to a superior enemy; he had truly been a light in the darkest hour of the nation. Yet his right-wing stance in prewar politics, especially during the 1926 General Strike, made many ordinary people ambivalent about his and his party's appropriateness to run the nation's affairs in peacetime. For its part, Labour had never formed a majority government and its experiences in minority governments had been less than convincing. As for the Liberals, they were confidently seeking once again to establish themselves as a major force. In these days when opinion polling was in its infancy and the broadcasting media were not extensively used in electioneering there was room both for universal optimism and uncertainty. In the event Labour won a massive victory with an overall majority of 147 seats. Their 393 MPs constituted an increase of no fewer than 239. The Conservatives returned 210 MPs, a decline of 219, and the Liberals won twelve seats, nine fewer than in 1935. In the House of Commons a basically two-party system had emerged, with the Liberals an irrelevance. In terms of votes the Labour Party took approximately 12 million, the Conservatives 10 million and the Liberals 2¼ million. Had this election been fought on a proportional system the Liberals would have won some fifty seats. But it was not, and the next general election, of 1950, confirmed that Britain had a two-party system, for in that election Labour returned 315 MPs, the Conservatives 298 and the Liberals nine. Even in such a close-run race the Liberals were an irrelevance, though the party polled over 2½ million votes.

These figures seem to speak for themselves, indicating a divided nation. That this represented a division primarily based upon social class is not in dispute (Westergaard and Ressler 1980: ch. 1), neither is the fact that the division was very sharply defined (as witness the opening doggerel). What is paradoxical is that this two-party system – based upon social divisions that were as sharp as they were irrefutable – should have been characterised for almost twenty years by consensus politics – the so-called postwar consensus. How to explain this paradox?

Perhaps the single most important fact was the common experience of the miseries, privations and eventual triumphs of war. Class barriers had not tumbled, as socialists like George Orwell had hoped, but they had been subsumed within patriotic sentiment. The nation had – with some notable exceptions – been united and single minded through six crucial years. The common feeling built up during those years was not easily dissipated. Moreover, as Eric Shaw has shown, the Attlee government had presided over a process of transformation:

> the economy had recovered from war-time dislocation, industrial output, productivity and investment all rose substantially, equilibrium in the external account was reached (until rearmament), inflation was well under control, a welfare state was created and, above all, for the first time, full employment was secured. (Shaw 1995: 47–8)

These were years when, according to the economist Sir John Cairncross, 'the government knew where it wanted to go and led the country with an understanding of what was a stake' (Shaw 1995: 59). No wonder, then, that the Conservative Party, to relocate itself in the new order and not to restructure the order itself, declared as its objective to establish 'an alternative policy to socialism which was viable, efficient and humane, which would release and reward enterprise' but which would do so 'without abandoning social justice or reverting to mass unemployment' (Norton and Aughey 1981: 128). With the promulgation of its industrial charter in 1948, committing it to a policy of full employment and Keynesian demand-led economic management, the Conservative Party publicly accepted the postwar consensus as providing a framework within which a modern brand of Conservatism could flourish. The point to grasp here is that the major parties were contesting for the right to manage the state without similar objectives in mind, and it was almost certainly the experiences of wartime, shared by the whole nation (or a very great part of it), which provided the framework of that consensus.

One of the crucial constituents of that consensus was the regular alternation of power between the major parties. After all, a party which believes it has little or no possibility of achieving power is unlikely to support the system which denies it. Now, in the period of the postwar consensus such an expectation could readily be entertained. The 1950 election brought victory to the incumbent Labour government by a hair's breadth and indeed the Conservatives formed the government in 1951. Nobody could question the viability of power rotation until the third successive Conservative victory in 1959, when (not for the last time) articles were written suggesting the possible demise of the Labour Party (Abrams 1961).

I have sought to show elsewhere (Ingle 1989) that in fact those thirteen years of Conservative rule were not an aberration from the long-term, two-party system with regular rotation of parties in office, but the reverse: rotation in power is the aberration. Any perusal of electoral statistics since the last Liberal government, of 1910, indicates the unmistakable dominance of the right in British politics: indeed, I have suggested that in party-modelling terms (Sartori 1976) Britain's is actually not a two-party system but a 'one-party dominant' system (Ingle 1994). There were two reasons, however, for most voters and indeed most practising politicians accepting the delusion of a two-party consensus system: first, it offered the voters an apparent choice without actually inviting major systems changes, and second in the cockpit of parliamentary debate there appears to be a general election campaign going on every day that parliament is in session. Let us consider these points in a little more detail.

Richard Rose (1984) argued persuasively that parties do not make a difference, in the sense, that is, of changes of government bringing major policy changes. I shall show later that I think he is incorrect in the broader perspective but as far as the period of postwar consensus goes, I believe that thrust of his argument is well directed. Andrew Gamble has also argued that Britain's party system was characterised more by consensus politics than by its opposite, adversarial politics. Indeed, political stability demands continuity, not change, of policy. What this meant was that the people had not a choice between policies at elections but a choice between political leaders. If these leaders were actually to change their party rhetoric for reality, Gamble continued, then a 'real rather than a symbolic polarisation' would take place, with unfortunate consequences for stability. 'If the two parties ever became genuine adversaries the system would cease to be

89

workable' (Gamble and Walkland 1984: 184). Gamble referred to this token adversarialism as a sham, and even at the time many commentators criticised 'me-tooism' or 'Butskellism' (an amalgamation of two senior political figures from the major parties during the 1950s, R. A. Butler and Hugh Gaitskell) and spoke of the two main parties as Tweedledum and Tweedledee.

Yet in the Palace of Westminster bitter political battles continued to be fought and not all of these were shams. The nature of parliamentary debate, and the cut and thrust of prime minister's questions, brought a ritual baying for blood. To say that it gave an appearance but not a reality of inter-party hostility would not be wholly accurate: the debate over the British and French invasion of the Suez Canal Zone in 1956 was fiercely real, for example.

In parenthesis ... the media

The 'continuous election' theme was augmented by a development which was to have profound consequences for politics in Britain as elsewhere: the intrusion of the mass media. If one is looking for events or developments which changed the nature of party politics in the last fifty years then the entry into the arena of broadcasting, more especially television broadcasting, has been the greatest. Because of its huge audience and immediate accessibility television has transformed party politics, giving ever-growing influence to media strategists (so-called spin doctors) in the packaging and deployment of policy. It was the Labour strategist and later MP Peter Mandelson who first publicly argued that the days when one did not sell politicians like tins of beans were gone for ever. Nowadays radio and television coverage of politics is so devouring that many have argued that the media create their own agenda. John Major's resignation as party leader and subsequent leadership re-election campaign in 1995, for example, was widely thought to have been a response to intense media pressure. Radio and television interviewers, as well as legitimately questioning political leaders over events and policies closely, seek to trap them into some inadvertent statement that might, used out of context, lead to the creation of an issue which can then be analysed at merciless length. The voracious media appetite for issues could, by its lack of balance, be said to have helped to engender much of the almost universal distrust of politicians which has become such a worrying feature of modern politics in most advanced countries. But back, now, to the 1950s.

The advent of mass-media coverage of political events did much to cement the concept of two-party politics, if for no other reason than the simple 'for' and 'against' format of presentation had a great appeal for programme producers because it made possible the treatment of political issues in an apparently fair and democratic manner. Allowing 'both sides of the argument' to be presented was so natural and easy to produce that it scarcely occurred to anyone that there might be more than two sides to a question. The model for the coverage of elections required the 'swingometer' – the 'swing of the pendulum' theory being given the solid form of an oscillating totem which kept score, but only the score between two teams. The fact that the viewer was both observer and participant (voter) added to the excitement. It was no coincidence that the inventor and original operator of the swingometer was the psephologist Robert McKenzie, whose seminal *British Political Parties* (1955) painted exactly the picture of two-party competition within a consensus frame which his device sought to portray and measure.

The interregnum: the emergence of multiparty Britain, 1962–79

Yet already the moles were tunnelling beneath the two-party consensus. As early as 1958 a Liberal candidate had won a handsome by-election victory against all expectations, even though he was related to Asquith and the constituency was in the Liberal's traditional West Country stronghold.[1] Four years later, however, a small part of the political landscape caved in: the Liberals won a by-election victory of stunning proportions in the London commuter constituency of Orpington. With a turnout of over 80 per cent the Liberal candidate secured 53 per cent of the vote, taking over 20 per cent from his Conservative opponent. And at the subsequent general election, of 1964, though the party returned only thirteen MPs, it secured over 3 million votes nationally. Three years later the two-party model received a further setback when Winifred Ewing captured Hamilton for the Scottish National Party (SNP). In the years 1972/73 the Liberals surged further forwards with a string of by-electoral victories and in the two general elections of 1974 the Liberals took over 5 million votes nationally, the SNP captured eleven seats in Scotland and in Wales Plaid Cymru won four seats. Psephologists and political commentators were, for the first time, recognising that the two-party model might have imploded altogether. Finer's *Adversary Politics and Electoral Reform* (1975) and Drucker's *Multi-Party Britain* (1979) assumed that Liberal and nationalist successes were not simply indications that the two-party system had begun to work inefficiently and needed to readjust itself, but that perhaps its days were numbered and that this was not necessarily such a bad thing. Drucker hit upon the paradox at the core of Britain's two-party system: its halcyon days coincided (as we have seen)

---

1 Mark Bonham Carter won the 1958 by-election in Torrington, Devon, taking 40 per cent of a turnout of more than 80 per cent and beating his Conservative opponent by 2.6 per cent.

with the absence of 'real' choices, coincided, that is to say, with the postwar consensus. To put it another way, two-party politics appeared to work best when they were not really working at all!

The politics of the 1970s were driven to some degree by the agendas of the minority parties: membership of the European Economic Community had originally been a Liberal policy at a time when both major parties opposed the idea. Britain's place in Europe was to become a pre-eminent party issue in the 1970s and one which the two-party system proved unable to handle: hence the non-partisan referendum of 1975. Devolution of power to Scotland and Wales had been a Liberal policy since the nineteenth century: it too, because of the pressure exerted by the nationalist parties (especially the SNP), became a major issue. It too proved impossible for the two-party system to accommodate and was also decided or at least addressed by non-partisan referenda. Moreover, Callaghan's minority Labour administration was able to hold on to office only because of a negotiated arrangement with the Liberal Party which lasted for eighteen months. Coalition government, an expected consequence of proportional representation but not of the two-party system, was also an objective favoured by the Liberals but not by either of the major parties.

We might feel drawn to conclude from all this that the two-party system seemed to have been part of the postwar consensus and that as that consensus began to crack, a multiparty system of sorts began to emerge. It represented both a manifestation of the end of consensus and also a means of confronting the problems of the post-consensus age. It would have to be said, however, that this small experiment in multiparty politics was hardly a success. After dominating the parliamentary timetable for three years, the government's devolution plans failed, and the attempt to run the economy through the neo-corporatist approach of tripartism ended in tears during the 'winter of discontent'. Yet, in fairness, this was no genuine experiment in multiparty politics but rather an attempt to patch up the two-party system by accommodations towards which the Labour rank-and-file had no affection and the leadership no commitment.

The one-party state? 1979 onwards

Consensus politics, then, of the two-party and multiparty varieties, were already dead when Margaret Thatcher dedicated her party to killing them in 1979. She did, however, produce an alternative means of handling post-consensus politics: one-party politics. In the process she transformed the nature of the British party system. By winning four successive elections – in 1979, 1983, 1987 and 1992 – Margaret Thatcher and John Major consigned a generation of leading Labour politicians to virtually a lifetime of opposition. Assuming that Labour wins office after the 1997 general election, none of its senior figures will have held a major portfolio in their entire political careers; indeed, only two will have held any office at all. In early 1996 potential Labour cabinet ministers were given introductory 'courses' by civil servants to help them grasp what their responsibilities might be – job-opportunity training, as Tony Benn dismissively described it. It would be wrong, as was hinted earlier, to imagine that one-party politics was unique to the post-1979 period or indeed to parliament: the Conservative Party has dominated British politics for the greater part of this century and in local government many areas have been governed by one party for generations.

Perhaps at Westminster what is in effect a one-party dominant system offers genuine advantages, balancing policy consistency against accountability through opposition vigilance. This is a line which Conservative ministers have argued since 1992; their party needed nearly twenty years in government to correct the drift towards collectivism, and the constant fear of parliamentary and eventually electoral defeat would keep the government accountable: policy consistency and accountability – not a bad combination if they are right.

But are they right? What are the disadvantages in a nominally two-party system of one-party dominance? The most obvious is that the opposition party loses heart; its whole *raison d'être* is to secure power and yet in Labour's case a generation of leaders is passing which has hardly experienced power; even the first Labour government, of 1924, was much better served. The majority simply no longer associates the Labour Party with government, or if they do it is not with the reforming government of Attlee, now a distant memory for older voters only, but with Callaghan and the 'winter of discontent'.

But one-party dominance is almost as bad for the dominant party. The British Conservatives, unlike their continental counterparts, never got round to devising an ideology; indeed, until Thatcher became leader they were proud of that fact. To be sure, the neo-liberal Thatcher agenda changed all that, but that agenda has now been largely fulfilled, and the Major government has foundered on the rock of Europe. The Conservatives have not been able to establish a comfortable compromise on European policy as they might have done in the quiet waters of opposition; in government they can find no position on which the party can unite. Moreover, the government's social and economic policies caused unprecedented internal dissensions as it became incontrovertible that under the Conservatives the rich had got richer and the poor poorer – the very opposite of the goal of traditional Conservatism. Indeed, the dissensions have reached such a state that two members of the parliamentary party crossed the floor of the House in 1995, one to Labour and the other to the Liberal Democrats.

So much for the party system since 1945. Let us now turn to the parties themselves, though it is necessary to point out that space precludes an investigation of the roles of the various Northern Irish parties.

The Conservative Party

One of the reasons that Conservative leaders were traditionally permitted such freedom of manoeuvre by the party was the relative certainty that they would pursue the proper objectives of Conservatism, which may be briefly summarised as sound administration and tight control of the economy. Not for Conservatives the grandiose aims of their opponents – to make society more equal or to empower ordinary people. Conservatives believed in what the *Guardian*'s Edward Pearce referred to as 'chug-chug' government, or so it had always been thought. As leader, Edward Heath, it is true, had attempted to give the party a radical agenda with his Selsdon programme, but he had subsequently felt obliged to withdraw behind the ideological safety barrier of the postwar consensus. Thatcher's aim, however, was nothing less than to 'roll back the state' so that government could concentrate on its historic functions, such as defence, security and justice, thus allowing the unrestricted flowering of the nation's entrepreneurial talents. And this leader was not for turning. Paradoxically, in order to recreate (or approximate) the minimal state it was to prove necessary for central government to take on substantially increased powers (for example in health, education and local government) and to implement a legislative programme as far reaching as that of the most radical of left-wing governments. It quickly became clear that Thatcher was driving a wedge between the Tory and Whig wings of the party (between the 'wets' and the 'drys'). Thatcherism could be said to have brought ideology into Conservative Party politics and in doing so helped to destroy the basis of unity, trust and loyalty which had been one of the party's most reliable (and envied) weapons.

In bringing ideology into the Conservative Party, Thatcher also put at risk the largely unconstrained power of its leader (Ingle 1989: ch. 2). Conservative leaders, it was believed, could count upon the loyalty of all levels of the party until they had become clearly recognised as electoral liabilities. The events of the Thatcher years have largely changed the balance of the relationship within the parliamentary party. Prominent among these events were the series of senior ministerial resignations and the resulting public recriminations, culminating in the fatal (for Thatcher's leadership) resignation of Sir Geoffrey Howe (Young 1989: 558). Most prominent was the unseating of the leader herself: not so much a body blow to the myth of the infallible leader and the loyal party as a nuclear explosion whose fallout engulfed her successor. Thatcher was not the first Conservative leader to be removed; indeed, history suggests this to be quite a normal process, but the manner of her fall and indeed the height from which she fell were, to say the least, unusual.

At the heart of Thatcher's disputes with her ministers and symptomatic of the relationship between them lay Britain's relationship with the European Community (EC), and there is no doubt that Conservative Party politics continue to be convulsed by the issue of Europe. It is not fanciful to speak of open warfare during the 1992 party conference, for example. After powerful anti-Maastricht (and by implication anti-government) interventions from Lord Tebbit and Lady Thatcher, Major's address to the conference filled the hall with hisses at the mere mention of Maastricht (Ingle 1995a). Never had such antipathy and division shown itself at a Conservative conference. The conference of 1993 was by contrast an anodyne affair, largely because conference managers had taken the greatest care to minimise opportunities for opposition to the leadership on contentious issues; European unity did not appear as an issue at all. Despite the cessation of open hostilities, few commentators believed that peace had broken out or that Conservative conferences had returned to their traditional status of the political equivalent of Balfour's valet.

Returning to the Maastricht issue, much had happened by the time the House of Commons was to debate the Treaty. The fissures which had manifested themselves at the conference had hardened and widened. Major discovered that the party in parliament was, like the annual conference, very much its own creature. The details of the debates need not detain us; it is sufficient to state that, even in what amounted to motions of confidence, the results of the debates frequently rested on a knife's edge. The Conservative Party leader's hold on the party in parliament had grown so tenuous that Major's credibility was likened to that of Neville Chamberlain during the early days of the Second World War. The government won its crucial votes with the support of the unequivocally pro-Europe Liberal Democrats and the Ulster Unionists (who would certainly have hoped for some quid pro quo), but these were intensely close-run things (*Daily Telegraph*, 26 October 1992).

Nevertheless, Europe was not the only issue on which the Conservative back benches have refused to be cowed by the government. When President of the Board of Trade Heseltine had declared the government's intention to close thirty-one pits in October 1992 the furore which ensued among his own backbenchers was so great that the government was obliged to retreat. The issues of the extension of VAT to domestic heating and the privatisation of British Rail rumbled on, with the government fighting a rearguard action in defence of generally unpopular policies. (Indeed, its plans to extend VAT to domestic fuel were defeated in the House in 1994.) In short, not since the Second World War has a Conservative leadership had such little control over the party in parliament or enjoyed such little sympathy from activists. Four disastrous by-election defeats by the Liberal Democrats, together with wide losses, both to Labour and to the Liberal Democrats, in all local government elections, indicated that disillusion with the party and its leaders stretched down to the voters.

The problems did not end here: the vaunted efficiency of the party organisation and its supposed financial stability could by this time no longer be assumed. During the Thatcher years Conservative Central Office had, in fact, become somewhat less 'central' in party affairs. The research department had been obliged to give ground, in terms of policy development, to the prime minister's policy unit and to outside bodies such as the Institute of Economic Affairs and the Adam Smith Institute. Moreover, Central Office had to contend throughout the 1990s with a financial crisis.[2] In 1991 the reformist constituency organisation, Charter, mounted a scathing attack on Central Office's 'stunningly incompetent' financial stewardship. Charter urged proper democratic control of the voluntary donations, which had come to provide the lion's share of income. 'We don't know what Central Office had to concede in return for this money but we can be absolutely sure that the interests of party democracy are not enhanced' (*Guardian*, 13 December 1992).

All in all, it is clearly the case that the party bureaucracy, far from offering a model of well healed efficiency for others to follow, is in a state of disarray and certainly no longer the predictable, obedient creature of the party leader. In short there seems to be no aspect in which the traditional strengths of the Conservative Party remain undiminished. Whether it is the habit of almost unrestricted power over a long period that is finally destructive, whether it is the corrosive issue of Britain's relationships with Europe (which all but broke a Labour government in the 1970s), whether it is the continuing economic malaise, or whether it is a combination of these factors, the Conservative Party today is in confusion.

The Labour Party

If 1979 was a watershed for the Conservative Party, so too it was for Labour. The left of the party felt bitterly thwarted by their own government's inability to pursue a socialist agenda, and the advent of a right-wing Conservative government presented the left with an opportunity to 'democratise' the party structure and challenge the control of the right-wing leadership. At the 1990 party conference decisions were taken to explore ways to relieve the leadership of control of the manifesto, to require all MPs to seek reselection and to broaden substantially the base on which the party leader was elected. Moreover, on Callaghan's resignation as leader the acknowledged leader of the right, Denis Healey, was defeated in the leadership election ballot by Michael Foot, a man whose leftist views (especially on nuclear disarmament) were well known. All this proved too much for a group of prominent right wingers who, along with more than twenty other

---

2 Labour accused the government of tackling its financial problems by offering 'privatisation' contracts to City firms that had contributed to party funds, though such claims are impossible to substantiate or refute with certainty (*Sunday Times*, 17 November 1991).

Labour MPs, decided to leave the party to form a new party, the Social Democratic Party (SDP). Seven of these MPs, however, stayed in the party long enough to vote in the leadership election. They voted for Foot, whose views they abhorred. In the event Foot won by ten votes. Had the seven voted for their natural ally, Healey would probably have won. Their reason for not doing so was deviously simple: 'It was very important that the Labour party as it had become was destroyed,' one later admitted (Neville Sandelson, in the *Sunday Telegraph*, 13 January 1996). They came to believe that the subsequent transformation of Labour vindicated their actions: Healey believed their actions resulted indirectly in nine more years of Thatcher government.

In 1983 the Labour Party secured its worst general election result for over half a century, losing 119 deposits. When, as a consequence, Foot resigned the leadership, it fell to Neil Kinnock to save the party from eclipse. He did so, as Shaw (1995: *passim*) has shown in detail, with general aplomb and very considerable managerial skill. Indeed, after the general electoral defeat in 1987, attributed to unpopular policies rather than a badly fought campaign, Kinnock initiated a series of policy reviews that were intended to have the cumulative effect of transforming Labour by modernising its image. The scope of these reviews was wide and their effect in transforming the party into something approaching a modern social democratic party on the west European model was profound (Smith and Spears 1992). Yet the party lost again in 1992, in the most propitious circumstances. What more could be done? Labour needed to question some of the most fundamental assumptions about its nature and objectives if it was again to achieve power. Perhaps the greatest and certainly the most pervasive of these assumptions was that Labour was the party of and for the working class. This relationship was assumed to manifest itself in terms of the membership of the parliamentary party and the party in the country, the link with the trade unions, and in the party's policies – 'socialism'. While Labour would never have claimed to be only a party for the working class, its very *raison d'être* was to support and further the interests of that class. Yet precisely because the working class has declined as a proportion of the total population, and will almost certainly continue to do so, working-class support will never again be sufficient to win elections for Labour (Curtice and Stead 1992). Moreover, in its failure to win wider support from the more affluent sector of the working class (especially in the south of England), Labour demonstrated its inability to hold on even to its natural constituency.

The justice with which Labour can claim to be the party of the working class is anyway nowadays challengeable. Not for a long time has the Parliamentary Labour Party (PLP) reflected that class (Ingle 1989: ch. 7). The 1992 parliament comprised 271 Labour members, of whom no fewer than 186 had university degrees (including forty from Oxford and eighteen from Cambridge) and eighteen had polytechnic qualifications. The occupational background of those Labour MPs is equally revealing: fifty were journalists or authors, forty-eight lecturers, forty-three teachers and forty-six trade union officials or party workers, and twenty-one barristers or solicitors (*Sunday Times*, 12 April 1992). A number of these would have been the sons and daughters of workers, but that is hardly the same thing, and it forces the observer to conclude that the PLP is nowadays no more representative of the working class than was the Liberal Party which Labour replaced over seventy years ago.

As for the party in the country, Seyd and Whitely (1992) indicated a similar position in some respects. They established that 49 per cent of activists were salaried and only 14 per cent were wage earners – yet more evidence of the 'embourgeoisement' of the party. Although there were working-class activists, especially trade unionists, many of their views would not be particularly welcome to party modernisers: 82 per cent were in favour of renationalisation, 68 per cent were unilateralists and 92 per cent favoured increased taxes. This contrast of policy preferences between leaders and activists could pose a problem for an incoming Labour government.

The conflicts during the early and mid-1980s over the activities of radical left groups such as Militant do not make headline news so frequently in the 1990s, but the problem has not gone away. At the Liverpool Walton by-election in 1991 the Militant ('Real Labour') candidate secured 2,613 votes and some had described this as a victory for socialism. In Glasgow, too, candidates standing as Scottish Militant Labour won seats from Labour on the city council and the Strathclyde regional council. Entryism in the 1990s was by no means as wide a problem as it had been in the 1980s, but defections in the party's heartland (Liverpool and Glasgow) clearly indicate a measure of grass-roots dissatisfaction.

Labour's relationship with the unions has usually been held to provide the party's main justification for considering itself the party of the working class, but even this relationship has changed and is likely to change more radically in the near future (Minkin 1991). As far as Labour is concerned there is strong evidence of public anxiety over the extent to which the unions act as Labour's paymasters. This public anxiety has been reflected within the party. Union influence, through the block vote at annual conference, through constituency candidate selection and reselection, through the leadership elections and on policy through conference and the National Executive Committee (NEC), was seen to be too great by many. The unions themselves were, by and large, not averse to the idea of change.

At the 1993 annual conference the new party leader John Smith promoted a compromise package of reforms of the relationship between the unions and the party. The aim was to abolish the union block vote in constituency selection and reselection ballots and to require trade unionists to pay a £3 levy to join the party before being able to vote. This reform became known as OMOV (one member one vote). Ballots for constituency and trade union representation on the NEC and for constituency delegates to conference were to be held on a similar basis. Moreover, the electoral college in leadership and deputy leader elections was henceforth to comprise equal representation of trade unions, the PLP (including MEPs) and constituencies, and finally the trade union block vote at conferences was to comprise not 90 per cent but 70 per cent of the total; in 1996 this was further reduced to 50 per cent.

Perhaps it was entirely coincidental that in December 1992, while Smith's reforms were brewing, the Transport and General Workers' Union, one of Labour's largest benefactors, decided to cut its subscription to the party by more than £500,000. The union decided to sponsor MEPs and so would support fewer than the traditional thirty-eight MPs. In 1992 one major union (GMB) opened an office in Brussels; others have followed. It has been argued that as the process of amalgamations continues (AEU and EEPTU followed by NALGO, NUPE and COHSE in 1992) perhaps by the end of the decade there will be five or six major unions, not all of which are likely to retain their links with the party (Holliday 1993).

Reform of the trade union link was only part of Labour's programme of modernisation. In 1990 Kinnock had initiated reforms which fundamentally changed the way the party made policy. In that year conference agreed to the establishment of a 170-strong national policy council, elected every two years from all sections of the party. From this would come seven commissions of about thirty members covering the whole gamut of policy and reporting on a two-year rolling programme. Annual conferences would debate the reports, and thus repetitive and damaging policy rows at conference would be minimised.

The task of modernising Labour, initiated by Kinnock, was incomplete at the untimely death of John Smith and the cause of reform was picked up with enthusiasm by the newly elected leader, Tony Blair. He immediately began a frontal assault on Labour's ancient shibboleth, clause four of the party's constitution, which sought the social ownership of the means of production, distribution and exchange. Working through the unions Blair was completely victorious and by 1995 Labour had ceased even nominally to be a socialist party. Blair showed a commitment to remodelling the party and he turned not so much to Europe as to Australia for his inspiration. The Australian Labor Party (ALP) had made a striking success of running a modern economy and of securing more than a single term in office. The ALP attempted to strike a balance between social justice and economic management. Described as 'assertively pragmatic, anti-utopian, non-socialist' (*Guardian*, 8 November 1995), the ALP deregulated banks and airlines, cut the top rates of tax, brought government expenditure down to 36.9 per cent of gross domestic product (the target of the Major government was

40 per cent) yet substantially increased the social wage, jobs programmes, family assistance, student loans, superannuation, health and insurance provision. Though real incomes increased by 21 per cent in Australia between 1981 and 1995, real earnings increased by only 7 per cent: the rest was targeted on the poor and needy. This is Blair's model for New Labour. What ALP leaders Hawke and Keating possessed, however, was a firm alliance with the powerful trade union movement (where Hawke's background in union leadership was an inestimable advantage) and the general support of the Australian press, neither of which is open to Blair.

Blair sought to position the Labour Party more centrally, and continued Smith's attempts to win the approval of the business community – the so-called 'prawn raids'. He emphasised the NEC's control over candidate selection when, in Leeds North East, Liz Davies was deselected because of her alleged left-wing views, with front-benchers warning once again of Trotskyist entryism. He attempted a stricter control of the party conference, abandoning the method of debating loose, composite motions in favour of fewer, better-focused debates. Suggestions have been made that conferences will, in future, become biennial. Moreover, delegates have been sent to regional training sessions on public speaking. So-called spin doctors, a 'platoon of sharp men with sharp suits, sharp haircuts and whispering sharp words' (*Daily Telegraph*, 7 November 1995), were employed to minimise adverse media coverage of the 1995 conference, the most stage managed ever. The days of the macho conference may be numbered.

The powers of the NEC, too, have been trimmed, and control of party strategy has moved towards the leader and his allies. Indeed, party general secretary Tom Sawyer sent the entire NEC away on a weekend management course. A leaked document in 1995 called for the establishment of a management team, headed by the leader, which would meet daily – an 'operations room at the heart of our campaigning'. What was sought was a 'directness of decision-making that is the hall mark of a successful political organisation' (*Guardian*, 12 September 1995). Perhaps the leak slowed the trend away from collegial decision making, a feature of the traditional party, but it certainly will not have stopped it. And the party's head office, too, is being modernised. It will have a mission statement and annual performance indicators and there will be sweeping reforms of the directorates. A group of management consultants have been employed to oversee these changes.

At the same time, Blair is constructing a new vocabulary for New Labour, the vocabulary of stake holding. It is in fact not new at all, nor so very distinctive from the aims of the policies of co-ownership and co-partnership which were Liberal Party policy in the late 1950s. It was no coincidence that this vocabulary and the concepts underpinning it were introduced by Blair in a speech to oversees business people in Singapore in January 1996. Although the speech offered a share to all in education, welfare, technology and corporate governance, it was aimed in large part at convincing overseas investors that they would have nothing to fear from a Labour government, which was promoted not as a nationaliser, nor even as an intervener, but as a facilitator.

All these changes were to prove too much for Arthur Scargill, leader of the National Union of Mineworkers, who, quite correctly, perceived that Labour was no longer a socialist party. He set up a new party, the Socialist Labour Party, and in February 1996 the party fought a by-election in the safe Labour seat of Hemsworth in the Yorkshire coalfield: Scargill country. In the event Labour won easily and the Socialist candidate managed only to save her deposit. As the press had remarked at the previous Socialist Labour Party conference, King Arthur had become King Canute.

In terms of policy, organisation and style, New Labour is similar to the defunct SDP. Indeed, a thorough survey of policy commitments (*Guardian*, 21 August 1995) indicated that New Labour policies are far more similar to SDP policies than they are to traditional Labour policies. Yet the modernisation of Labour is not complete and it is difficult to be certain how enduring the changes will prove. When Blair's adviser and arch moderniser Peter Mandelson had been director of communications, clause four had unaccountably been left off party membership cards – a printer's error. If only, from the modernisers' perspective, changes could be made so easily!

The Liberal Democrats

In contrast to the two major parties, the Liberal Democrats and their forerunners have, on the whole, made solid progress since 1979. By far the most significant event of the period was the emergence of the SDP, a competitor for Liberal votes in the centre of the political spectrum. That the two parties were able to act in alliance was an inestimable advantage to both, and candidates in the 1983 election stood as either Liberal Alliance or SDP Alliance candidates, as a result of a nationwide division of seats that few commentators thought possible. In that election the Alliance received 25 per cent of the national vote, only 2 per cent less than Labour, but it managed to return only twenty-three MPs to Westminster. In a sense the Alliance was at once within a whisker of a major breakthrough (a higher popular vote than Labour) and yet as far from power as the centre had been for a long time (so few parliamentary seats). That election represented the Alliance's zenith – 1987 represented at best a consolidation but no further advance. Many members of both parties saw a need to merge and immediately after the election, Liberal leader David Steel took the necessary steps to begin a merger debate. Although this bore fruit and a new party, the Social and Liberal Democrats (eventually the Liberal Democrats), emerged, a rump SDP under the leadership of David Owen survived for a brief period. The 1992 general election result (twenty seats won) could hardly be represented as a triumph but since the party had been decisively beaten into fourth place by the Greens in the European elections only three years earlier it was hardly a failure either. After the general election the party gained four stunningly successful by-election victories at the expense of the Conservatives and benefited from the defection of Conservative MP Emma Nicholson but there have been other changes in the relationship between the two parties.

In May 1995 party leader Ashdown announced that his party would not be prepared to prop up a minority Conservative government after the next election, thus heralding the demise of the traditional stance of equidistance (Ingle 1995b), according to which the Liberal Democrats were no further in policy terms from the Conservatives than they were from Labour. While previously the party could have realistically declared itself willing, after an inconclusive election, to try to work with whichever had secured most seats, Ashdown now declared: 'People must know that if they kick the Tories out through the front door, we will not allow them to sneak in through the back door' (Ingle 1995b). His theme was clearly spelt out: Britain's success depended upon the defeat of the Major government, and 'every vote for the Liberal Democrats is a vote to remove this Conservative government and the policies they stand for'. The concept of equidistance was therefore unambiguously jettisoned.

The historic function of the Liberal Party in the twentieth century, as articulated for example by Lloyd George in the first election of 1910, was not to hold an equidistant position: it was to provide a non-socialist radical alternative to Conservatism. When, some fifty years later, Jo Grimond was helping to re-establish the Liberals as a major, national party he called not for equidistance but for a realignment of the left much along Lloyd George's lines, adding significantly that he 'didn't give a tinker's cuss what such a party should be called' (Ingle 1995b). Later still, after the 1992 election, David Marquand (then a Liberal Democrat) argued that the party should have 'come clean' to the voters: it was a left-of-centre party and should not have masqueraded as an equidistant, centre party. (He has subsequently chosen to rejoin Labour, a party which is now pleased to be considered a centre party.) The problem for the Liberal Democrats in 1992 was exactly what it had been since 1950: it professed a preponderance of left-of-centre policies but in the main was supported by disgruntled centre and right-of-centre voters. It was simply not expedient for the Liberal Democrats to do what Marquand wanted: to campaign vigorously and openly 'as a part of a broadly-based progressive coalition, essentially democratic in inspiration' (Ingle 1995a). The Liberal Democrats may well have needed then, as they do now, a Labour victory to have any hope of sharing power but they continue to rely now, as then, principally on defecting Conservative support for the electoral successes to provide the basis on which they could bargain with Labour about power. We should be clear, though, that what Marquand criticised was electoral strategy rather than equidistance.

It is true that in the 1950s agreements were reached, in Huddersfield and Bolton for example, in which Liberals and Conservatives allowed each other a free run against Labour opponents; true also that in the 1987 election one of the Alliance leaders, David Owen, made clear his belief that a post-electoral arrangement with Margaret Thatcher's Conservative Party was perfectly plausible: but by and large since the 1950s and arguably for the whole of the century the Liberals, the Alliance and the Liberal Democrats have not located themselves equidistantly between the two major parties. In 1974 the Liberals refused to make a post-electoral arrangement with Heath's Conservatives despite their having received most votes at the previous election, though in 1978 they were willing to keep a minority Labour government in office.

Why should Ashdown signal the end of a policy which had never really existed? To abandon the myth of equidistance was, for Ashdown, to signify a change in the ideological or policy stance not of the Liberal Democrats but of the other parties. The party sought to build on this notion of having marked out its independent position by publishing the Liberal Democrat Guarantee in 1995, which boldly advocated a programme of increased government spending and a measure of public ownership. In the Littleborough and Saddleworth by-election the Labour Party had denounced the Liberal Democrats as a high-spending, high-taxation party. The party stuck to its guns, however, in the by-election, declaring that taxation was the price of membership of a civilised society.

Although the Liberals and Liberal Democrats have always sought to eschew the classical descriptions of left and right, they have frequently claimed to be more radical than the Labour Party, and so should take some pleasure at being described by commentators as 'left of New Labour'. Most commentators see this as a consequence of New Labour's move to the right. Indeed, it has been argued that this is a common feature of socialist politics, quoting the examples of Lange and Keating in the Antipodes and Gonzalez and Craxi in western Europe. What seems to have escaped the attention of commentators, however, is the leftward shift of the Liberal Democrats. In the 1992 general election Ian Aitken considered that Liberal Democrat policy amounted to 'a neo-Thatcherite commitment to the free market' (Ingle 1995b). More recently, a new journal, *The Reformer*, established chiefly by former SDP members of the Liberal Democrats, declared its opposition to 'any false impression that we are a laissez-faire party' and called for a party commitment to a 'clear and active role for the state in creating a dynamic economy and extending individual opportunity'. Ashdown's May statement on equidistance, the Guarantee and Glasgow 1995 have moved party policy a long way from a position in which it could be described as neo-Thatcherite or laissez faire.

To recapitulate, in abandoning the myth of equidistance the Liberal Democrats have signalled a move not towards Labour but to the left; they have also suggested that there are no longer fixed referents in modern British politics. By attempting to 'fix' the party's policy position, however, Ashdown has been able at least to retain the prospect of coming to some arrangement with Labour after an inconclusive election without alienating a considerable section of the party.

The Liberal Democrats are stronger than at any time since the war but the party's successes have been the consequence principally of an almost total collapse of the Conservative vote, thus allowing scope for both the Liberal Democrats and Labour to enjoy electoral successes. Should Conservative fortunes improve, the Liberal Democrats may, as often before, find themselves losing ground and consequently holding few counters to bargain with. If the party is in a position to bargain after a general election, however, it could find common ground with Labour on many policies. Moreover, agreement between the parties on the structure and functions of the proposed Scottish parliament offers an example of what is possible. The party's best prospect for achieving a position from which it might bargain requires the maintenance of party unity and a continuing capacity to attract disgruntled Conservative voters. The party must continue to portray itself, in Ashdown's words, as 'an alternative to both Conservative and Labour parties' (Ingle 1995b) and it must not be deflected by considerations of pacts, hung parliaments and the like. In a world of flux, independence, not equidistance, is the key to success.

The nationalist parties

What of the nationalist parties? Unbroken rule from 1979 weakened the Conservative Party in both Scotland and Wales almost beyond repair and in both countries the nationalists have been the chief beneficiaries. Though it has not yet repeated the success of 1974, when it returned eleven MPs, the SNP consistently enjoys poll support of between 20 and 30 per cent. 'Free in '93' was the 1992 electoral slogan for the SNP and if this always seemed over-ambitious the party nevertheless was riding higher in the opinion polls before that general election than for many years. The election result, however, was desperately disappointing for the SNP. Though securing 21.5 per cent of the Scottish vote, the SNP actually lost one of its seats, thus leaving the party, as its opponents were quick to note, not 'free' but 'three' in '93. Nevertheless, if the call to independence was rejected by over three-quarters of Scots, the unreformed union was rejected by an almost equally high number. The mass demonstrations in Glasgow (and later in Edinburgh) after the election indicated not only a dissatisfaction with undiluted rule from Westminster but also an inability on the part of Labour, SNP, Liberal Democrat and other reformers to combine on a common programme. The Scottish constitutional convention has since reached agreement on the putative shape and powers of a Scottish parliament, but the SNP took no part in these deliberations.

In Wales Plaid Cymru, far less vociferous, has been electorally more successful, returning four MPs on 8.8 per cent of the vote in the Principality.

Neither of the nationalist parties has managed to sustain a consistently high profile since the general election and the government's decision not to extend the privatisation of water to Scotland unquestionably diffused a potentially damaging issue. The extension of VAT to domestic heating in 1994, however, hitting the Scots particularly hard, proved grist to the nationalist mill and brought the politics of devolution (and indeed independence) on to the political agenda once again.

Future developments

All in all, the British party system of the 1990s, despite intervening vicissitudes, despite the rise of the Liberal Democrats and to a lesser extent of the nationalist parties is, if not the same as in the 1940s, at least recognisable. Yet perhaps all is not as permanent and immutable as it might appear, and perhaps we should finish this account with some speculation.

A Gallup poll for the *Daily Telegraph* in September 1993 showed that more than 90 per cent of respondents thought British politicians to be evasive, dishonest, predictable, partisan and untruthful. This was certainly not the case in 1945, and no doubt the change in attitude reflects many concerns, but it is clearly the case that a system which actually requires parties to seek to outbid each other at general elections, requires governments to defend and oppositions to attack every policy decision come what may, views information as a partisan commodity not a public right, and builds adversarialism into the warp and woof of its policy-making procedures, is almost destined to lose public sympathy and support. The ability of an adversarial system to cope with long-term and increasingly technical decisions must be open to doubt anyway. Britain is now the only major two-party adversarial system in the world. The only other, New Zealand, fought its last first-past-the-post election in 1993. In 1996 it fought under a German-style additional-member system and a coalition government subsequently took office. Now the whole world is out of step with Britain. The expectation in New Zealand, very clearly expressed and documented (Ingle 1995c), was that a multiparty system would make it impossible for one party's ideological agenda to dominate the policy-making process and, by the same token, to encourage the development of consensual policies.

If Britain were to opt for a proportional electoral system, the immediate effect would almost certainly be to transform the fortunes of the Liberal Democrats, who might then be expected to gain between fifty and a hundred seats, thus giving the country what would be, in effect, a three-party system. Three-party parliaments in Britain have not been an unqualified success, to say the least, yet in the past each of the parties was jockeying for position in the belief that, in a first-part-the-post system, only two would be likely to survive. If three main parties were seen to be permanent features of the system then that situation would need to be accommodated by coalition or minority governments. In either case policies would be driven not by partisan ideology but by compromise between at least two parties, and would thus reflect majority electoral support. Already a number of county and district councils operate unofficial local arrangements between the Liberal Democrats and Labour and many more have considerable experience of running hung councils. The local government system seems to have coped. With coalition or minority governments in power at Westminster it would prove far more difficult for any single party to maintain the kind of ascendancy that the Conservatives have established this century, pursuing policies to which the majority of people were clearly opposed, such as the poll tax, pit closures, and rail privatisation.

Britain's adversarial political structure, with its day-to-day parliamentary clashes, gives the appearance of two-party politics and the reality of one-party dominance.

Electoral reform could encourage the emergence of a coalition-based system in which adversarial procedures would be transformed, thus helping to re-establish the trust between citizens and politicians, the absence of which is an indictment on modern British democracy. Britain's retention of its present system is, some would argue, the result of a misconception: that the days of the postwar consensus, McKenzie's swingometer, politicians deemed to be trustworthy and alternations of power were, indeed are, the norm. They were not and moreover they ceased before 1979, and without electoral reform there is no reason to expect their return.

References

Abrams, M. (1961), Class and politics: another look at the British electorate, *Encounter*, October, 14–20.

Curtice, J. and Stead, M. (1992), The results analysed, in D. Butler and D. Kavanagh (eds), *The British General Election of 1992*, London, Macmillan.

Drucker, H. (1979), *Multi-Party Britain*, London, Macmillan.

Finer, S. E. (1975), *Adversary Politics and Electoral Reform*, London, Anthony Wigram.

Gamble, A. M. and Walkland, S. A. (1984), *The British Party System and Economic Policy 1945–1983*, Oxford, Oxford University Press.

Holliday, I. (1993), Organised interests after Thatcher, in P. Dunleavy *et al.* (eds), *Developments in British Politics 4*, London, Macmillan.

Ingle, S. (1989), *The British Party System*, Oxford, Blackwell.

Ingle, S. (1994), Is Britain a one-party state?, *Talking Politics*, 7:1, 17–23.

Ingle, S. (1995a), The political parties, in R. Pyper and L. Robins (eds), *Governing the UK*, London, Macmillan.

Ingle, S. (1995b), The Liberal Democrats and equidistance, *Parliamentary Brief*, 4:2, 32–4.

Ingle, S. (1995c), Electoral reform in New Zealand: The implications for Westminster systems, *Journal of Legislative Studies*, 1:4, 76–92.

McKenzie, R. (1955), *British Political Parties*, London, Macmillan.

Minkin, L. (1991), *The Contentious Alliance*, Edinburgh, Edinburgh University Press.

Norton, P. and Aughey, A. (1981), *Conservatives and Conservatism*, London, Temple Smith.

Rose, R. (1994), *Do Parties Make a Difference?*, London, Macmillan.

Sartori, G. (1976), *Parties and Party Systems: A Framework for Analysis*, Cambridge, Cambridge University Press.

Seyd, P. and Whitely, P. (1992), Labour's renewal strategy, in M. J. Smith and J. Spears (eds), *The Changing Labour Party*, London, Routledge.

Shaw, E. (1995), *The Labour Party since 1945*, Oxford, Blackwell.

Smith, M. J. and Spears, J. (eds) (1992), *The Changing Labour Party*, London, Routledge.

Westergaard, J. and Ressler, H. (1980), *Class in a Capitalist Society*, Harmondsworth, Penguin.

Young, H. (1989), *One of Us*, London, Macmillan.

6

The promise of reform

Philip Cowley

'The rule is, jam tomorrow and jam yesterday – but never jam today'.
'It *must* come sometimes to "jam today",' Alice objected.
'No it can't,' said the Queen.
(Lewis Carroll, *Through the Looking Glass*)

This chapter is emphatically *not* an analysis of the rights and wrongs of the various shopping lists of constitutional or institutional reforms that have been or still are being presented to the British public. In part, this is because plenty of other people have written such works: one of the few growth industries of the last fifty years has been books and pamphlets dissecting the British state and offering solutions.[1] But mainly it is because it is unlikely that the rights and wrongs of particular reforms had or have very much to do with their chances of implementation. It is better to see reform as akin to fashion: when flared trousers become popular, it is not because the logical argument for flares (they are loose and comfortable) has beaten the argument against (they use up too much material and flap around in the wind); it is just that people need trousers, and they happen to be the sort of trousers that other people are wearing.

To committed reformers (or preservers of the status quo) who would wish their position to win on the strengths of their well rehearsed arguments this may seem like heresy. But over the last fifty years it is possible to identify clear fashions in the reform debate in Britain, and it is doubtful whether these fashions had much to do with the rights and wrongs of particular causes. Linking these fashions has been either an attempt to reverse (or at least ameliorate) Britain's economic decline or explicitly party political pressures. This chapter explains these fashions, concentrating largely but not exclusively on three institutions that have been almost ever-present targets for reformers in the last fifty years – parliament, the civil

---

1   For a good summary, and critique, of many of the currently proposed reforms, see Norton (1991). Norton comes to the conclusion that everyone else is wrong and he is right.

service, and local government – as well as those areas – such as the electoral system – that have attracted attention only more recently.

Busy doing nothing

The first fashion, which lasted for some fifteen years after the end of the war, was to avoid reform. Despite the reforming zeal of the Attlee government in many areas of British life (chapter 3) many of the central institutions of the British state were left untouched. Britain was glowing (perhaps somewhat smugly) in the aftermath of victory and few saw any need to tamper with the institutions responsible for delivering that victory. Nevil Johnson's comment on parliament – 'The impact of the Second World War on parliamentary institutions in Britain was favourable. Their survival and that of the country wiped out the critical mood of the previous decade' (1979: 446) – could be applied with neither caveat nor qualification to almost every other institution of state. Indeed, not only had these institutions delivered victory, but they also showed every sign of winning the peace. As Pollard (1982: 2) argued:

> At the end of the war ... [Britain] was still among the richest nations of the world, ahead by far of the war-shattered economies of Europe.... The problem that exercised the statesmen of the day was whether the rest of Europe, even its industrialised parts, would ever be able to come within reach of, let alone catch up with, Britain.

Although this belief was soon to be shattered, the lack of significant institutional innovation is surely understandable given the circumstances.

There were some reforms. Attlee, Churchill and Eden did not pickle the state in aspic. There was some minor procedural tinkering in the Commons; some of the functions of local government changed; and the period saw the first electoral reform of the postwar era: the 1948 Representation of the People Act abolished the business and university votes for parliamentary elections (which had allowed some plural voting, with some people having more than one vote, by a system of proportional representation in the university seats). It also removed all remaining double-member constituencies and abolished the six-months residence qualification. This finally established the system of single-member geographic constituencies – with one voter having one vote – that we have today. And, finally, the 1949 Parliament Act reduced the time that the House of Lords could delay legislation from two years to one.

There are three differences between these reforms and those that followed after 1960. First, in some cases these reforms were the opposite to those desired in other periods. Later concerns about the Commons (and prewar concerns) focused on its ability to hold the executive to account. Yet the reforms of the immediate postwar period – including the reform of the

Lords – were designed to expedite the massive legislative programme of the Labour government. They created, in other words, a more effective legislative machine rather than a machine that necessarily produced more effective legislation. Second, some were by-products of other reforms rather than being intended in their own right. Most of the functions lost by local government, for example, such as electricity or hospitals, went as a consequence of nationalisation. (Concomitantly, as these functions were acquired by the centre, the role of the civil service was enhanced.) And third, they were far from radical.

There were also some calls for greater reform. The 1947 local government boundary commission made some very strong criticisms of the structure of local government, but had its recommendations rejected because they would have put the governing Labour Party at an electoral disadvantage. The civil service still attracted some criticism. And there were the first postwar calls for parliamentary reform as early as 1949 with the publication of Christopher Hollis's *Can Parliament Survive?*, but compared with either what had gone before, or what was to come, this was thin reformist gruel. In 1960 the structure of local government in England and Wales was nearly identical to that of 1894 (in Scotland to that of 1929); the basic structure of parliament had not undergone any major reform since 1911; the electoral system had been tweaked but had still not seen any major upheavals since 1918; and the civil service owed more to the nineteenth than twentieth century.

Doom and gloom

It is difficult to identify exactly when or why people began to feel that things were not quite so rosy. The two causes are probably the Suez debacle of 1956 and a growing sense that despite the 'age of affluence' Britain was not doing as well economically as its rivals. The difficulty of finding a precise cause and starting date does not prevent us being clear that some change was under way. Although one social historian points out that there is never 'an era in which no writers or artists are expressing criticism of the society in which they live,' he continues by concluding that in the 1960s there was a 'transformation in British ideas and modes of behaviour which can, without slipping into bathos, be described as forming a "cultural revolution"' (Marwick 1990: 120).

The 'decline literature' of the period saw national self-doubt replace self-satisfaction. Bryan Magee was not upbeat in 1962: '[W]e drag along, knowing and caring little about the world we live in, falling farther and farther behind most other advanced countries, and yet still supposing that others share our view of our own importance. It is a pathetic spectacle' (Magee 1962: 184). Tony Crosland (1962: 127) rather dryly pointed out that things were not all bad: '[n]o doubt we still lead the world in certain traditional spheres – merchant banking, classical scholarship, trooping the colour, or sailing the Atlantic single-handed'.

The blame for this decline from mighty power to failed anachronism was laid firmly at the door of Britain's 'establishment'. The targets for blame were numerous, but included – just to take the chapters from Thomas's *The Establishment* (published in 1959) as a fairly representative example – public schools, the army, the civil service, the City, parliament and the BBC. Selected examples of the decline genre would include Sampson's *The Anatomy of Britain* (1962), Koestler's edited collection *Suicide of a Nation* (1963) and Michael Shanks's *The Stagnant Society* (1961), which was the first in a series of Penguin paperbacks looking at various British institutions, from hospitals to the church, collectively entitled 'What's wrong with Britain?' This brief list is illustrative rather than exhaustive: parliament alone attracted a voluminous literature which there is not the space to discuss here. And these complaints were cross-party: the problems with the civil service identified by the Fabian Society's *The Administrators* (1964) were remarkably similar to those in *Change or Decay* (1963), a pamphlet written by a group of Conservative MPs. In short, each aspect of British political hardware – and much of the software too – was examined, critiqued – and then damned. The 1960s were clearly not a time of optimistic bedtime reading.

The nature of the complaints and suggestions for improvement varied between authors and institutions, and went wider than simple institution bashing, but there was a basic message: the institutions of the state – including their culture – were simply not up to administering Britain in the late twentieth century. The state needed to be modernised.

Modernisation

During the two decades from 1960 onwards there were attempts to modernise parliament, the civil service, local government, and many other parts of the public sector. Three features distinguish these reforms. First, the reform was often preceded by and based upon a thorough investigation of the problems. Second, much of the reform failed to be implemented fully. And third, even if implemented fully, the reform failed to deliver the economic prosperity that was expected.

Civil service reform is a perfect example. The Fulton report of 1968 – which famously declared that the 'Home Civil Service today is still fundamentally the product of the nineteenth century philosophy of the Northcote-Trevelyan Report [of 1854]' – echoed much of the reformist literature in its critique of the civil service (cmnd 3638: para. 1). But in the short term Fulton failed. Most of the recommendations were only half implemented. Some – like the preference for 'relevance' – were rejected altogether. The medicine may have been strong, but the patient refused to take it and no one forced it down the throat (Kellner and Crowther-Hunt 1980).[2]

A similar lack of longevity occurred with the reforms introduced by the Heath government of 1970–74, which had come into power armed with a wide range of proposed changes to the machinery of government (cmnd 4506). Heath had a 'managerial view' of the world, a belief that 'structural reforms would make ideological measures unnecessary' (Butler and Pinto-Duschinsky 1971: 19). But one of his new 'super departments' (Trade and Industry) had been partly dismembered even before he had left office (a process Wilson completed after returning to Number 10). The Programme Analysis and Review project had petered out by 1973. The commitment to 'hive off' some functions of government to semi-autonomous bodies also achieved little. The impact of the think tank, probably the most successful of his Whitehall innovations, was more varied but even this only lasted as late as 1983.

Most of the local government reforms of the 1960s and 1970s (see chapter 11) were at least fully implemented. By 1975, local government in all of Great Britain (and in Northern Ireland too, following the Macrory review of 1970[3]) had been structurally reorganised. It is worth noting how typical of the contemporary approach to modernisation the local government reforms were. First, there were three royal commissions involved: Herbert for London, Redcliffe-Maud for England, and Wheatley for Scotland.[4] Second, there was a belief that the structure was not modern enough (Redcliffe-Maud's phrase that 'local government areas did not fit the pattern of life and work in modern England' or Wheatley's that things had remained 'basically the same for forty years, when everything around ... has changed'). Third, there was a faith in planning: to cite Redcliffe-Maud again, the old, fragmented system made 'proper' planning 'impossible'. And fourth, as with government ministries, there was a belief that bigger is better. Ken Young (1994: 404) sums it up well: '"Modernisation" for its own sake, strategic planning, and the effective management of the (unquestioned) growth in public expenditure took priority over local attachment and popular consent as the [Conservative] party stumbled along the road to Peter Walker's Local Government Act of 1972'.

A similar approach (for similar reasons) was taken to the reorganisation of the National Health Service in England at the same time. Although enacted by the second Wilson government after 1974, the plans were drawn up by Keith Joseph, ironically later to be a great scourge of such planning.

---

2 There is however an argument about the long-term impact of Fulton. See Dowding (1995).
3 Although this was implemented to prevent gerrymandering rather than for 'modernisation'.
4 Local government in Wales was initially to be investigated by a Welsh Office departmental inquiry, but their proposed reforms were dropped after the Redcliffe-Maud Commission reported.

Parliament (another favourite target of reformers) also saw its failures in the period up to 1979. A series of new select committees was set up. Few lasted or were considered a great success while in existence. Other reforms of the era were similarly short lived: morning sittings were soon abolished and live sound broadcasting of parliament was not a success. The introduction of 'Short' money (state aid to opposition parties) failed to achieve the desired and expected growth in opposition competence. There were some successes, but, as Philip Norton (1981: 207) observes: 'Overall, the picture was not an impressive one from the point of view of those seeking to rectify the imbalance in the relationship between Parliament and the executive'.[5] Offsetting this slightly, both Houses became more assertive. In the Lords, the cause was a combination of one failed and one successful institutional reform. The successful reform was the 1958 Life Peerages Act, which allowed men (and, for the first time, women) into the Lords for their lifetime, but with the title not passing on through the generations. Equally important was the failure of the 1969 Parliament (No. 2) Bill, which would have removed the hereditary principle from the Lords altogether, and which was abandoned by the government after encountering opposition from an unholy alliance of the left of the Labour Party (because it did not go far enough) and the right of the Conservative Party (because it went too far). This led to an attitude among peers that because they had not been reformed they had better get on with making the most of the status quo (Baldwin 1995). By 1979, then, against some failed institutional reforms could at least be set some notable behavioural reforms that went some way – but only some way – towards meeting the complaints of critics that parliament failed to check the executive.

Finally, there was Britain's membership of the European Community (EC, later the European Union, EU). David Sanders deals with this in more detail in chapter 1 than is possible here. However, discussing reform of the British state without mentioning Europe is akin to discussing the Second World War and not mentioning Hitler. It is sufficient to note how the issue of membership of the EC is similar to many of the other reforms discussed here. Initially, it is either ignored or rejected. But then, in the 1960s, as doubt about Britain's economic performance and political significance sets in, so the prospect looks more appealing, eventually resulting in membership.

However, the membership of the EC aside, many of the reforms of the 1960s and 1970s were short lived. Most failed to last even a decade. Those that did rarely matched the longevity of the institutions they had replaced. More importantly, however, as will become apparent, they failed to stem Britain's economic decline.

5 The successes are the European Legislation Committee (1974) and the Joint Committee on Statutory Instruments (1972), which both continue to fulfil useful, but strictly limited, functions.

Democratic reform

Beginning around 1970, a new reform fashion emerged that ran alongside modernisation: concern about the state's *democratic* performance. This had a different set of targets: in place of the civil service or parliament, the reformers aimed for the electoral system and the unitary state. In each case the targets, the complaints and the solutions were not original. There had always been criticisms of the electoral system. Equally, neither the use nor the advocacy of referenda was born in the 1970s. And pressures for a devolution of powers to Wales and Scotland have been ever present in the twentieth century. However, in the immediate postwar period they had been a background hum, away from the forefront of political debate. That changed in the 1970s. Electoral reform, devolution, referenda, and, to a lesser extent, a bill of rights, and reform of the judiciary and the House of Lords all became important political issues (Norton 1982: part 2).

The electoral reform debate in the last fifty years has been dominated by the question of how votes cast should be translated into seats.[6] That debate became more urgent in the 1970s – particularly after the 1974 elections – for five reasons.

First, the disproportionality (or 'unfairness') created by the system became more dramatic. In 1951 the Liberals gained 1 per cent of seats in the Commons but since they had received just 2 per cent of the votes they had little complaint. However, in 1974 the Liberals gained almost a fifth of the votes, but only 2 per cent of the seats. This was the largest imbalance since the war.

Second, the winning party (Labour) in 1974 achieved office with the support of only 39 per cent of the vote (or 29 per cent of the electorate). This was another postwar record: the lowest share of the vote received by any victorious party. The fears of a government 'imposing' its policies on the nation with such a flimsy 'mandate' worried many, even those hostile to electoral reform.

Third – another postwar first – the 1974 election had failed to produce a clear winner. This had both an intellectual and a practical impact. Intellectually, it strengthened the case for change, because it showed that one of the supposed virtues of the system – that it produced 'firm' or 'stable' government – was far from certain. Practically (and more importantly), it made change more likely because it ensured that the Liberals – firm supporters of electoral reform – would play a prominent role in the 1974–79 parliament.

6 However, *actual* electoral reform in the last fifty years has been dominated by decisions concerning who should vote and the rules governing elections. As we have seen, the franchise was altered in 1948. The 1969 Representation of the People Act altered it again, extending the vote to those over eighteen (previously it had been twenty-one). There have also been periodic amendments to the constituency boundaries.

The fourth factor was the failure of parliamentary reform. 'External' reformers argued that the internal reforms of parliament (discussed above) had failed because the party system in Britain was too entrenched; what was needed therefore was something that would break down the party blocs. That 'something' was electoral reform.

Fifth, and finally, there was a growing belief that electoral reform could cure Britain's decline. The argument, crudely put, went like this: the British plurality voting system generates a large majority for one party. A small change of votes at the next election then produces a large majority for the other party. The incoming party rips up everything that the outgoing party has begun to achieve. Then another small change in votes returns the original party to government and they in turn replace all of the outgoing party's policies, and so on. This mantra soon became part of the standard case for proportional representation (PR) put forward by reformers, achieving its academic apotheosis in S. E. Finer's *Adversary Politics and Electoral Reform* (1975). Electoral reform, it was argued, by almost certainly leading to a form of coalition government, would remove both the excess variation encouraged by the plurality system (a small swing in votes would no longer lead to a large swing in seats) and the excess power enjoyed by the parties in power ('extremist' policies pursued by one of the coalition's partners would lead to the other partner leaving, bringing down the government, preventing extremist policies being imposed without a mandate). If you changed the electoral system, you produced both a more democratic government and one that performed well. About the only thing not claimed was that electoral reform could produce English cricket victories.

This again demonstrates the centrality of decline and realpolitik to the politics of reform. Electoral reform became attractive because it would cure British decline, and it became a possibility because the government was dependent upon the Liberal Party (buying their support with the promise of a free vote on the use of PR for the European parliament). But by 1979 nothing had been achieved. The House of Commons defeated plans for PR for the European parliament (the government had promised a vote on PR, but not that their backbenchers would support its use), and with the exception of Northern Ireland, where the single transferable vote (STV) is used for sub- and supranational elections, PR was a non-reform.

Much the same can be said for referenda. The 1970s saw referenda used on four occasions on a nationwide basis: in Northern Ireland in 1973 (on continuing membership of the United Kingdom); in the United Kingdom in 1975 (on continuing membership of the European Community); and in both Scotland and Wales in 1979 (on devolution). By 1979, therefore, the entire population could have voted in one referendum, and anyone living anywhere other than England could have voted in two. However, although there may be good democratic reasons for having referenda (itself a matter of debate) in both the two main cases (1975 and 1979) these were not the motivations of those calling for a referendum. There were important party political reasons why the referenda occurred: in 1975, the Labour cabinet was so split that the referendum on Europe became a 'life-raft' (Tony Benn's famous phrase) into which they could clamber; in 1979, the minority Labour government had the referendum forced on it by anti-devolution backbenchers who did not want to be responsible for voting against the government. Although the 1970s saw a handful of referenda, as soon as the political pressures disappeared (as soon, in other words, as we ceased to have a minority government) so too did referenda. Referenda appeared to be a fad of the seventies, just like the Bay City Rollers, Chopper bikes, and Charlie George's sideburns.

Similar political reasons explain the rise of devolution as an issue in the period. In chapter 11 Roger Levy details and explains the rise in nationalism in Scotland and Wales from the mid-1960s onwards, which peaked in October 1974. The grandly titled Royal Commission on the Constitution (under first Lord Crowther and then Lord Kilbrandon) had actually spent most of its time examining just one aspect of the constitution – the position of Scotland and Wales[7] – and had just reported, recommending a devolution of powers. Perhaps as importantly – as with referenda – the Labour government from 1974 onwards did not enjoy a Commons majority and so was dependent upon the goodwill and votes of both nationalists and Liberals (who made devolution one of the foundations of the Lib–Lab pact). But the referenda results of 1979 meant that devolution became one of the great 'nearly reforms' of the last fifty years.

The 1970s also saw early calls for a bill of rights, criticism of the judiciary, and renewed calls for the reform of the House of Lords. The attempt in 1969 to reform the House of Lords has been mentioned above. Eight years later Labour's 1977 party conference voted for the abolition of the House of Lords. But this pledge was not acted upon by the Labour government, and was not in the 1979 manifesto. The calls for a bill of rights came from those who were worried about what Lord Hailsham called the emergence of an 'elective dictatorship'. Ironically, given more recent developments, such calls came mainly from the right. And 1977 saw the first edition of J. A. G. Griffith's highly critical *The Politics of the Judiciary*.

Changing everything?

There is a tendency to overstate the importance of the arrival of Margaret Thatcher in Downing Street in 1979. We are not helped by her own claim to have changed 'everything'. Thankfully, there is now a considerable amount of revisionism as academics and others examine exactly how much

---

7 Devolution has also been suggested for regions within England. Two dissenting members of the Kilbrandon Commission argued just such a case, as did the Redcliffe-Maud report.

changed after 1979 and how much of it would have changed anyway. In retrospect, 1976 – when the Labour government was forced to cut public spending – may prove to be as important a date in British history as 1979. There are, however, four reasons for picking 1979 as an important date in the reform debate.

First, 1979 marked the end of minority government. Thatcher's first Commons majority was not huge, but it was sufficient to allow her to dispense with favours to nationalists, Liberals and other undesirables.

Second, there was a new style of policy making: the 'names' disappeared. The earlier era had seen Fulton, Redcliffe-Maud, Kilbrandon, Wheatley, *et al.* Mackintosh argues that by the end of the 1950s the pressures for reform had become obvious but 'there was no strong ideology to provide guidelines for the necessary reforms,' and so the governments of the 1960s and 1970s 'either tended to hand the task over to a royal commission or begin piecemeal pragmatic changes in the hope that such difficult and unanswered questions would resolve themselves' (see Richards 1984: 32–3). Margaret Thatcher was prime minister for eleven years, yet did not establish a single royal commission.[8]

Third, the purpose of reform changed. In the 1960s and 1970s, the idea of reforming the institutions of the state was to make them perform better. From 1979, the idea of reform was either to (try to) make the state do less or, failing that, to make it perform more cheaply.

Fourth, 1979 marks what was (at the time of writing) seventeen years of uninterrupted Conservative hegemony at a national level. This has had several consequences. It has allowed governments to pursue their plans to fruition, which has had noticeable effects on the reform of the state. And it has meant that the 'outs' of British politics no longer rotate, which has had dramatic effects on the politics of democratic reform.

Heath's 'managerial view of the world' ('the belief that structural reforms would make ideological measures unnecessary') was noted above. Thatcher, by contrast, had a more explicit ideological view of the world, a belief that ideological reforms would make structural measures unnecessary. This ideological belief – crudely described as 'new right' – was itself born out of the perceived failures of the governments of the 1960s and the 1970s. The project of modernisation launched in the 1960s seemed to have failed by 1979. Not only had it not reversed British decline (as it was supposed to) but Britain seemed to be declining ever faster. Articles began appearing discussing 'overload' and 'ungovernability' (see for example King 1975; Rose 1979). The year Margaret Thatcher entered Downing Street, a book was published called *Is Britain Dying?* (by Kramnick). She thought she knew how

---

8 Departmental committees – such as those producing the Franks report on the Falkland Islands or the Scarman report – were still used however.

to stop it dying.[9] Indeed, in one of the more vainglorious parts of her memoirs she comes close to claiming that she was the only person who knew:

> Chatham famously remarked: 'I know that I can save this country and that no one else can'. It would have been presumptuous of me to have compared myself to Chatham. But if I am honest, I must admit that my exhilaration [at winning the 1979 election] came from a similar inner conviction. (Thatcher 1993: 10)

Watching the pennies

One of the most important policies pursued by the Thatcher government in its mission to save Britain was privatisation. This is covered in more detail by Martin Burch and Bruce Wood in chapter 2, but it is important here to note how typical the privatisation programme was of many of the reforms of this period. First, there was no grand privatisation plan, thought out in advance. Second, perhaps as a result, it began slowly: by 1983 few industries had been privatised. Even by 1987 some of the biggest privatisations were still to come. And third the over-riding aim of the scheme was to save money. Nigel Lawson was quite open about this: 'No industry should remain under State ownership unless there is a positive and overwhelming case for it so doing. Inertia is not good enough. We simply cannot afford it' (Sked and Cook 1990: 339). Later the privatisation programme came to be imbued with all sorts of talk of 'extending popular capitalism' but the initial spur was hard cash.

Almost exactly the same process was at play in the civil service. Thatcher did not like the civil service, seeing it as both expensively bureaucratic and consensual. But there is a difference between not liking something and knowing what to do with it. Accordingly, early reforms concentrated on efficiency gains. Sir Derek (now Lord) Rayner was brought in from Marks and Spencer to identify savings. The Rayner 'scrutineers' were told to ask three questions: 'What is it for? What does it cost? What value does it add?'. Similar motivations lay behind the Management Information System for Ministers (MINIS) and the Financial Management Initiative (FMI), a more coordinated drive to improve financial management in departments launched in 1982. The National Audit Office (itself strengthened during the first Thatcher term) began to conduct value-for-money (VFM) audits of government departments. And the process of slimming down the civil service began: by the time Margaret Thatcher left Downing Street it was 23 per cent smaller than when she arrived, and by early 1995 it was smaller still, down by 28 per cent on 1979.

9 Thatcher (1993: 3–15) gives about as good a flavour of the Thatcher/new right analysis of the problems of British decline as you will get anywhere.

Local government was no different. Rod Rhodes describes earlier stages of centre–local relations as being characterised by 'partnership' (1970–74) and 'corporatism' (1974–79). From 1979 to 1983 they were characterised by 'direction' (Rhodes 1992a). Elsewhere he has described the explicit motivations for such direction:

> The first objective was to control local expenditure as part of its broader strategy of reducing public expenditure.... The second objective was to strengthen local accountability by introducing a clear link between the provision of services, paying for them and voting in local elections. (Rhodes 1992b: 51)

However, the second was also seen almost totally in terms of the first: the purpose of strengthening local accountability was to 'encourage efficiency and safeguard against extravagance' (cmnd 8449). This led to a piecemeal approach to reform, largely concentrating on the funding of local authorities: cash limits, rate capping and so on. Even when the government did introduce some structural reform – the abolition of the Greater London Council (GLC) and the other metropolitan authorities in 1986 – the reason was precisely the same. As Norman Tebbit famously admitted, the GLC was being abolished because it was Labour dominated and therefore high spending.

Similarly, apart from the 1982 replacement of area health authorities by district health authorities (probably the last attempt to make the existing system work better) the National Health Service saw:

> efficiency savings, cost improvement programmes, the Rayner scrutinies, restrictions on GP prescribing, management/clinical budgets, performance indicators, competitive tendering and the requirement to dispose of surplus property. The centre-piece of these initiatives, however, has been the introduction of general management and an annual review process; and *underlying all of them has been a cost effectiveness imperative*. (Wistow 1992: 63; my emphasis)

Now nobody understands the system[10]

By the late 1980s the Thatcher governments began to believe that the savings they wanted could not be achieved within the existing institutional structures. It is then, around 1988, that institutional reform began to be implemented. This should not, however, be confused with the earlier structural reforms, because there was no belief that structural reform in itself could work. It was merely the means to an end. That end was the market.

An almost identical process went on in nearly every part of the state. Services that could be were privatised. If they could not actually be put into the market, then they were at least exposed to the market. And failing

10 This is lifted (shamelessly) from Rhodes (1991).

that, they were made to perform in an artificial market or be managed by people who were from the market. One of the most obvious examples of this (again) is the civil service. The year 1988 saw the publication of the Efficiency Unit's report *Improving Management in Government: The Next Steps*, which argued for a 'quite different way of conducting the business of government':

> The central Civil Service should consist of a relatively small core engaged in the function of servicing Ministers and managing departments, who will be the 'sponsors' of particular government policies and services. Responding to these departments will be large numbers of agencies employing their own staff, who may or may not have the status of Crown servants, and concentrating on the delivery of their particular service. (Efficiency Unit 1988: para. 44)

Next Steps (as it became known) was described by the Treasury and Civil Service Committee as 'the most ambitious attempt at Civil Service reform in the twentieth century'. It began slowly. But by mid-1994 over 60 per cent of the civil service worked in organisations run along *Next Steps* lines.

Running alongside *Next Steps* were several other reforms: the Citizen's Charter, launched in 1991; the launch of market testing, which tests the in-house service against external competition and, if necessary, contracts out; and the privatisation of agencies if the government feels that their functions could be better carried out in the private sector. Indeed, *Next Steps* agencies are set up only if the three 'prior options' of abolition, privatisation and contracting out have been considered and rejected.

Also in the late 1980s, local authorities shifted from being 'providers' (actually providing services themselves) to 'enablers' (ensuring that others provide the service). Compulsory competitive tendering (CCT) required authorities to allow private firms to carry out of a wide range of services if they could do so more cheaply than the in-house organisation. In addition, many powers – over policing, transport, housing and education – were taken away from local authorities and given to other (almost always unelected) bodies. The urban development corporations took over control of the authorities' planning and regeneration functions. The 1988 Education Reform Act delegated management of the schools from the local education authority (LEA) to the governors of a school and allowed schools to opt out of LEA control altogether if they so wish (and the introduction of the national curriculum diminished the influence that LEAs had over those schools that remained). The 1989 white paper *Working for Patients* set out the plans for an internal market in health care: separating 'purchasers' from 'providers'. In addition, more and more 'providers' now have trust status, making them more independent. In some cases these trends had begun earlier (such as the sale of council houses, for example) but it was the late 1980s that experienced the more dramatic changes.

Local government also saw the poll tax (community charge) and structural reorganisation. Both were extensions of the principle that greater account-ability would lead to lower expenditure. The poll tax was an attempt to make all local electors aware of the full cost of their services, and thus vote for those that cost less (Butler *et al.* 1994: 58–9). It was not an unqualified success and was replaced by the council tax in 1993, which traded accountability for popularity. Local government reorganisation was supposed to lead to unitary authorities, also seen as improving the lines of account-ability. Such unitary authorities began functioning in Scotland and Wales in 1996. In England a local government commission was established in 1992 under Sir John Banham to investigate, area by area, the shape and structure of local government, to see whether unitary authorities should be introduced. However, many of its solutions – few of which were unitary authorities – were not those favoured by the government. Banham was dismissed in March 1995, and at present very few unitary authorities have been proposed or implemented.

Among all this change, one institution has remained relatively stable: parliament. The most dramatic change came with the introduction of a system of departmental select committees in 1979. Even allowing for (understandable) hyperbole, Norman St John-Stevas (then Leader of the House, and now Lord St John of Fawsley) was probably right when he said that the Commons was 'embarking on a series of changes that could constitute the most important parliamentary reform of the century'. Since their inception, the committees have changed slightly in number and style, and have not fulfilled all of people's (often over-inflated) expectations (Jogerst 1993). But they are certainly an improvement on what went before. Perhaps as importantly, they are now embedded: they have lasted for over seventeen years, and show no signs of disappearing. In addition, parliament became better resourced, more professional, and, with televising, more open. The rise of the 'career politician' – which had begun in the 1970s – continued unabated through the 1980s and 1990s. The 'constituency face' of the MP in Britain became increasingly important, as constituents made more use of their MPs, themselves more proactive in their links with the constituency (Cowley 1996). However, it is a comment both on these changes and on the other reforms of the postwar era that the introduction of select committees count as the most important.

Parliament notwithstanding, the period since 1979, and in particular since the late 1980s, has seen the most radical reforms to the state in the last fifty years. Ironically, it has been a Conservative government that initially explicitly eschewed institutional reform that has actually delivered it.

There is one other constant that links all these changes: they have fragmented the state, making it *extremely* complicated. The following exchange, which occurred between Sir Robin Butler, the cabinet secretary, and a Labour MP during a select committee sitting on the civil service, sums it up well:

> John Garrett MP: Is it not the case that we are in the process of moving from a unified Civil Service of some 30 main departments to a Civil Service which consists of 30 ministerial head offices, about 150 executive agencies and units, hundreds of quangos like TECs, trusts and corporate bodies and thousands of contracts with private contractors, all of whom are trying to make a profit? Would you agree with that description?
>
> Sir Robin Butler: Yes, I do not think that is an inaccurate description.

The British state is turning into a version of the famous nineteenth-century Schleswig-Holstein question, which it was said only three people understood: one was dead, another insane, and the third had forgotten.

The effect of exclusion

The years of Conservative electoral hegemony since 1979 had four consequences – two obvious, two less obvious – for the politics of democratic reform in Britain.

First, that with one or two minor exceptions, there was no democratic reform.[11] Although some Conservative politicians had been toying with reform prior to victory in 1979, victory itself soon dissuaded them: with very few exceptions proposals for political reform tend to come from those who are 'out'.

Second, because for all this period only one party was 'in', the party that was out (Labour) began to have doubts about the workings of the system. Before 1979, although parties that were out of power complained about the system, they thought that they might have a good chance of re-entering government at the next election under the existing system.

As well as being less obvious, the third and fourth consequences are not as self-serving. The third consequence was, without wanting to be melo-dramatic, that the period of one-party dominance changed Labour's view of history. Before 1979, many Labour politicians had (whether they knew it or not) a teleological view of the history of citizenship: the battle for rights in Britain had progressed from civil rights (in the eighteenth century) to political rights (in the nineteenth) to social rights (in the twentieth). The first two battles were over; socialists in the twentieth century had to fight the third, which they could do within the existing framework because that framework was egalitarian. The longevity of Conservative rule threw that

---

11 In 1985 the franchise was extended to British citizens living overseas if they had left the country in the last five years; in 1989 this was extended to twenty years. At the time this was a consensual measure, with cross-party support. It has since become far more controversial.

assumption open to question, as Labour politicians saw (what to them were) attacks on basic civil and political rights (Marquand 1992: 44–58).

Closely associated with this comes the fourth and final consequence of one-party dominance. Britain used to be described as a two-party (or sometimes a two-and-a-half party) system; as Conservative election victory followed election victory, it was better described as a one-party dominant system (King 1992: 223–48; Heywood 1994: 10–25). As Hutton (1995: 3–4) argued:

> The only formal check on executive power is the notion of a government-in-waiting – Her Majesty's Opposition – but four successive Conservative election victories have devalued even that threat.... In some respects the concentration and centralisation of power resembles that of a one-party state.

This one-party state, so the argument went, led to a breakdown in standards in politics, increased corruption, and a decline in civic culture (as described by Bill Jones and Lynton Robins in the Conclusion). The creation of the 'quangocracy' or 'magistracy' – the unelected members of quangos – and the rise in the concerns about political 'sleaze' have both been seen as resulting from one-party dominance.[12]

As a consequence, there has been a recent dramatic growth in books about the need for constitutional 'renewal', all of which poke fun at all sorts of British political institutions and declare them unfit in much the same way as Shanks and others ridiculed the 'establishment' in the 1960s. Examples of this genre would include Holme and Elliot's *1688–1988 Time for a New Constitution* (1988), Graham and Prosser's *Waiving the Rules* (1988), almost anything by Charter 88 (itself a good example of the phenomenon), Brazier's *Constitutional Reform* (1991), Marr's *Ruling Britannia* (1995), and Will Hutton's best-selling *The State We're In* (1995). As always, there are plenty of solutions aimed at plenty of targets: parliament, quangos, local government, the police, the judiciary, the monarchy. And, as always, these reforms are linked with Britain's economic decline. Large parts of the British left now view as almost a truism the belief that political change will lead to economic change (Wright 1987).

But most importantly, this is now the view of the Labour Party. Changes in the position of the Labour Party on democratic reform took a long time coming, and for all practical purposes began after the 1987 election, and continued with force after the 1992 election. Take electoral reform as an example. In 1984 the Labour Campaign for Electoral Reform (LCER) had just thirty-five members. Even as late as 1989, Labour's policy review document *Meet the Challenge, Make the Change* described the present system

---

12 Two special issues of *Parliamentary Affairs* in 1995 (volume 48) analyse quangos and the rise of sleaze in depth.

as producing 'the most honest, the most efficient and the most effective form of government'. But between 1989 and 1991, in a series of conference decisions – beginning with the rejection of plurality voting for a Scottish parliament – Labour's position on electoral reform shifted from outright opposition to agnosticism. By 1990 LCER had 1,000 members; and by 1993 that had doubled again (Linton 1993). The Labour Party is now committed to a referendum on electoral reform should it gain power. But it is also committed to a lot more: House of Lords reform, various measures of parliamentary reform, devolution to both Scotland and Wales (with the Scottish parliament using proportional representation rather than plurality), and the incorporation of the European Convention of Human Rights into British law as the first step towards a bill of rights. Together these reforms would be 'more substantial *in toto* than any carried out by any British Government since the First World War' (Marquand 1992: 47). For the first time since 1945 a political party would enter government with plans to change the democratic arrangements of the state.

It is also the policy of both main parties (along with the Liberal Democrats) to offer a referendum on the issue of a single European currency. But, as in the 1970s, they will be offered to get the parties out of political holes. Labour supports a referendum on electoral reform because many of its own backbenchers are deeply unhappy about the plan. Both parties support a referendum on a single currency for the same reason. And Labour's plan to have referenda on devolution allows it (partially) to deflect Conservative charges about the costs and powers of devolved government.

Reformers should not get carried away with excitement. Labour's commitment to constitutional reform is broad but not deep. Tony Blair is not a supporter of electoral reform (Rentoul 1995: ch. 19). There are considerable doubts about whether Labour has any real desire to create a wholly elected second chamber and about whether it will find time in its legislative programme for even removing the right of hereditary peers to vote. Doubts about the wisdom of incorporating the European Convention on Human Rights run throughout the party. Even devolution – which of all the reforms promised by Labour is probably the most likely to be enacted – is causing the party all sorts of headaches.

Conclusion

Compared with the nineteenth century, which saw the Great Reform Act of 1832, or even the first half of this century, which witnessed the suffragettes and the clash over the 'people's budget' of 1909, the last fifty years at first look bland by comparison. In 1945 Britain had an asymmetric bicameral legislature, one chamber of which was elected almost exclusively by a simple plurality system in single-member constituencies. The passage of fifty years just requires you to take the word 'almost' out of the last sentence: the second house – a majority of whose members are still there by birthright rather than merit – is now slightly weaker in formal terms than it was in 1945 (but has reasserted itself marginally in informal terms), and the few minor exceptions to the electoral system have been removed. In 1945 there were complaints that the legislature was not an adequate check on the executive; direct democracy was used only for some local matters and then rarely; and Britain had a unitary political system. *Plus ça change....*

This chapter has shown that this is too simplistic a picture. Apart from the first decade and a half after the war, the remaining thirty-five years can be summed up without exaggeration as years when the promise of reform has been continually dangled before the British people. That promise came in two instalments. The first, from 1960 to 1979, saw attempts to make the existing system work better. Most failed. Those that were implemented were replaced as a new reformist fashion took hold after 1979: a fashion to make the system do less. This process began slowly, but the last decade has seen the implementation of reforms that have dramatically altered the structure of the state. It is always easy to throw words like 'revolution' about, but it seems a fair description of the recent reforms of the public sector.

It is too early to see if these reforms have achieved their desired end, and halted British decline (although it seems doubtful at present). In his *Britain in Decline*, Andrew Gamble lists the different types of explanations for this decline. Many have nothing to do with the institutions of the British state, individually or collectively. British decline may be historical, or cultural, or just plain inevitable (Gamble 1990: ch. 1). If so, then the 'leave it alone' approach of the Attlee, Churchill and Eden governments after the war may have been right, albeit right for the wrong reasons.

But the thesis of this chapter is that 'right' or 'wrong' does not help explain what has gone before. Nor does it explain what may be about to come. Pressures for democratic reform have been ever present since the 1970s, but little has been done. We now may be about to enter a new period of reform. Labour's policies include the most wide-ranging package of constitutional reform since 1945. That package is the result both of almost two decades of exclusion from the corridors of power and of a belief that democratic constitutional reform will deliver economic success where modernisation and the market failed. It will be interesting to see what – if anything – happens. Despite the Queen's objections, Alice may yet get her jam.

References

Baldwin, N. D. J. (1995), The House of Lords and the Labour government 1974–79, *Journal of Legislative Studies*, 1, 218–42.

Butler, D., Adonis, A. and Travers, T. (1994), *Failure in British Government: The Politics of the Poll Tax*, Oxford, Oxford University Press.

Butler, D. and Pinto-Duschinsky, M. (1971), *The British General Election of 1970*, London, Macmillan.

Cowley, P. (1996), Good value for 19p? The consequences of MP–constituent post, *Politics Review*, 5, 12–15.

Crosland, C. A. R. (1962), *The Conservative Enemy*, London, Jonathan Cape.

Dowding, K. (1995), *The Civil Service*, London, Routledge.

Efficiency Unit (1988), *Improving Management in Government: The Next Steps*, London, HMSO.

Finer, S. E. (ed.) (1975), *Adversary Politics and Electoral Reform*, London, Anthony Wigram.

Gamble, A. (1990), *Britain in Decline* (3rd edn), London, Macmillan.

Griffith, J. A. G. (1977), *The Politics of the Judiciary*, London, Fontana Paperback.

Heywood, A. (1994) Britain's dominant party, in L. Robins, H. Blackmore and R. Pyper (eds), *Britain's Party System*, Leicester, Leicester University Press.

Hutton, W. (1995), *The State We're In*, London, Vintage.

Jogerst, M. (1993), *Reform in the House of Commons*, Lexington, University Press of Kentucky.

Johnson, N. (1979), Select committees and administration, in S. A. Walkland (ed.), *The House of Commons in the Twentieth Century*, Oxford, Oxford University Press.

Kellner, P. and Crowther-Hunt, Lord (1980), *The Civil Servants*, London, Macdonald.

King, A. (1975), Overload: problems of governing in the 1970s, *Political Studies*, 23, 284–96.

King, A. (1992), The implications of one-party government', in A. King *et al.*, *Britain at the Polls 1992*, Chatham, Chatham House.

Linton, M. (1993), *Labour's Road to Electoral Reform*, Guildford, LCER.

Magee, B. (1962), *The New Radicalism*, London, Martin, Secker and Warburg.

Marquand, D. (1992), Half-way to citizenship? The Labour Party and constitutional reform, in M. J. Smith and J. Spear (eds), *The Changing Labour Party*, London, Routledge.

Marwick, A. (1990), *British Society Since 1945* (2nd edn), Harmondsworth, Penguin.

Norton, P. (1981), *The Commons in Perspective*, Oxford, Martin Robertson.

Norton, P. (1982), *The Constitution in Flux*, Oxford, Blackwell.

Norton, P. (1991), In defence of the constitution: a riposte to the radicals, in P. Norton (ed.), *New Directions in British Politics*, Aldershot, Edward Elgar.

Pollard, S. (1982), *The Wasting of the British Economy*, London, Croom Helm.

Rentoul, J. (1995), *Tony Blair*, London, Little, Brown.

Rhodes, R. A. W. (1991), Now nobody understands the system: the changing face of local government, in P. Norton (ed.), *New Directions in British Politics*, Aldershot, Edward Elgar.

Rhodes, R. A. W. (1992a), Local government, in B. Jones and L. Robins (eds), *Two Decades in British Politics*, Manchester, Manchester University Press.

Rhodes, R. A. W. (1992b), Local government finance, in D. Marsh and R. A. W. Rhodes (eds), *Implementing Thatcherite Policies. Audit of an Era*, Buckingham, Open University Press.

Richards, P. G. (ed.) (1984), *Mackintosh's The Government and Politics of Britain*, London, Hutchinson.

Rose, R. (1979), Ungovernability: is there smoke behind the fire?, *Political Studies*, 27, 351–70.

Sked, A. and Cook, C. (1990), *Post-War Britain* (3rd edn), Harmondsworth, Penguin.

Thatcher, M. (1993), *The Downing Street Years*, New York, Harper Collins.

Wistow, G. (1992), The health policy community, in D. Marsh and R. A. W. Rhodes (eds), *Policy Networks in British Government*, Oxford, Clarendon Press.

Wright, A. (1987), British decline: political or economic?, *Parliamentary Affairs*, 40, 41–56.

Young, K. (1994), The party and English local government, in A. Seldon and S. Ball (eds), *Conservative Century*, Oxford, Oxford University Press.

7

Elections and voting behaviour

David Denver

In surveying changes in elections and voting behaviour in Britain over the past half century or so, the 1950 general election marks a better point of departure than 1945. When the 1945 election was held – the first for ten years – the war with Japan was still in progress and millions of electors were still serving overseas with the forces. The 1950 election was, then, the first 'normal' postwar election and a simple comparison of the results in the 1950 and 1992 general elections (table 1) illustrates some of the major changes that have occurred during this period.[1]

The data show, first of all, that Labour had a much lower level of support among the voters in 1992 than it had in 1950. This reflects a long-term trend. After 1951 Labour support in general elections fell steadily – although there was a slight reversal of the trend in the mid-1960s – to just 28.3 per cent in 1983. In the 1987 and 1992 elections Labour recovered somewhat but, even so, their share of the vote was still significantly smaller than it had been in the 1950s.

Second, in contrast, the Liberal Democrats in 1992 gained almost double the share of votes that their predecessors had in 1950. This too reflects a gradual change but in this case it dates from the 1970s. The 1950 election marked almost the last gasp of the old Liberal Party and during the 1950s they were almost eliminated as a serious force in electoral politics. In February 1974, however, the Liberal share of the British vote increased sharply to almost 20 per cent and in 1983 the Alliance between the Liberals and the Social Democratic Party gained 26 per cent. Since then, electoral support for the centre has declined somewhat, but in the 1990s the Liberal Democrats remain much more serious contenders for votes than the Liberals had been at the start of the period.

Third, table 1 shows that the part played in elections by the nationalist parties is now much more significant than it used to be. This development

---

1 The figures given in the table and referred to in the text exclude Northern Ireland.

Table 1 Results of the 1950 and 1992 general elections in Britain

	1950			1992		
	% of votes	No. of candidates	No. of seats	% of votes	No. of candidates	No. of seats
Conservatives	43.0	607	288	42.8	634	336
Labour	46.8	612	315	35.2	634	271
Liberals[a]	9.3	475	9	18.3	632	20
SNP	0.03	3	0	1.9	72	3
Plaid Cymru	0.06	7	0	0.5	35	4
Communists	0.3	100	0	–	–	–
Others	0.5	41	1	1.3	842	0
Turnout	84.0			77.9		

The figures shown exclude Northern Ireland.
Sources: Craig (1981); Rallings and Thrasher (1993).
[a]Liberal Democrats in 1992.

dates from the late 1960s. In 1950 the Scottish National Party (SNP) and Plaid Cymru were generally regarded as rather eccentric parties on the fringes of British politics, but now both contest almost all seats in their respective countries and are major players in the electoral game. In 1992 the SNP gained 21.5 per cent of the Scottish vote and Plaid 8.8 per cent of the vote in Wales.

Fourth, there has been a massive increase in the number and variety of 'others' participating in British elections, although the support that they attract remains at a very low level. In 1950 there were 100 Communist Party candidates but these have now all but disappeared. They have been more than replaced, however, by new parties, such as the Green Party and the Natural Law Party, which put forward 256 and 300 candidates respectively in 1992, and by a variety of other concerned, aggrieved or eccentric groups and individuals. Increased participation by, and support for, Liberal Democrats, nationalists and others has not greatly affected the composition of the House of Commons, however. In 1950 the two major parties held 98.4 per cent of seats in mainland Britain. By 1992 this had fallen only slightly, to 95.7 per cent. This reflects, of course, the operation of the electoral system, which benefits parties which have geographical concentrations of support.

The final point worth noting from table 1 is that the turnout of electors was six percentage points lower in 1992 than in 1950. This does not reflect any long-term trend, however, and, indeed, the two figures are not exactly comparable. The voting age was lowered from twenty-one to eighteen just before the 1970 general election and the 1992 turnout figure is based on a much larger electorate, containing many more young people (a group which does not have a very good turnout record) than the 1950 figure. In fact, turnout in 1992 was slightly higher than the average for all thirteen general elections since 1950.

A second set of changes in British elections since 1950, which is not revealed by an examination of the results, is in the nature and style of election campaigning. Modern campaigns are sophisticated exercises in political marketing (Scammell 1995; Kavanagh 1995). The parties employ professional experts to give advice on the content of party political broadcasts on television, on the images of party leaders and how they should be improved, on the design of posters and logos, on the slogans to be employed and even on the policies to be stressed. There is a strong focus on the party leaders, who jet around the country, accompanied by teams of aides, minders and security personnel, as well as a media scrum of radio and television crews and press reporters; they address large meetings and rallies of supporters, visit hospitals, schools and factories and occasionally meet and talk to ordinary voters. The primary purpose of engaging in these activities is to be *seen* doing them on television. Daily press conferences are carefully managed and other campaign events planned to ensure the best possible media coverage. Public opinion polls appear almost daily – and the parties conduct their own private polls – and the progress of the parties is carefully charted. Television coverage of the campaign reaches saturation point with daily news programmes, campaign reports and analyses, discussion programmes and extended formal interviews with the party leaders. These interviews are now major campaign events and the leaders prepare for them very thoroughly.

All of this is a far cry from election campaigning in the 1950 election. Television hardly existed. There were party election broadcasts on the wireless – all on the Home Service, with some repeated on the Light Programme – but these consisted simply of leading party figures making speeches to the microphone. Apart from these broadcasts, as Nicholas (1951: 126) noted, 'the BBC kept as aloof from the election as if it had been occurring on another planet'. After the election was called, 'virtually all mention of election politics disappeared from the British air,' until the sober reading out of constituency results on election night.[2] The results of only six opinion polls were published during the campaign (one a week by two companies) and for the first time the parties began, tentatively, to use poll results to assist with their campaign strategies. Perhaps the most

---

2 Coverage of the election was avoided by the BBC because it was believed that any coverage might conflict with its commitment to neutrality and be in contravention of the current Representation of the People Act. An extraordinary consequence, noted by Nicholas (1951), was that every broadcasting service in the world reported a speech by Winston Churchill proposing talks on the atomic bomb with the USSR, except for the BBC and the USSR's radio service.

extraordinary comparison with modern campaigns concerns the activities of the party leaders. In 1950, the prime minister, Clement Attlee, undertook a 1,000-mile tour of the country. He was accompanied only by his wife and a single detective and travelled in his prewar family saloon car (with Mrs Attlee doing the driving). His campaigning consisted of making speeches at large public meetings in the major cities. If the little group was ahead of schedule they stopped by the roadside and Mrs Attlee caught up with some knitting while the prime minister smoked his pipe and did a crossword puzzle (Nicholas 1951: 93–4).

Clearly, there has been a revolution in election campaigning over the past half century. Largely this is due to the growth of television. It is generally agreed that 1959 was the first 'television' election, with the BBC overcoming its earlier inhibitions about political coverage, and from the 1960s campaigns were dominated by television. In addition, changes have resulted from associated developments in what might be called campaign 'technology' – the extensive use of polls (both public and private), computers, targeted direct mailing, advertising and marketing techniques and so on. In contrast with the early postwar years, election campaigning in the 1990s is a highly professional activity to which the parties devote enormous effort and resources.

A third area in which there have been major changes since 1950 is in the study of elections and the analysis of electoral behaviour. As noted above, there were six published opinion polls during the 1950 campaign and these received relatively little attention. By the 1970s about twenty-five campaign polls was the norm and this number continued to increase during the 1980s. In 1992 there were at least fifty-seven national polls together with regional polls, constituency polls, polls of specific groups of voters and three 'exit' polls on election day itself. The campaign polls were themselves a major feature of media reporting of the campaign and the exit polls enabled instant analysis of voting behaviour by television pundits, which was communicated to viewers by sophisticated computer graphics. Academic studies of voting behaviour have also changed. The 1950 election saw the first-ever survey study of voting behaviour in Britain – some 850 voters in the constituency of Greenwich were interviewed before, during and after the election. Partly because of the rudimentary nature of the technology available to analyse survey returns (there were no computers) the book reporting the results of the study was not published until six years later (Benney *et al.* 1956). Although the topics covered have remained central concerns for electoral analysts – the role of social class and policy opinions, voters' attention to the local and national campaigns, vote switching, and so on – the report was very much an exploratory and mapping operation, and the analysis was confined to what would now be regarded as the elementary technique of cross-tabulation. Further constituency surveys followed in the 1950s but it was not until 1963 that the first nationwide academic survey was undertaken. Although 1963 was not an election year, this was the first of a series of national surveys carried out at every general election since 1964 and reported in a series of major election studies (Butler and Stokes 1969, 1974; Sarlvik and Crewe 1983; Heath *et al.* 1985, 1991, 1994). The availability of these data, together with the development of computers and of statistical techniques, has given rise to an explosion in the number of books and articles presenting highly sophisticated analyses of British electoral behaviour over the past twenty years or so.

This literature has charted major changes in voting behaviour in Britain. Despite the relative paucity of relevant data from the 1950s, most analysts suggest that, compared with those of the 1950s and 1960s, the bases and processes of party choice among voters from the 1970s onwards were significantly different. Four main changes can be identified – from alignment to dealignment, from stability to volatility, from uniformity to variability and from habitual to 'judgemental' voting – each of which is explained and discussed in what follows.

From alignment to dealignment

To describe the electorate as being 'aligned' has two distinct meanings. First, it suggests that there is an alignment between the social groups or categories to which people belong and the parties that they vote for. Second, it means that individual voters align themselves with parties by identifying with them – by thinking of themselves as party supporters rather than as people who vote for the party from time to time. In both cases, the story of the past fifty years is one of a move from alignment to dealignment.

In their research on the 1950 election in Greenwich, Benney *et al.* were much influenced by previous research in the United States, which emphasised the extent to which party choice appeared to be determined by social characteristics. Among other things, therefore, the British team set out to describe the 'social geography' of party choice, and this 'social determinism' approach has continued to figure prominently in voting studies ever since. Benney *et al.* investigated the effect of social class, age, sex, education, religion and union membership and found that alignment by class was by far the strongest (1956: 103–5). Every subsequent study of voting in the 1950s and 1960s agreed and, on the basis of their national surveys in the 1960s, Butler and Stokes (1974: 77) argued that while class did not entirely determine party choice, 'its pre-eminent role can hardly be questioned'.

The situation today is rather different. From about 1970 observers began to detect a weakening of the alignment between class and party – a class dealignment. Although there has been considerable debate about the precise meaning and measurement of class dealignment, most analysts agree that

132

there has been a decline in the proportion of middle-class electors voting Conservative and of working-class electors voting Labour. Changes in the definition of classes and the move from local to national surveys – themselves reflecting the increased sophistication of voting studies – make it difficult to compare the strength of the class alignment in the 1950s and the 1990s. In table 2, however, the figures for manual and non-manual workers presented by Benney *et al.* (1956) are compared with those found in surveys by the national British Election Study at the 1964 (Crewe *et al.* 1991) and 1992 elections.

The data from the Greenwich survey showed that over 70 per cent of both groups voted for the expected party. By 1964 national figures suggested that the class alignment was somewhat weaker but still significant, with over 60 per cent of respondents voting along class lines. By 1992, however, only around half of manual workers voted Labour while just over half of non-manual workers voted Conservative. In this sense, therefore, there has been a clear class dealignment. The data in table 2 also suggest that the decline in middle-class Conservative support seems to have been to the advantage of the centre parties and others, whereas in the working class there has been a clear increase in support for the Conservatives as well as others. This interpretation is consistent with the trends in election results discussed above, which showed steady support for the Conservatives, a decline in Labour support and an increase in support for other parties.

No new social cleavage has emerged to replace class as the primary basis of party support. Region of residence has become more important but within-region variations remain very substantial. Ethnic minority voters were practically non-existent in the early 1950s and are now a strongly Labour-supporting group. But, since members of ethnic minorities constitute only about 5 per cent of the electorate, ethnicity fails to discriminate among the vast majority of voters. Patrick Dunleavy (1980) has suggested that sector of employment and of consumption of services (public or private)

Table 2 Party choice of non-manual and manual workers, 1950, 1964, 1992 (%)

	Non-manual			Manual		
	1950	*1964*	*1992*	*1950*	*1964*	*1992*
Conservatives	74	64	54	23	31	34
Labour	19	21	23	73	60	49
Liberals/other	7	16	23	4	9	16
No. of respondents	109	464	1,299	500	1,048	1,045

Sources: 1950 figures calculated from Benney *et al.* (1956: table 9); 1964 figures from Crewe *et al.* (1991: table 1.13); 1992 figures calculated directly from British Election Study data.

may have replaced the class cleavage but the evidence for this is patchy. Taking a variety of social characteristics together – class, age, sex, religion and housing tenure – our ability to predict party support on the basis of social location is now significantly less good than it was even in the 1960s (Rose and McAllister 1990).

The second form of alignment relates to party identification. Although it had long been recognised that voters had enduring attachments to political parties – derived, for example, from family and community traditions – from which they rarely deviated, the concept of party identification was developed in the United States in the 1950s. In 1964, 81 per cent of the electorate had a 'partisan self-image' that was either Labour or Conservative while 40 per cent described themselves as 'very strongly' Conservative or Labour. By 1992 generalised attachment to the two main parties was still common – 78 per cent identified with one of them – but the strength of attachment had declined significantly. Only 18 per cent of the electorate were very strongly Labour or Conservative. This weakening of the psychological alignment between voters and the major parties had a variety of causes – the performances of the parties in government and the extent and nature of television coverage of politics, for instance – and has important consequences. Strong party identification acted like an anchor, binding the voter securely to a party and thus ensuring stability in party support over lengthy periods (for a lifetime in many cases). When the anchor is loosened the voter is likely to drift on the electoral sea, being pushed backwards and forwards by temporarily prevailing winds. Electoral volatility increases and stability decreases.

From stability to volatility

Given the strength of class and partisan alignment in the 1950s, it is not surprising to find that students of voting behaviour tended to emphasise the stability of party choice among voters, both from election to election and in the run-up to a specific election. At this time the British Institute for Public Opinion estimated that about 80 per cent of the national electorate always voted for the same party (cited in Milne and Mackenzie 1958: 77). Individual constituency surveys also produced evidence of impressive stability in voting. Milne and Mackenzie, for example, found that three-quarters of their respondents in Bristol North East had made their minds up about how to vote in the 1955 election by the time of the 1951 election, and commented upon the 'rock-like fidelity of the British voter' (Milne and Mackenzie 1958: 36–7). These studies also exploded the myth that 'floating voters' (those who switched) came closest to fulfilling the ideal of the democratic citizen. On the contrary, floaters were found to be less interested in politics, less well informed about politics, and less concerned about the outcomes of elections than those who always voted for the same party. As early as the 1960s, however, Butler and Stokes detected an increase in electoral volatility, which they believed was a consequence of incipient class dealignment (Butler and Stokes 1974: 206–8, 268–75).

In order to explore the extent and nature of the growth in volatility more systematically, however, we need to consider the meaning of volatility more closely. At its simplest, volatility refers to the extent to which voters switch parties in successive elections. Unfortunately, measuring this is not straight-forward, since there can be no guarantee that survey respondents will accurately remember what they did in an election four to five years before. A broader definition of inter-election volatility would include as volatile voters not only those who switch parties but also those who move between voting and not voting at either of the relevant elections, even though they were eligible to vote. Table 3 shows figures for these two definitions of volatility at four elections from 1950 to 1992.

Benney *et al.* reported that among those who voted in both 1945 and 1950 only 13 per cent changed parties; Milne and Mackenzie found a very similar level of switching (14 per cent) between 1951 and 1955. In the first national survey study, Butler and Stokes suggested that 18 per cent of those who voted in both 1959 and 1964 switched parties. From the 1970s, however, the proportion of switchers was regularly greater than 20 per cent, and was 22 per cent for the 1987–92 elections. Not unexpectedly, the broader definition of volatile behaviour produces higher volatility estimates. Given the circumstances of the 1945 election we would expect a great deal of movement from non-voting in 1945 to voting in 1950 and that is what the Greenwich study found. The volatility figure including all eligible voters is 35 per cent. By 1955, however, things had settled down and Milne and Mackenzie's data suggest that 22 per cent of their sample were volatile in this wider sense between 1951 and 1955. Between 1959 and 1964 the figure was rather higher, at 35 per cent, and in 1992 higher still, at 37 per cent. More detailed analysis shows that switching between Labour and the Conservatives is usually the least common form of inter-election volatility. Switching between major and minor parties is more

Table 3 Trends in electoral volatility

	1945–50	*1951–55*	*1959–64*	*1987–92*
Percentage who switched parties	13	14	18	22
Percentage who switched (including non-voters)	35	22	35	37

Sources: 1945–50 figures are calculated from Benney *et al.* (1956: 221) and 1951–55 from Milne and Mackenzie (1958: table 3, p. 42). 1964 and 1992 figures are from Heath *et al.* (1994: 281).

frequent and moving between voting and non-voting is usually the most common type of change in successive elections. Nonetheless, the data in table 3 suggest that there was somewhat more inter-election volatility from the 1960s onwards and that electoral change involved not a small minority of floaters but a large section of the British electorate.

This conclusion is supported by an examination of general election results. If we compare the period from the 1950 election to the 1970 election with elections from February 1974 to 1992, we find that there has been greater variability in the shares of votes received by the major parties in the later period. The range of Conservative vote share (the difference between the maximum and the minimum) was 7.8 percentage points between 1950 and 1970 and 8.1 percentage points from 1974 to 1992. For Labour the respective figures are more striking – 5.8 and 11.6, while for the Liberals and their successors they are 8.7 and 11.6.

A second type of volatility might be called 'campaign swithering'. This refers to the extent to which voters change their minds about which party to support, or delay making up their minds, or are hesitant about coming to a decision during the campaign. One simple indicator of this is the percentage of voters who report that they did make up their minds about which party to support during the election campaign itself. In the earliest election for which data are given (1955) 15 per cent of respondents claimed that they decided which way to vote during the election campaign. By 1964 this had fallen to 11 per cent but from 1974 the figure was regularly over 20 per cent and was almost a quarter of all voters in 1992. A more detailed and complicated analysis of campaign volatility from 1964 also suggests that it rose sharply from 1970 and peaked in 1983. The 1987 election saw unusually low volatility but in 1992 there was a return to the levels of the mid-1970s (see Farrell *et al.* 1995).

A third dimension of volatility is 'mid-term movement'. Between general elections some electors have the opportunity to vote in by-elections, many in local elections and all, nowadays, in European elections. In addition, monthly opinion polls keep track of movements in voters' opinions. Academic surveys of voters between elections are rare, however, and a relatively recent innovation. Nonetheless, those that have been undertaken all find that the proportion of voters which can be described as constant declines sharply if mid-term attitudes to the parties are taken into account. Thus, in the 1983 and 1987 general elections and an interview in 1986, 71 per cent of Heath *et al.*'s (1991) panel of respondents voted for the same party in the two elections, whereas only 61 per cent supported the same party on all three occasions.

To compare the extent of mid-term volatility today with volatility in the early part of the period we can use the results of by-elections and opinion polls. Although analysis is complicated by the precise point in the inter-election cycle at which by-elections occur, it does seem clear that by-elections now produce much greater swings in votes than they used to (Norris 1990). A rough indication of the change is given by calculating the average drop in support for the governing party in by-elections held during its period in office. During 1945–51, sixty-two by-elections produced an average decline of 2.2 per cent in Labour's share of the vote. Between 1951 and 1964, 154 by-elections saw the Conservative share fall by 8.7 per cent on average. During the Conservative governments from 1979 to December 1996 the average fall was 13.8 per cent (in seventy-two by-elections). Another rough indication of increased mid-term volatility comes from a comparison of monthly opinion poll results during two lengthy periods of Conservative government – from 1951 to 1964 and from 1979 to 1992. Ignoring three months on either side of a general election, the difference between the maximum and minimum proportion of voters intending to vote Conservative throughout the first period was 19 percentage points; in the later period it was 29 points. Similarly, the range of Labour support rose from 15 to 29.5 points; for the Liberals during 1951–64 the range of voting intentions was 23 points while for their successors from 1979 to 1992 it was a huge 45.5 points.

Some commentators reject the view that the British electorate has become more volatile over the past fifty years (Heath *et al.* 1994: ch. 15) but their position rests largely on a restricted definition of volatility and the argument that the increased participation of third and fourth parties in elections caused (rather than reflected) increased volatility. When we take a wider definition it is apparent that in aggregate, as well as at the individual level, electors are more volatile today than they were in the 1950s.

From uniformity to variability

The third clear change in electoral behaviour over the past fifty years has been a move from relative uniformity of party support over the country as a whole to considerable geographical variability. This can be illustrated by comparing regional differences in party support in the elections of 1955 and 1992 – two elections which were won handily by the Conservatives. Table 4 shows how six broad regions of Britain deviated from the overall results. In 1955, only Wales deviated sharply to Labour and the south of England to the Conservatives. By 1992, however, only the Midlands and London did not differ markedly from the national picture in the division of votes between Labour and the Conservatives. Ignoring signs, the mean deviation in 1955 was 9.2 while in 1992 it was 15.5.

As the figures in table 4 show, there was already something of a 'north–south' electoral divide in 1955. But by 1992, as a result of steady trends away from Labour in the south and away from the Conservatives in the north and Scotland, which had accelerated in the 1980s, the divide was stark. After the 1992 election the Conservatives held only 70 of the 273

Table 4 Regional deviations from national result in 1955 and 1992 general elections

	1955		1992	
	Conservative lead over Labour	Regional deviation	Conservative lead over Labour	Regional deviation
Nationally	+2.3		+7.6	
North of England	-2.1	-4.4	-9.1	-16.7
Midlands	-2.2	-4.5	+10.3	+2.7
South of England	+16.1	+13.8	+31.1	+23.5
London	+0.7	-1.6	+8.2	+0.6
Scotland	+3.4	+1.1	-13.3	-20.9
Wales	-27.7	-30.0	-20.9	-28.5

seats in Scotland, Wales and the north while Labour held only 10 of the 177 seats in the south outside London.

Three main explanations have been suggested for this increased variability in party support in different parts of the country. First, Curtice and Steed (1982) suggest that there have been slow changes in the make-up of regional electorates. Broadly speaking, patterns of population movement have meant that the proportion of middle-class people has tended to increase in the south and, relatively speaking, to decrease in the northern regions. While this appears plausible, detailed research has been unable to confirm that migration has contributed significantly to the growth of the regional divide (see Denver and Halfacree 1992). Second, Curtice and Steed also make the point that as third parties, such as the Liberal Democrats or SNP, have increased in popularity this has generally been at the expense of the locally weaker major party. Thus, since the Conservatives were already weaker than Labour in Scotland and the north they suffered more from the advances of third parties after 1970 whereas in the south Labour was the party which suffered more. Comparing support for the two major parties suggests, therefore, an accentuated regional divide. Third, the most popular explanation for the north–south electoral divide focuses on economic wellbeing. Put simply, Scotland, Wales and the north have just not been as prosperous as the south. This explanation is particularly associated with the work of the political geographers, Johnston and Pattie (see, for example, Pattie *et al.* 1991, 1993). They suggest that the acceleration of the regional divide since 1979 is closely related to uneven economic development. Government policy had a differential regional impact, including effects on unemployment levels, the occupational and industrial structure and property values, and this resulted in regional variations in satisfaction with the country's economic performance and in optimism about economic prospects. In turn this was reflected in divergences in regional voting patterns. Pattie *et al.* give a convincing account of developments since 1979, but the trend of a widening regional divide was previously visible under Labour governments – which were just as unsuccessful in reversing economic divergence – and regional differences in party support have existed for a very long time. At root, these differences seem to reflect deep cultural and historical differences and cannot simply be explained in economic terms.

The trend towards greater regional variability in party support over the past thirty-five years has been overlain by another divergence, between more urban and more rural areas. The latter have moved steadily away from Labour and the former away from the Conservatives. When the two trends are combined, the long-term geographical divergences in party support – between the rural south and Scottish cities, for example – have been truly enormous. The most comprehensive way to demonstrate the increased variability in party support across the country, however, is to consider the distribution of the Conservative (or Labour) share of the two-party vote across all British constituencies. In 1955 this distribution had a standard deviation (which is a measure of the amount of dispersion or variation in a set of scores) of 13.5; by 1992, having steadily increased election by election, the statistic was 20.3.

The increased variability in levels of party support from constituency to constituency was itself the product of increased variability in change in successive elections. 'Swing' is a simple summary measure of electoral change and in the 1950s it tended to be uniform – about the same size across all constituencies. As Ivor Crewe noted with reference to the period 1945–70:

> In every election but one (1959) at least three-quarters of the constituency swings were within 2 per cent of the national median and only a handful of seats bucked the national trend. To know the swing in Cornwall was to know the swing in the Highlands; to know the results of the first three constituencies to declare was to know not only which party had won – but by how many seats. (Crewe 1985: 101–3)

Much earlier, Butler and Stokes had commented that 'no electoral phenomenon in Britain has been more widely remarked on than that of uniform national swing' (1969: 203). As the discussion in Butler and Stokes makes clear, the fact that swing tended to be uniform is something of a puzzle, and it has never been satisfactorily explained. The reasons why swing was uniform in the 1950s need not detain us here, however, since over the past fifty years it has become steadily less uniform. This is again best illustrated by the use of standard deviations and table 5 shows how the standard deviations of swings have increased over the years. The data show that there was more than twice as much variability in constituency swings in the 1980s and 1990s as there had been in the 1950s.

Table 5 Standard deviations of constituency swings, 1951–92

Elections between:	1951 and 1959	1964 and 1970	1974 and 1979	1983 and 1992
Mean SD	1.8	2.6	3.1	4.4

The figures shown are the mean standard deviations of the two-party swing for the elections during the periods specified.

As implied by the preceding discussion, the increased variability in constituency swings was not random. Compared with the national swing, Scotland, Wales and the north of England and more urban areas consistently tended to move away from the Conservatives while more rural areas and the rest of the country consistently moved away from Labour. The cumulative effects are partly seen in table 4 but, in addition, these trends had important consequences for the operation of the electoral system. In the 1950s it was found that the share of seats in the House of Commons that a party would obtain on the basis of a given share of the national vote could be predicted fairly well using the 'cube rule'. If the share of votes between the two leading parties were in the ratio $a{:}b$ then the division of seats between them would be in the ratio $a^3{:}b^3$. The winning party's lead in terms of votes was thus greatly exaggerated in terms of seats. In fact, however, this rule works only when the standard deviation of the major parties' shares is approximately 13.7. As we have seen, this is no longer true. The increased geographical variation in party support has had the effect of making Labour seats more safely Labour (and more hopeless for the Conservatives) and Conservative seats more safely Conservative (and hopeless for Labour). There are now many fewer marginal seats and so the exaggerative effect of the electoral system has declined sharply. In 1992, indeed, the ratio of Conservative to Labour share of the two-party vote was 55:45 and the ratio of their shares of seats was also 55:45. The electoral system completely failed to exaggerate the largest party's lead when translating votes into seats.

From habitual to judgemental voting

When the electorate was aligned by class and party identification, it would be fair to describe the party choice of voters as a matter of habit rather than anything else. For most voters, indeed, the idea that they made a 'choice', in the sense of a conscious decision about which party to support as election day drew near, is misleading. Rather, they had a 'standing decision' derived from class, family tradition and so on, which made voting for the appropriate party almost automatic. In the dealigned era, however, the prevalence of this kind of habitual voting decreased.

Most commentators agree that this is the case but there is some disagreement about what has replaced aligned or habitual voting. Some have suggested that 'issue voting' is now much more important, with electors making up their minds on the basis of the parties' policies on important contemporary issues, such as taxation, defence, the National Health Service and education (Sarlvik and Crewe 1983). Others emphasise that it is voters' opinions about the performance of the government in office that is important and, in particular, the success or failure of the government in running the economy (Sanders 1992). There is a widespread impression that the electors' reactions to the party leaders are now more influential in determining party choice than they used to be. Rose and McAllister (1990) and Heath *et al.* (1985) are critical of what they understand to be issue voting and argue that it is the long-term political values, principles or ideologies of voters that lead them to support one party or another (Denver and Hands 1990).

What ties these various strands together, however, is the suggestion that, compared with the period of alignment, voters have become increasingly likely to base their choice of party on judgements – whether about current issues, ideologies, party leaders, government performance or the state of the economy. We might say, then, that habitual voting – which predominated in the 1950s – has declined and in more recent elections has given way to what we might term 'judgemental' voting.

Evidence for this interpretation is given in table 6. The upper part of table 6 shows the percentage of the variation in party choice in 1964 and 1987 that could be explained by family loyalties and socio-economic interests on the one hand, and by political judgements made by voters on the other. The data suggest that the influence of family and social characteristics declined over this period while the influence of judgements increased, so that by 1987 the latter outweighed the former in importance. The data in

Table 6 The influence of judgements on party choice

	1964	1987
Variance explained by:		
Family loyalties and socio-economic interests	38.9	29.0
Political judgements of respondents	25.2	38.4
Index of concentration between party choice and:		
Parents' party preferences	0.24	0.19
Parents' party preferences + respondents' attitudes	0.49	0.62

Variance data are from Rose and McAllister (1990: table 9A). 'Judgements' are a combination of what Rose and McAllister describe as 'political values' and 'current performance of parties and leaders'.
Index-of-concentration data are from Heath *et al.* (1991: 44). The 'index of concentration' is analogous to r^2 and can be interpreted as the proportion of variance explained.

the lower part of table 6 can be interpreted in the same way and show that when survey respondents' political attitudes were added to their family tradition the proportion of variation in party choice that could be explained rose by 0.25 in 1964 but by 0.43 in 1987. Remembering that the heyday of habitual voting was likely to have been in the 1950s, this evidence of change since 1964 strongly suggests that there has been a significant shift from habitual to judgemental voting over the past half century.

Conclusion

British elections in the 1990s are clearly different from elections in the 1950s in a number of ways – the style of campaigns and the techniques used in campaigning, the nature and extent of media coverage, the number of and prominence given to public opinion polls. In one respect, however, there appears to be an element of continuity – the Conservative and Labour parties still dominate. To some extent this reflects the operation of the electoral system, which makes it difficult for other parties to 'break the mould' of the party system. To some extent also, it reflects the power of inertia. Despite the fact that from at least 1900 to 1945 the British party system was relatively complicated, the idea that a two-party system was somehow 'natural' became fixed in the public mind during the 1950s. Parliament is organised around a party duopoly, one in government and the other as the 'official' opposition, and media attention has focused on these. Although, as we have seen, two-party dominance appears to be crumbling somewhat – at least among the electorate – the established major parties continue to be at an advantage in terms of funding and resources and in having a core of traditional supporters upon whom they can rely.

Despite this surface continuity, the reality is that electoral behaviour over the past fifty years has changed a good deal. The dominance of the two major parties has been much reduced and the bases on which voters support them have altered. The clear class and partisan alignments that existed in the 1950s have given way to a dealigned electorate; electoral stability has been replaced by volatility, national uniformity by variability and habitual voting by a more judgemental approach. In these respects the British electorate of the 1990s is very different from the electorate of the 1950s.

References

Benney, M., Gray, A. P. and Pear, R. H. (1956), *How People Vote*, London, Routledge and Kegan Paul.
Butler, D. E. and Stokes, D. (1969), *Political Change in Britain* (1st edn), London, Macmillan.
Butler, D. E. and Stokes, D. (1974), *Political Change in Britain* (2nd edn), London, Macmillan.
Craig, F. (1981), *British Electoral Facts 1832–1980*, Chichester, Parliamentary Research Services.

Crewe, I. (1985), Great Britain, in I. Crewe and D. Denver (eds), *Electoral Change in Western Democracies*, London, Croom Helm.

Crewe, I., Day, N. and Fox, A. (1991), *The British Electorate 1963–1987*, Cambridge, Cambridge University Press.

Curtice, J. and Steed, M. (1982), Electoral choice and the production of governments: the changing operation of the electoral system in the UK since 1955, *British Journal of Political Science*, 12:3, 249–98.

Denver, D. and Halfacree, K. (1992), Inter-constituency migration and party support in Britain, *Political Studies*, 40:3, 571–80.

Denver, D. and Hands, G. (1990), Issues, principles or ideology? How young voters decide, *Electoral Studies*, 9:1, 19–36.

Dunleavy, P. (1980), The political implications of sectoral cleavages and the growth of state employment, *Political Studies*, 28:3,4, 364–83, 527–49.

Farrell, D., McAllister, I. and Broughton, D. (1995), The changing British voter revisited: patterns of election campaign volatility since 1964, in D. Broughton et al. (eds), *The British Elections and Parties Yearbook 1994*, London, Frank Cass and Co.

Heath, A., Sarlvik, B. and Crewe, I. (1983), *Decade of Dealignment*, Cambridge, Cambridge University Press.

Heath, A., Jowell, R. and Curtice, J. (1985), *How Britain Votes*, Oxford, Pergamon Press.

Heath, A., Jowell, R., Curtice, J., Evans, G., Field, J. and Witherspoon, S. (1991), *Understanding Political Change*, Oxford, Pergamon Press.

Heath, A., Jowell, R., Curtice, J. with Taylor, B. (eds) (1994), *Labour's Last Chance? The 1992 Election and Beyond*, Aldershot, Dartmouth Publishing.

Kavanagh, D. (1995), *Election Campaigning: The New Marketing of Politics*, Oxford, Blackwell.

Milne, R. S. and Mackenzie, H. C. (1958), *Marginal Seat 1955*, London, Hansard Society.

Nicholas, H. G. (1951), *The British General Election of 1951*, London, Macmillan.

Norris, P. (1990), *British By-elections: The Volatile Electorate*, Oxford, Clarendon Press.

Pattie, C., Fieldhouse, E., Johnston, R. and Russell, A. (1991), A widening regional cleavage in British voting behaviour, 1964–87: preliminary explorations, in I. Crewe, P. Norris, D. Denver and D. Broughton (eds), *British Elections and Parties Yearbook 1991*, Hemel Hempstead, Harvester Wheatsheaf.

Pattie, C., Johnston, R. and Fieldhouse, E. (1993), Plus ça change? The changing electoral geography of Great Britain, 1979–92, in D. Denver, P. Norris, D. Broughton and C. Rallings (eds), *British Elections and Parties Yearbook 1993*, Hemel Hemptstead, Harvester Wheatsheaf.

Rallings, C. and Thrasher, M. (1993), *Britain Votes 5*, Aldershot, Dartmouth Publishing.

Rose, R. and McAllister, I. (1990), *The Loyalties of Voters*, London, Sage.

Sanders, D. (1992), Why the Conservatives won – again, in A. King et al. (eds), *Britain at the Polls*, Chatham, Chatham House.

Sarlvik, B. and Crewe, I. (1983), *Decade of Dealignment*, Cambridge, Cambridge University Press.

Scammell, M. (1995), *Designer Politics: How Elections are Won*, Basingstoke, Macmillan.

8

Political and cultural change in postwar Britain

Bill Jones and Lynton Robins

Class, politics and society

The working classes in the 1950s

Ferdynand Zweig published a portrait of the British worker in 1952. Using informal methods of social investigation, he produced an intuitive account of working-class life which at the time had no rival outside the English novel. He made the point, more than once, that within 1950s working life were many cultural threads that led directly back to the 1930s and even earlier. Even in the nearly full-employment conditions of the early postwar years, there were still to be found the 'chronically unemployed' (Zweig 1952: 23–4), living in hostels, struggling against adversity. Many others experienced 'poverty, slummy conditions, unsatisfactory working conditions, and educational backwardness' (p. 67). Although jobs were plentiful, even the higher-paid workers' families of the early 1950s were still 'hard pressed for money' (p. 71), had little or nothing in the way of savings, and spent little on leisure outside the pub, sport, or personal hobbies. In his interviews, Zweig found that the 1930s were still salient; the General Strike remained a strong class memory among workers in the 1950s, and even he was astonished by a group of cotton workers who recalled strikes in the 1890s and the lessons that could still be learnt from them.

The emerging welfare state offered workers only limited protection from life's vagaries. Zweig took great pains to record what he described as the 'fluidity of the position of men in the working class' (p. 23). Above all, prolonged illness or injury, either of which may have been job related, could result in a working-class family's frugal lifestyle being replaced by an outright struggle against poverty. Fear, from incapacity or other threats from unforeseen sources, never seemed far from the thoughts of Zweig's interviewees.

Industrial life, too, was a struggle, but here the worker had a strong ally in the form of the union. In what was essentially a low-level class struggle between radical managers and traditional unions, the loyalty of the worker was unquestioned. For not only did the union provide collective strength for individual workers, but in so doing provided each worker with individuality. Zweig found that where workers were critical of some aspects of their union's policies, this never resulted in a withdrawal of support for their unions. Frequently, he observed, workers saw in their unions 'something sacred' (p. 175).

Zweig's portrait of the working classes was not monochrome; he recorded a diversity of scale and differentiation in detail, observing that 'every industry breeds its own type of man' (p. 33). Not only that, but a social ladder, based on skill, grade, strength, and wage spanned all industries and types of worker, and consisted of 'innumerable rungs' (p. 21), from those in dead-end jobs to the powerfully defended artisan. Nevertheless, this diversity was contained within a common culture. In some industries, these cultural bonds took on a sharper social, political, and economic significance. In the case of miners, he noted that 'They all live in closely-knit communities where there is a strong projection of the group upon the individual.... The pit and the village control their habits and rules of conduct' (p. 34). In terms of the general workplace culture, Zweig observed norms of solidarity expressed in defence of the weakest or slowest worker, with the qualification that 'A man's work should be as near the average as possible' (p. 92).

In terms of the politics of the 1950s working class, Zweig offered an informal explanation of Labour support. Almost two decades before the 'deviance' of the working-class Tory fascinated political scientists, Zweig observed that the 'popularity of socialist ideas among workers differs according to the industrial group'. He agreed with the observation of an interviewee that most workers were 'intuitive socialists' (p. 189), with the trade union movement forming the core of their socialism. Since working-class life in the early 1950s was characterised still by struggle, what the union did for the underdog at work, Labour did nationally. There were deviants, however, who failed to fit neatly into this formula. Among hotel workers, shop assistants, hairdressers and those many other workers in the distribution trade, Zweig found 'a much greater tolerance for what is called capitalism and they often think of socialism as impracticable' (p. 187).

The affluent worker

Zweig conducted a second, more social-scientific survey of working-class culture a decade later and discovered that 'a deep transformation of values ... new ways of thinking and feeling' had taken root alongside 'a new ethos, new aspirations and cravings' (Zweig 1961: ix) during the intervening years. He believed that improved housing conditions, including an increase in owner occupation by working-class families, was 'one of the most potent factors' (p. 5) in this transformation. Inside the home he noted the increase of consumer durables, particularly television, which, among other things, resulted in 'the kitchen mentality' being gradually replaced by 'the living-room mentality' (p. 5), as well as making the increased shift work of husbands tolerable to their wives. Congruent with a more meaningful focus on the home and family, Zweig recorded what might be seen as the prototype of 1980s 'new man'; the once commonplace working-class male, 'the stern, bullying, dominating, and self-assertive father or the absent father who took no interest in the children ... whose life oscillated between the works and the public house' was fast being replaced by the 'benevolent, friendly, and brotherly' father figure (p. 23).

The 1960s witnessed among workers what Zweig referred to as the 'acquisitive instinct' as a new hard-edged money-mindedness was brought to bear on a wide range of decisions, including industrial and political ones. This theme is developed in the two-part study of Goldthorpe *et al.* (1968), *The Affluent Worker*. Generally speaking, it was found that less-skilled workers employed in modern production processes sought specifically economic gratification from work. Promotion, for example, to the position of supervisor tended not to offer the pecuniary rewards that the new working class was seeking. Self-esteem, status, responsibility or greater job satisfaction failed to take priority over the size of the wage packet; the majority 'appeared to concentrate their aspirations on securing a continued improvement in their standard of domestic living rather than an advancement of any kind in their occupational lives' (Goldthorpe *et al.* 1968: 146). Money-minded thinking resulted in the new working class adopting 'a largely instrumental view of unionism' (p. 98) combined with minimal participation in branch activities. Even security in life was seen in terms of long-term income maximisation rather than in terms of permanent employment.

While Goldthorpe *et al.* failed to substantiate the embourgeoisement process described by Zweig, other findings supported in large part the new home-based, or 'privatised', lifestyles of the new working class he described. Where the two surveys differed in detail, however, was in the emphasis given to the importance of overtime working to the affluent condition. Goldthorpe and his colleagues paid little attention to the topic while Zweig, sensing the crucial link between overtime worked and the size of the final pay packet, devoted a substantial section to the 'quest for overtime' (Zweig 1961: 70–6). He noted that few workers liked overtime, but most clamoured for it. He cited an example, *in extremis*, of a Vauxhall worker who had done thirty-three hours of overtime in a week. However, such hours were not exceptional in the early 1960s. For example, the norm in Pirelli Cables was twenty-eight hours of overtime a week on the early shift (two double-shift days plus Saturday and Sunday mornings), which would be alternated with thirty-two hours of overtime on the late shift (four double shifts, which would include nights). The importance of overtime for Pirelli workers was its twofold multiplier effect on pay: first, most overtime was worked at time and a half or double time, depending on the shift; and second, a production bonus was paid pro rata with the total of paid hours. Little wonder, then, the desperate quest for overtime working and the consequent panic should there be little or none available.

In terms of the political behaviour of the new working class, Goldthorpe *et al.* found that no process of embourgeoisement was evident. In terms of percentages supporting Labour, there were no significant differences between members of the old and new working classes. Labour was perceived generally in terms of being a class party, but support was given more for instrumental reasons rather than as expressions of solidarity when compared with the old working class.

In a case study of local politics, Hindess (1971) presented a far more pessimistic account of working-class participation in Labour. He found that conventional wisdom held true, with councillors being generally drawn from a higher social class than activists, who, in turn, were members of a higher class than constituents. Within this stratification, however, was a process of working-class decline. Reflecting the decline of working-class represent-ation inside the Parliamentary Labour Party (PLP), Labour's grass roots were becoming less working class. He observed that it was not uncommon for such working-class politics as did exist locally to get marginalised by a powerful alliance between middle-class Labour and the party bureaucracy. Working-class representation was further diluted by councillors belonging to a ward party located in middle- or lower-middle-class areas representing a predominantly working-class ward.

Postwar affluence, further fired by an increasing number of working wives, increased educational opportunities, urban living, and the culturally levelling influence of television, reshaped the class structure. Roberts *et al.* (1977) found that while the working/middle-class dichotomy remained a useful distinction, there had been a general fragmentation of classes within and across the old divide. For example, where once there may have been one common culture, as defined by Lewis and Maude in their 1949 study of *The English Middle Classes*, incorporating a coherent set of values and an easily recognisable lifestyle, by 1977 there were several. Alongside the traditional middle class, now 'compressed' (Roberts *et al.* 1977: 111), might be added the bourgeois manual worker, the salaried manager, the new middle class based principally but not exclusively on an expanding public sector, and a highly unionised white-collar proletariat. The last group was created by a number of complex processes, including deskilling, promotion limitation and:

> shop-floor conditions ... being extended into white-collar work situations. Open-plan offices, 'pools' of clerks, and drawing rooms where individuals work alongside dozens of similarly placed peers are replacing the traditional smaller bureaux with their intricate hierarchies. (Roberts *et al.* 1977: 125)

In something of a mirror image of Hindess' findings regarding embourgeoise-ment, Roberts *et al.* reported on the 'shallow anchorage of middle class political loyalties' (p. 165). Speaking generally they noted that 'the party loyalties of working class Conservatives appear especially unreliable, while white-collar Conservative support does not exhibit anything approaching the solidity characteristic of the blue-collar Labour vote' (p. 166). Nevertheless, within two years of publication, Conservatives were to begin nearly twenty uninterrupted years in office.

The political meaninglessness of class

The Thatcher years witnessed a campaign against trade unions, which included the defeat of the miners after a year-long strike, at a time of mass unemployment. A more subtle attack was made on the autonomy of some middle-class professions, particularly those of education and medicine. The 'Thatcher revolution' was set on replacing the so-called dependency culture of postwar popular socialism with the enterprise culture of popular capitalism. Electoral support for this project was drawn from all social classes. Margaret Thatcher, projected heroically by the tabloid press, finally killed off the lingering belief of some Marxists that the working class was about to embark on a revolutionary adventure. The skilled working class, the C2s of 'Essex man', swung to the Conservatives more than any other class in 1979, thereby winning the reputation of being the 'shock troops of Thatcherism'. In following general elections, undeservedly so in electoral terms, support from the C2s was seen by most political commentators as critical in deciding who was returned to Number 10 Downing Street.

The complex changes that had taken place within the social structure left political scientists disagreeing on how social class should be measured operationally when analysing voting behaviour. Some political scientists dismissed orthodox measures of class since they were no longer seen as being realistic, while others criticised the inadequacies of the proposed alternative classification. Rather different conclusions were drawn by political scientists about voting trends, which seemed to depend in substantial part on the methodology employed.

The increasing fluidity in the occupational and class structure of Britain, as well as frustration with the orthodox conceptions of class, resulted in many political commentators referring to the loosely designed concept of 'middle England'. It is no longer the support of the C2s which is seen as crucial in deciding general elections, but the support of an increasingly disaffected middle England. Sometimes middle England is used as a term that substitutes for the 'middle class' plus the 'respectable' working class; sometimes, when considering the location of critical marginal seats, it refers to the Midlands plus adjoining areas to the North; at other times it refers to neither-rich-nor-poor 'middle-earning' Britain.

Will Hutton's (1995) conception of a 30/30/40 society is a useful summary of the fundamental changes that occurred during and after the Thatcher years. The impact of globalisation, and the deregulation and casualisation of work, has put British people increasingly at risk: it is no longer the simple distinctions between rich and poor, between employed and unemployed, that form the basis of social inequality, but the new risks of distress and exclusion. The disadvantaged comprise 'the bottom 30 per cent of unemployed and economically inactive who are marginalised'. For them, 'the risk is that poverty will turn into an inability even to subsist, and that marginalisation will change into complete social and economic exclusion' (Hutton 1995).

A further 30 per cent are made up from the 'newly insecure', who are in forms of employment that are at risk. Legislation has reduced their employment protection; many are women. They are the temporary, part-time and contract workers, agency workers, and self-employed workers, who are taken on and laid off as the demand for their labour ebbs and flows.

The 'advantaged 40 per cent' are in what are normally understood as full-time permanent or 'tenured jobs' in the great organisations of the public and private sectors. But even here there is risk in the form of various managerial innovations – market testing, contracting out, down sizing and delayering – which erode the advantaged 40 per cent by around 1 per cent a year. Hutton (1995) argues that 'by the year 2000, full-time tenured employment, around which stable family life has been constructed along with the capacity to service 25 year mortgages, will be a minority form of work'. Middle England, largely located within the advantaged in society, is, in the words of one broadsheet, 'bruised, battered, bewildered,' not only by employment insecurity but by falling property prices and negative equity, an increasing tax burden and increasing crime, with the 'feel-good factor' of the Thatcher years replaced by the symptom of 'feeling bad'. According to opinion polls, the residents of middle England are prepared to make an historic realignment as they leave the Conservative fold, with many bypassing the Liberal Democrats, to give their support direct to new Labour.

The debate about the British 'underclass'

A lumpen, possibly inevitable, group in the British working class has long been discerned. In the late eighteenth century a hopelessly illiterate and criminalised group in London was perceived as a threat to civilised life in the capital. In response, sentences were pushed to ever-higher degrees of severity until death sentences were being handed down for negligible offences. Magistrates became so loath to apply this draconian code that they increasingly began to take the option of transporting offenders to Australia, thus taking the first steps in founding a brand new (and, for the most part, law-abiding) nation. Later in the nineteenth century, when a similar problem arose with a worrisome urban proletariat, intellectuals devised a new solution: eugenics. This approach sought to eliminate such problems by breeding out, possibly via compulsory sterilisation, that

149

incorrigible element in society, the 'undeserving poor' section of the lower working class.

In the autumn of 1989 a new twist occurred in this almost familiar story. An American sociologist, Charles Murray, already well known for his analyses of the working class in his own country, visited Britain at the invitation of the *Sunday Times*. His report appeared on 26 November and provoked considerable controversy. In May 1994 another article appeared by him, claiming the trends he had earlier identified had intensified; it was entitled 'The New Victorians and the New Rabble' (*Sunday Times*). His analysis of the underclass was not based on a quantitative measure but on a 'type of poverty', a form of behaviour. He made the distinction between the decent, hard-working poor and the 'undeserving' or 'feckless' poor, who are spendthrift, poor parents, neglect their property, often have an addiction to drink or drugs, are involved in crime and have an aversion to work. His analysis focused on three criteria by which an underclass could be identified: illegitimacy, violent crime and dropout from the labour force.

Illegitimacy

Murray calls illegitimacy the 'best predictor of an underclass in the making'. He notes that the rate in Britain had shot up to 25.6 per cent by 1988 (figure 1) but finds its location in the lowest social classes, invariably in the inner cities, the more worrying statistic. He believes these communities have suffered a 'catastrophe' because 'Communities need families. Communities need fathers'. In the USA, he points out, single mothers tend to stay on welfare nearly five times as long as women who have been married but have divorced. Furthermore, he maintains, communities with a high incidence of single mothers tend to be difficult or impossible to live in because children

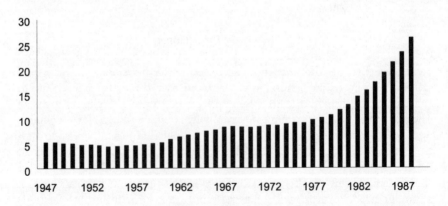

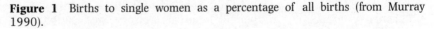

Figure 1 Births to single women as a percentage of all births (from Murray 1990).

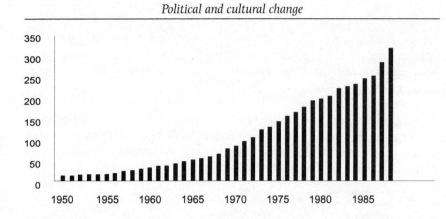

Figure 2 Crimes of violence per 100,000 population (from Murray 1990).

in such circumstances tend to 'run wild'. What is worse for the future is that male children do not see any examples of role models who are good fathers. In Birkenhead, he says, he met a father of a child who went to her school concert, where he was the only father present; he alleges the child was so embarrassed she asked him not to come again.

Violent crime
'Crime is the next place to look for the underclass,' says Murray, who produces the surprising statistic that property crime is higher in Britain than in the USA. Violent crime is much lower but is rising dramatically (figure 2). Once again, he insists the criminals are concentrated in the poorest communities in the inner cities: in the underclass. Young males, therefore, already without role models of good fathers, are provided instead with the worst possible alternatives: figures whose exploits are antisocial and destructive. Taken together with other interacting influences, children in these inner-city areas tend to grow up unprepared for study and unsocialised in the ways of considerate behaviour. Instead they tend to: retaliate against anyone who shows them disrespect; sleep with and impregnate as many women as possible; regard violence as a sign of strength; and view worrying about tomorrow as weakness. And these are more than mere tendencies, Murray insists, they are a code of behaviour in the inner cities.

Employment
Murray feels the economic slump of the late 1970s and early 1980s created a 'lost generation' of young long-term unemployed people in those areas hardest hit; he elaborates with contrasting quotations from their unemployed fathers – desperate to find a job, desolate being without one – and the unconcerned younger generation: contemptuous of the 'slave labour' of

151

youth training schemes and of any job paying less than £200 per week. And if they do get a job, they tend not to turn up or to drop out early on, unused to and unable to cope with its rigours of punctuality and periods of inevitable boredom.

Murray stresses the importance of work as the 'centre of life'. Without it young men remain 'barbarians', without an identity and a 'vantage point from which they can make sense of themselves'. Without work experience, young people remain uncivilised and unlikely to become supporters of a family, itself an 'indispensable civilising experience'.

Further features of the underclass

Murray rejects Frank Field's (1989) explanation of the underclass as the rational outcome of recession and high-interest-rate, tax-cutting Thatcherism; rather he traces the origins back into the 1950s and '60s. At this time two things began to happen. First, welfare strategies were constructed that elevated having a baby without being married just above the 'economically feasible threshold'. Given that young women quite naturally like sex and babies this change was highly instrumental in creating the single-parent-dominated underclass. Second, he points out that since the 1950s committing crime has also been getting safer and safer. The clear-up rate for robberies, for example, fell from 61 per cent in 1960 to 21 per cent in 1987. Moreover, in 1960, 50 per cent of all cleared up crime resulted in convictions; by 1987 it had fallen to 30 per cent and in the 1990s even lower: 'Committing crimes has been getting safer for more than three decades and the trend continues,' Murray concludes.

More up to date, *The Economist* (3 February 1996) reported on a manifestation of the underclass in Meadowell, on the outskirts of Newcastle: 'The main occupation is crime: the professionals travel around the country, the amateurs burgle their neighbours. Kids hijack the odd bus. There are almost no two-parent families'. Even large investment, by Siemens, in the area has not helped much, as most of Meadowell residents do not have the education nor the skills to gain employment: 'Meadowell's people have drifted so far away from the job market that the council is putting together a pre-training scheme for its teenagers which would explain, for instance, what work is, what is expected at a job, what responsibility is'.

Where is all this leading, according to Murray? His answer is apocalyptic; he foresees the erosion, even breakdown, of civil society, with a polarisation into the new Victorians – educated professionals, more self-denying and socially concerned – and the new rabble – poorly educated, dreadful parents, non-community minded, welfare dependent, high levels of addiction and criminality, impervious to all remedial welfare programmes. Even worse, these two groups are destined physically to separate into middle-class (social groups A and B) 'ghettos' and council estates riddled with drug abuse, crime and uncaring single-parent families whose children turn schools into zoos.

Skilled workers (C1s and C2s) would opt for the middle-class areas, which will increasingly take the form of 'closed or gated' suburbs, guarded by walls and security guards, leaving the unskilled (Ds and Es) to end up in the same boat as the underclass, increasingly contaminated by their social maladies. Inevitably this would have a revolutionary and destructive effect on political parties, especially Labour, which draws the majority of its support from the working classes, but the Conservatives too would be thrown into disarray, not to mention Britain itself. Murray suggests the best way to solve the problem is not by throwing money at it; this has been tried in the USA and has failed disastrously. Rather he urges tough action to remove 'state interference' with the natural logic of child rearing, which requires two rather than one parent: in other words, end state benefit for single mothers, a recommended course of action that has already influenced the Clinton administration and the Conservative Party in Britain. Murray also advises a 'massive dose of self government', on the grounds that if they had the power, local communities would not allow these abuses to health, education and personal property and safety, and make their own arrangements accordingly.

Ralf Dahrendorf (1987), an experienced, sympathetic and highly perceptive observer of British society, shares some of Murray's analysis regarding the growth of disaffected and hostile values and sees the underclass as representing 'the greatest single challenge to civilised existence' in Britain: 'Any group which does not have a stake in the values of society tends to undermine that society quite systematically'. However, other commentators on British society and politics are less in agreement with the German and American sociologists' perceptions and conclusions.

Critiques of Murray

In the paperback publishing Murray's essay, a number of critical essays also appear (Murray 1990). Professors Alan Walker and Nicholas Deakin make it clear they place Murray in the same tradition as those right-wingers who have traditionally 'blamed the victim'. The causes of unemployment and poverty – high interest and exchange rates, new technologies – have not been fully addressed but the poor have been blamed for their own misfortune. They attack the notion that the underclass is self-perpetuating by pointing out studies initiated by Sir Keith Joseph – who produced a 'cycle of poverty' argument in 1973 – that proved that 'at least half the children born into a disadvantaged home do not repeat the pattern of disadvantage in the next generation' (Murray 1990). Moreover, other studies, they claim, prove the so-called 'generation gap' over employment to be illusory; long-term unemployed people continued to search for work 'in the face of repeated failure and disappointment'. But it is on Murray's claims relating to illegitimacy that they direct their most scornful fire: half the children born to 'single' parents in 1986 had parents who were living together; in Britain it is single, not divorced mothers who spend the shorter time on welfare; and in Denmark and Sweden, the illegitimacy rate is twice that of Britain with no apparent erosion of the social fabric in those exemplary stable societies.

Finally, the critics focus on the actions of government: if government causes unemployment, why not change policies to create employment in problem areas? In the *Economist* article cited above, evidence is given that urban development policies have born encouraging fruit in terms of job creation, especially in areas where traditional industries have declined or disappeared (though, it adds, tough, irremovable pockets of poverty – what Murray would dub underclass pockets – stubbornly remain). Further, it is often local government that causes concentrations of the so-called underclass by directing problem families to the 'sink' areas of the city (Moss Side and Hulme, for example, in Manchester), thus creating the 'ghettos' of alienated long-term unemployed youth with their associated antisocial behaviour.

At the end of his book, Murray returns with a spirited rejoinder, arguing: that even half of each generation repeating a pattern of disadvantage is serious; that cohabitation is rarely in the long-term interests of children; and that the jury is still out on Scandinavian societies. Indeed, the jury is also still out on Murray's thesis, though there is enough evidence presented every day in the media about poor schools in the inner city, rising violent crime, drug-related crime and wild uncivilised behaviour by young working-class males to lead us to consider his analysis seriously and worry about the future of our civic culture.

Women, politics and society

The women's movement

In the history of feminism, the postwar Labour years were ones of unfulfilled promise. At the time, many feminists believed that equality of the sexes had been, or soon would be, achieved through the construction of a welfare state. Thinking equality near at hand, women accepted the necessity of giving priority to the continuance of their traditional child-rearing and domestic roles. Militant feminism was seen as inappropriate. Randall commented that, however:

> [by] the 1950s the contradictions in women's actual role and in normative conceptions of that role multiplied and intensified ... women's domestic role was in turn contradicted by the increased production of labour-saving domestic devices and more crucially by the availability of reliable and relatively untroublesome means of contraception. (Randall 1987: 222)

The conditions were in place for the resurgence of the 'second wave' of militant feminism of the 1960s, triggered by a variety of social factors. One such trigger was the impact of women's liberation in the USA and Germany which, it is generally agreed, burst upon many British women, suddenly making sense of their simmering resentments and frustrations.

The history of the women's movement can be understood in terms of the rise and demise of various feminist tendencies in setting the agenda and taking action. Randall identified the Marxist or socialist feminists, who dominated the early years of women's liberation in Britain. Marxist feminists 'though still insistent upon the primacy of the class struggle ... accepted that the struggle between the sexes could not be reduced to its parameters, but had a history of its own and would not automatically disappear with the overthrow of capitalism' (Randall 1987: 8). Marxist feminist groups were anxious to reach out and raised the consciousness of working-class women and, by the late 1970s, there was 'a veritable influx of socialist feminists into the Labour Party' (Randall 1987: 233) and trade union movement.

The absorption of socialist feminism into the political and industrial wings of the labour movement enabled the radical tendency of feminism to dominate the other parts of the women's movement. Radical feminism was defined principally by 'its insistence that sex is the fundamental division in society to which all other differences, such as social class or race, are merely secondary' (Randall 1987: 6). Essentially men are the enemy and there can never be an accommodation between the sexes. 'Increasingly however the strand of radical feminism, variously called political lesbianism or radical lesbianism, has come to insist the separatism be extended to sexual relations' (Randall 1987: 7). Radical feminist ascendancy occurred in the rapid growth of women's aid groups, refuges, and rape crisis centres.

Finally, feminism embraced a reformist or liberal tendency, which generally conceded that women are suffering 'only a minor and temporary handicap' (Randall 1987: 9) subject to remedy by equal rights legislation. This tendency was the heir to the 'moderate' and 'acceptable' aspects of feminism that sought liberation through equality. Since waged employment and responsibilities outside the home were seen as giving men their freedoms, it was assumed that once women were in a similar situation they, too, would find liberation.

Disillusionment with the results of mass female employment in raising income, alongside welfare cuts for women made acceptable by a changed moral climate, has resulted in something of a crisis for contemporary feminism. Some see the crisis as having resulted in deradicalisation, others in further fragmentation. Certainly an aggressive radical Conservative feminism of the 1990s has played the role of the enemy within, highly dismissive of 'sisterhood' since it is a barrier to the truly liberating forces of the free market and individuality.

Women in the workforce

Zweig's account of 'the British worker' focused on the world of men, and the Luton study of 'the affluent worker' (Goldthorpe *et al.* 1968) surveyed only men. At the time this methodology reflected male dominance of the

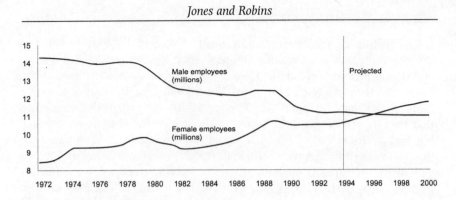

Figure 3 The rise of women in the British labour force (from Wallace 1995, and Institute of Employment Studies, University of Warwick).

workplace. However, structural changes in the British economy have resulted in the erosion of full-time male employment and an increase in part-time female employment. As figure 3 indicates, by the end of this century there will be more women at work than men. The workplace will have become a woman's world.

The early feminist demand for 'a woman's right to work' has not, however, brought liberation for many women in part-time, casual and discontinuous employment. Much of such work is repetitive, boring, low paid and insecure. At the same time, the entry of large numbers of women into the labour market has pushed down wage levels for men and women alike. Consequently, many families now rely on the employment of all adults in the household for a reasonable standard of living. In other words, rather than liberate women, the labour market has resulted frequently in the exploitation of women and the consequent 'feminisation' of poverty.

Many feminists are rethinking the core of their ideology and appear to be moving towards a revised logic, which concludes that real equal opportunities for women must, in future, take gender differences into account. Past thinking that female equality would be based on women having what men had is seen as being flawed since it did not take into account the different needs women have. Treating women in equal ways to men ignores such differences, and thereby frustrates achieving true equality. Creating new equal opportunities that are defined to take account of gender differences is the challenge now confronted by British feminists.

Youth, politics and society

Britain's youth culture

It has been argued that the emergence of a youth culture in Britain occurred during the early postwar years. Those commentators who were more cautious, believing that something akin to a youth culture could be found in the late nineteenth and early twentieth century, nevertheless accepted 'that there were distinctively new historical features in the 1950s' (Clarke *et al.* 1976: 18) that gave the period special importance. First, postwar affluence gave young people a level of spending power that their prewar counterparts did not enjoy. Young people became consumers and stimulated the growth of youth-oriented leisure industries. Second, the development of a mass culture, particularly the mass media, made cultural icons of youth accessible to the many. Third, the extension of schooling brought about by the 'Butler' Education Act of 1944 kept young people together longer, delaying the impact of adult workplace socialisation, thereby enabling the development of adolescent culture. Finally, some distinctive features of the new youth culture resulted from 'the disruptive effects of war on children born during that period – absent fathers, evacuation and other breaks in normal family life, as well as the constant violence – was responsible for the "new" juvenile delinquency of the mid 50s' (Clarke *et al.* 1976: 19). The arrival of rock'n'roll music, an expression of youth 'folk art', articulated the desired mood of rebellion against adult authority. Some commentators felt that by the 1950s, Britain's youth formed what was essentially a new 'class' and lived in a world apart from that of their parents.

An alternative interpretation was that youth culture, or more specifically youth subcultures, developed from the specific contexts occupied by young people. Many young people led 'ordinary' lives; they were touched by the youth culture to varying degrees, picking and choosing which aspects, such as music or fashion, they would incorporate into their own lifestyles. For others, however, the youth culture was total. It has been argued that subcultures such as teddy boys, rockers, mods and skinheads created subcultures that corresponded to their respective parents' culture and attempted to solve, perhaps through imagery or fantasy, the contradictions that social change had brought upon their parents' world:

> Thus the 'Teddy Boy' expropriation of an upper class style of dress 'covers' the gap between largely manual, unskilled, near-lumpen real careers and life chances, and the 'all-dressed-up-and-nowhere-to-go' experience of Saturday evening. Thus in the expropriation and fetishisation of consumption and style itself, the 'Mods' cover for the gap between the never-ending-weekend and Monday's resumption of boring, dead-end work. Thus, in the resurrection of an archetypal and 'symbolic' (but, in fact, anachronistic) form of working-class dress, in the displaced focusing on the football match and the 'occupation' of the football 'ends', Skinheads reassert, but 'imaginarily', the values of a class. The essence of a style, a kind of 'fan-ship' to which few working-class adults any longer subscribe: they 're-present' a sense of territory and locality which the planners and speculators are rapidly destroying. (Clarke *et al.* 1976: 48)

Citing Cohen (1972), Clarke *et al.* argued that these different subcultures all represented, in their different ways, an attempt to retrieve some of the socially cohesive elements destroyed in the parent culture.

Consistent with the parental culture, middle-class youth subcultures, sometimes referred to as countercultures, 'are diffuse, less group-centred, more individualised' than working-class youth subcultures (Clarke *et al.* 1976: 60). Typically, the middle-class counterculture found expression in the 'beatnik-peacenik' the period of the late 1950s and the hippies of the 1960s, which, in turn, fed into a variety of associated 'dropout', 'drug' and 'student protest' cultures.

It is a matter of conjecture whether the subcultures and countercultures discussed here developed in a linear or disjointed manner from the 1950s and 1960s through to the 1990s. Do any elements of the teddy boy or skinhead subcultures exist in contemporary youth culture? Can any similarities be found between the mods of the 1960s, the glamrock which followed, and the ravers of the 1990s? Or, alternatively, with the demise of acid house in the late 1980s, has the authentic expression of youth culture succumbed, albeit temporarily, to commercial production?

The politics of youth

The moral panic that focused on the original teddy boys and subcultures that followed them suggests that such youth subcultures must comprise a threat to the established political order. Despite being defined by deviance, lawlessness and generally aggressive behaviour, the political dimension of youth subcultures is, however, circumscribed and limited. Moreover, where it is expressed explicitly, it tends to be conservative.

A study of motorbike boys in the early 1970s portrayed a particularly aggressive, chauvinist and racist subculture with ideas expressed in restricted code. Despite the shock and offence the boys delighted in giving to adult society at large,

> it would be wrong, however, to read any real political significance into this. They were not in the end challenging the *structures* of society. Indeed, finally, they were, unexpectedly and surprisingly, reproducing them. Furthermore, it is possible to draw a continuity between the bike boys and what might be called the traditional respectable working class. A profound corollary of their simple, unreflective morality and concrete view of the world was that their spontaneous opposition fell much short of a political critique or attempt to change the larger society. (Willis 1978: 43)

Willis discovered in the bike boys' subculture a clear attachment to conventional working-class ideology. Much the same might be said of the skinhead subculture, which 'selectively reaffirms certain core values of traditional working class culture' (Clarke 1976: 99) with 'Paki bashing' and 'queer bashing' representing an ultra-conservative territorial defence of community and its values. By the early 1980s, researchers found that support for fascist parties – the National Front and the British Movement – had extended beyond the hard-core skinhead subculture. Of the working-class school leavers interviewed:

> over 30 per cent were expressing some sympathy for a fascist party ... support for the fascist parties was not disproportionately higher amongst those whose own parents were unemployed ... support was also related to a belief that the expulsion of non-whites from Britain would lead to an increase in job vacancies ... in many respects, their views resembled those expressed by the middle class members of the Young Conservatives who took part in the study. (Billig and Cochrane 1987: 48–9)

Black youth would appear to have most to gain from a struggle to replace the established political order, for many suffer multiple inner-city deprivations, which are seen as the result of white domination and discrimination. Not surprisingly, they react with a style perceived as 'arrogant, rumbustious, contemptuous towards whites' (Cashmore and Troyna 1982: 17), but, as with bike boys and skinheads, this has no substantial political significance. While there has been protest in the form of rioting, there has been no militant political organisation equivalent to the American Black Panthers or Nation of Islam. Shunning both revolutionary and oppositional forms of political behaviour, many young British blacks escape from what they see as white domination by disengaging from that society. In the Rastafarian subculture, such a strategy was evident in the idea of 'Babylon', a term which referred to the society within which West Indians lived, and which made sense of the multiple deprivations they experienced through their blackness. As Cashmore and Troyna have argued:

> if you believe in Babylon, one implication is that you believe it cannot be conquered through conventional political measures. It exists as a massive, immutable structure and has a capacity to repel or absorb attacks. Such is its nature which has been refined for the best part of four hundred years. You also believe that to organise politically and attempt to change the position of blacks through prescribed means is futile and self-defeating. (Cashmore and Troyna 1982: 30–1)

Rather than challenge the political order or even attempt piecemeal improvement through political negotiation with Babylon, Rastafarians accept their lot, preferring detachment and remoteness. Such an orientation was infectious and commentators believed that it tended to undermine the political activity of non-Rastafarian black youths.

Detachment from society of rather a different kind, together with an absence of political action, has been and still is exhibited by youth subcultures in which the use of recreational drugs plays a significant role. The hippies of the 1960s and 1970s, an articulate subculture based on an alternative mode of living that 'implied a decisive rejection of capitalism as such' (Willis 1978: 126), was characterised nevertheless by limited politics. Willis observed that the hippy critique of conventional politics 'remained silent, and finally, tragically, unorganized. There was no political analysis or expression behind the radical life-style' (p. 125). He concluded that it was their use of drugs that limited their potential for political action, since:

> Drugs put them through a symbolic barrier into a subjective world which underwrote their sense of the unreality of things, and of their powerlessness to affect the 'real' world. Drug-taking also induced a release from personal guilt and a general sense of being determined which made political action irrelevant and anyway impossible. (Willis 1978: 129)

Similarly, in the late 1980s and 1990s, the by now more widespread use of recreational 'dance' drugs was reported as undermining the political potential of youth. As before, the critique of the contemporary political order was present in the thinking of the young, but not acted upon. For example, it has been argued that the acid house movement was 'a genuine expression of dissatisfaction by a youth culture rejecting the popular 80s ideal of a capitalist society,' where success was based on the possession of yuppie trappings, measured by high profits, all gained 'at the expense of more humanitarian priorities such as the improvement of public welfare services' (Russell 1993: 93). Additionally, it might be argued that with more limited 'private space' resulting from legislation inspired by the new moral right, and heavier police surveillance, the feeling of oppression felt by contemporary youth is greater than that experienced by their counterparts twenty or thirty years ago. In which case, it might also be expected that the reasons for political organisation and political activity would be more acute. But, as with the hippies of the past, it is drug usage that limits the possibility of political behaviour. Rietveld described how dance drugs such as ecstasy made the user return to 'a stage in psychological development which is before the acquisition of language, thereby undoing the self that is constituted in and by language ... a break is caused with the established symbolic order at a basic level.' Under such circumstances, 'it is difficult to find an opposition with regard to politics. By dissolving the self, no counter-culture was established which offered an alternative' (Rietveld 1993: 65–6).

The popular notion that the postwar youth culture in Britain was accompanied by the emergence of radical left-wing politics is little more than a myth. There is much evidence of rebellion against parental values, adults in authority and the political order generally, but this is neither organised nor mobilised into action to replace old structures and processes with new. While some youth subcultures have resorted to ultra-conservative and fascist solutions, others retreat to inhabit worlds untouched by a reality they are unprepared to confront and engage. Recent studies have confirmed this increasingly bleak picture of political youth. A National Youth Agency survey (Wilkinson 1995) estimated that over 100,000 young people formed an underclass which had hardly attended school after the age of twelve or thirteen, and which had not received any vocational training. Up to 10 per cent of sixteen- to eighteen-year-olds interviewed had no substantial contact with official society, and many were caught in a vicious circle of truanting, crime, bad childhood experiences, drug abuse, poverty and homelessness. A report published by Demos (Wilkinson and Mulgan 1995) found that more than a third of the 'Thatcher generation' were alienated, living in an environment of personal freedom mixed with relationship instability, disinterest in politics, and an inclination towards lawlessness.

References

Billig, M. and Cochrane, R. (1987), Adolescents and politics, in H. McGurk (ed.), *What Next?* London, ESRC.

Cashmore, E. and Troyna, B. (1982), Black youth in crisis, in E. Cashmore and B. Troyna (eds), *Black Youth in Crisis*, London, Allen and Unwin.

Clarke, J. (1976), The skinheads and the magical recovery of community, in S. Hall and T. Jefferson (eds), *Resistance Through Rituals: Youth Subcultures in Post-War Britain*, London, Hutchinson.

Clarke, J., Hall, S., Jefferson, T. and Roberts, B. (1976), Subcultures, cultures, and class, in S. Hall and T. Jefferson (eds), *Resistance Through Rituals: Youth Subcultures in Post-War Britain*, London, Hutchinson.

Cohen, P. (1972), *Sub-cultural Conflict and Working Class Community*, Working Papers in Cultural Studies, no. 2 (spring), Birmingham, CCCS, University of Birmingham.

Dahrendorf, R. (1987), The erosion of citizenship and the consequences for us all, *New Statesman*, 12 June.

Field, F. (1989), *Losing Out: The Emergence of Britain's Underclass*, Oxford, Blackwell.

Goldthorpe, J. H., Lockwood, D., Bechhofer, F. and Platt, J. (1968), *The Affluent Worker: Industrial Attitudes and Behaviour*, London, Cambridge University Press.

Hindess, B. (1971), *The Decline of Working Class Politics*, London, MacGibbon and Kee.

Hutton, W. (1995), High risk strategy, *Guardian*, 30 October.

Murray, C. (1990), *The Emerging British Underclass*, London, IEA.

Randall, V. (1987), *Women and Politics: An International Perspective*, London, Macmillan.

Rietveld, H. (1993), Living the dream, in S. Redhead (ed.), *Rave Off: Politics and Deviance in Contemporary Youth Culture*, Aldershot, Avebury.

Roberts, K., Cook, F. G., Clark, S. C. and Semeonoff, E. (1977), *The Fragmentary Class Structure*, London, Heinemann.

Russell, K. (1993), Lysergia suburbia, in S. Redhead (ed.), *Rave Off: Politics and Deviance in Contemporary Youth Culture*, Aldershot, Avebury.

Wallace, P. (1995), Women win a pyrrhic victory at work, *Independent on Sunday*, 7 May.

Wilkinson, C. (1995), *The Drop Out Society*, Leicester, National Youth Agency.

Wilkinson, H. and Mulgan, G. (1995), *Freedom's Children: Work Relationships and Politics for 18–34 Year Olds*, London, Demos.

Willis, P. E. (1978), *Profane Culture*, London, Routledge and Kegan Paul.

Zweig, F. (1952), *The British Worker*, Harmondsworth, Penguin.

Zweig, F. (1961), *The Worker in an Affluent Society: Family Life and Industry*, London, Heinemann.

9

The mass media and politics

Kenneth Newton

Fifty years ago there was rather little to say about the mass media in British politics. Now the topic not only merits a chapter of its own, but the role of the mass media in politics is so widespread that the topic threads its way through many other chapters as well. The growth of media importance is not a new phenomenon in Britain, but it has been increasingly significant in the past twenty or thirty years. Nor is Britain unique in this respect; the trend is notable throughout the west, and no doubt in other parts of the globe as well (see, for example, Davis 1995). The result is that from modest beginnings in 1945, the daily output of the press, radio and television now exercises a huge and pervasive influence throughout the political system.

The mass media have never simply reported the news in the sense of acting as a faithful messenger passing on facts and opinion in a disinterested manner – this is impossible, for all sorts of practical and theoretical reasons – but what is notable is that the media have moved far beyond the messenger role to become independent political influences in their own right. Their importance is manifest in three different ways: first, they are major political players in their own right; second, they are major influences in the lives of other major political players; and third, they are the focus of a good deal of policy-making controversy about how the media should be organised, what they should do, and how they should do it.

How and why this has happened in Britain between 1945 and 1995 is the theme of this chapter. The main part of the chapter is divided into three sections, which deal first with the press, then with the second medium on the scene, radio, and last with television. There is good reason to distinguish between the press, on the one hand, and radio and television on the other. As we shall see, the press has not been regulated by the state as much as the electronic media, and therefore its history and impact on politics are rather different. Radio and television have more in common, but for practical reasons they will be treated separately here. An appendix gives a chronology of postwar media events.

The press

In some ways the national press has not changed much between 1945 and 1995. In 1945, as in 1995, national dailies outsold combined provincial morning and evening papers. In 1945 there were nine main national daily papers (excluding the small, specialist *Financial Times* and the still Manchester-based *Manchester Guardian*), with a circulation of around approximately 12 million, and eleven Sunday papers, with a circulation of almost 20 million. Fifty years later the figures were similar. At the end of 1995 there were ten main national dailies (*Today* closed in November 1995), and nine Sundays. Total circulation was around 14 million and 15 million respectively (tables 1 and 2). Behind these simple, overall figures there have been large and important changes in the British press that may be grouped under eight general headings.

Number of pages

The size of the papers has grown by leaps and bounds. Newspapers of 1945 were pathetically thin, due partly to wartime newsprint rationing (not fully lifted until 1955), which limited them to a few pages. They now run to thirty or forty pages, many more on Sundays.

Space devoted to politics

The amount of space devoted to politics has grown enormously. Compared with today's papers the postwar press devoted relatively few column inches to politics, and these tended to be dry, factual and dull. For example, the 1945 general election campaign was covered in a rather summary way. Although full election results were reported (it took a few days to collate them), there was little in the way of comment or analysis on either the campaign or the results, outside rather brief leader columns. In 1995 politics still accounted for a relatively small portion of newspaper content, but the amount of space devoted to the subject in one way or another (news, comment, analysis, photographs, banner headlines, and cartoons) was vastly greater than in 1945. Election coverage ran to millions of words, and detailed public opinion poll results on almost every aspect of the 1992 election campaign were presented in the serious papers.

Change in titles and ownership

Simply counting the number of newspaper titles conceals a fair amount of turnover, both of titles and ownership. Table 3 organises national papers into three groups according to whether they lasted the fifty years, died during the period, or were successfully floated.

Overall, twelve papers survived the period, eighteen ceased publication, and seven were successfully launched, although by 1996 two or three of these looked as if they might not survive the decade. Most of the new titles were launched by big companies, especially those with established dailies

Table 1 National daily papers: titles and sales, 1945–95 (sales in millions)

	1945	1995
Broadsheets		
Daily Telegraph	0.82	1.05
The Times	0.20	0.68
Guardian	0.08	0.40
Independent	–	0.30
Financial Times	0.04	0.03
Total sales	1.14	2.46
Number of titles	4	5
Average sales	0.29	0.49
Middle market		
Daily Express	3.24	1.25
Daily Herald	2.00	–
Daily Mail	1.75	1.85
News Chronicle	1.45	–
Today	–	0.57[a]
Total sales	8.44	3.67
Number of titles	4	3
Average sales	2.22	0.92
Mass market		
Daily Mirror	2.00	2.52
Daily Sketch	0.88	–
Sun	–	4.06
Daily Star	–	0.75
Daily Record	–	0.74
Total sales	2.88	8.06
Number of titles	2	4
Average sales	1.44	2.02
Total sales	12.46	14.19
Number of titles	10	12
Average sales	1.25	1.18

[a]*Today* ceased publication 17 November 1995.
Sources: Seymour-Ure (1991: 28–9); *Guardian*, 11 December 1995.

that needed a Sunday complement to keep them running seven days a week. Some of the fatalities were suffered by the big names, but more were launched by minor figures who were unable to get a foothold in the business – the *Recorder*, the *New Daily*, the *Post*, *Today*, and *Sunday Today* (the last three were Eddie Shah ventures). There were some newcomers to the scene (Robert Maxwell, Conrad Black and Lord Stevens), but most of the new ventures were those of established newspaper interests, or of large companies with substantial resources.

There was not just a turnover of numbers and titles of papers, however, for they also changed ownership, sometimes with rather bewildering

Table 2 National Sunday papers: titles and sales, 1945–95 (sales in millions)

	1945	1995
Broadsheets		
Sunday Times	0.46	1.27
Observer	0.30	0.48
Sunday Telegraph	–	0.67
Independent on Sunday	–	0.33
Total sales	0.76	2.75
Number of titles	2	4
Average sales	0.38	0.69
Middle market		
Sunday Express	2.11	1.35
Sunday Dispatch	1.37	–
Sunday Chronicle	1.15	–
Reynold's News	0.58	–
Mail on Sunday	–	2.03
Total sales	5.21	3.38
Number of titles	4	2
Average sales	1.30	1.69
Mass market		
News of the World	5.00	4.47
People	3.45	2.10
Sunday Pictorial	2.50	–
Empire News	1.81	–
Sunday Graphic	1.03	–
Sunday Mirror	–	2.51
Total sales	13.79	9.08
Number of titles	5	3
Average sales	2.76	3.03
Total sales	19.76	15.21
Number of titles	11	9
Average sales	1.80	1.69

Sources: Seymour-Ure (1991: 28–9); *Guardian*, 11 December 1995.

frequency. Of the titles that survived throughout the fifty years, most changed their proprietors at least once, and usually two or three times. Only the *Mail* and the *Guardian* did not do so, although the latter, controlled by the Scott Trust, dropped 'Manchester' from its title when it started printing in London in 1959.

Oligopolistic trends

Change in the newspaper business in the 1970s and 1980s was hardly surprising. Computer technology has caused a revolution in the industry, but, contrary to some expectations, it has not broken up the increasing

Table 3 Changes in the composition of the British press, 1945–50

	Title	Year
Survivors		
Dailies	*Daily Telegraph*	
	The Times	
	Guardian	
	Financial Times	
	Daily Express	
	Daily Mail	
	Daily Mirror	
Sundays	*Sunday Times*	
	Observer	
	Sunday Express	
	News of the World	
	People	
Total 12		
Successful newcomers		
Dailies	*Sun*	1970, absorbed and relaunched version of the *Daily Herald*
	Daily Star	1978
	Independent	1986
Sundays	*Sunday Telegraph*	1961
	Sunday Mirror	1963, absorbed and relaunched version of the *Sunday Pictorial*
	Mail on Sunday	1982
	Independent on Sunday	1990
Total 7		
Fatalities		
Dailies	*Daily Graphic*	1952, became *Daily Sketch*
	Recorder	1954
	News Chronicle	1960
	Daily Herald	1964, absorbed and relaunched as the *Sun*
	New Daily	1966
	Daily Sketch	1971, merged with *Daily Mail*
	Today	1986, lasted only a few months under Eddie Shah
	Post	1988, closed after four weeks
	Morning Star	1995
Sundays	*Sunday Chronicle*	1955
	Empire News	1960
	Sunday Graphic	1960
	Sunday Dispatch	1961, absorbed by *Sunday Express*
	Sunday Pictorial	1963, absorbed and relaunched by *Sunday Mirror*
	Sunday Citizen	1962, incorporated with *Reynold's News* 1967, closed
	News on Sunday	1987
	Sunday Today	1987
	Sunday Correspondent	1990
Total 18		

trend towards media oligopolies. On the contrary, these have become enlarged and strengthened. New printing technology makes it possible to print and experiment with a widening array of specialist publications, but the economics and distribution of mass newspapers and magazines has encouraged the concentration of their ownership and control. It also seems to have created a rather standardised range of tabloids, rather than diversity. Just as the world market for family cars has resulted in a cloning of designs produced by a handful of mass producers, so the competition for tabloid sales has produced few publishers printing similar papers with large sales.

The oligopoly has been occasionally challenged but not with great success. The most conspicuous attempt was Eddie Shah's much publicised giant-killing act with *Today*, the first computerised, colour national daily, launched in 1986. It was intended to challenge both the Fleet Street barons and the print unions by outflanking them with the latest computer-driven print technology. Within months of his first issue, Shah was forced to sell the paper to Lonrho, the multinational corporation of 'Tiny' Rowland, who already owned the *Observer*. He then sold it to Rupert Murdoch in 1987, who closed it down in 1995. Of the outsider ventures, only the *Independent* has survived in recent times. It was the first quality daily to be launched for 113 years (Negrine 1994: 49–50), and began with shoestring finances of only £18 million in 1986, although it still has a circulation of less than a third of a million, and its future is not certain. The main beneficiaries of the new technology were not new entrants into the market hoping to exploit new production methods, but the old hands. Rupert Murdoch led the way when he moved to his new, fully automated plant at Wapping (Whitaker 1987: 236–48). Many national papers followed suit by moving out of Fleet Street. As a result the term 'Fleet Street' is now technically a misnomer (Melvern 1986).

The consequence of change in the titles and ownership of national, regional and local newspapers over 1945–95 has tended to be further concentration of ownership and control. All the daily papers in 1945 were separately owned. By the 1990s eight companies controlled the national dailies. Five controlled over 80 per cent of national daily circulation, and over 90 per cent of national Sunday sales. Concentration of ownership and control of the British press is not at all new: in 1910 Lord Northcliffe controlled almost 40 per cent of London morning sales; in the 1980s, the biggest player in town (the Australian Rupert Murdoch) controlled only a third.

The main difference now is that the national dailies take an even bigger share of total daily newspaper sales. In 1945, sales of provincial morning and evening papers were almost two-thirds those of national dailies; by the 1990s the figure had fallen to less than a half. Many (London) national papers printed regional editions in 1945 centred on Manchester and Scotland, but this practice gradually disappeared. The number of independent local proprietors has also declined, as national chains and companies have taken a greater financial stake in the provincial and local press. In theory the Monopolies and Mergers Commission is charged with the job of preventing the creation of monopolies, but in practice it has not done so in the media business (Curran and Seaton 1985: 293). In 1981 it agreed to Murdoch's purchase of *The Times* and the *Sunday Times*, which brought his share of the national daily market to 30 per cent, and of national Sundays to 36 per cent.

Moreover, this concentration in press power has been accompanied by the absorption of the newspaper industry into the larger world of multimedia and multinational finance and business. The ownership and control of the press now extends far beyond newspapers to general publishing, television, radio, films, recording, entertainment, and a wide variety of other business interests. Thus the British business has been integrated into international finance capitalism. This is the process of what Seymour-Ure calls 'concentration, conglomeration, and internationalization' (1991: 107–17).

Politicisation

The growing concentration of ownership and control might not be important but for its political implications. Although the papers of 1945 were partisan – in the sense that their party sympathies were clear – they were far less party political than they are now. Throughout modern times, most newspapers in Britain have followed their own political line. Indeed, many of the Fleet Street barons of the early twentieth century made their political and party preferences publicly clear in their private and business lives. Most big business is highly technical, bureaucratic, and impersonal, and ownership is invariably spread among many different shareholders and interests. In contrast, the newspaper business tends to remain in personal hands; share holding is not widely spread, and as Seymour-Ure puts it: 'The newspaper is the natural tool for the autocrat' (1991: 34).

Compared with their modern counterparts, the papers of the 1940s and 1950s drew a clearer line between news and comment, and were much less inclined to present the news with a party political slant. The arrival of television as a major political medium in the 1960s and 1970s pushed newspapers into a more overtly partisan role. Television news attracts large audiences and, moreover, it is up to the minute with the latest news. Since news is a highly perishable commodity, instant television news represents a serious challenge to the slower print medium. It threatens newspaper circulation, and therefore their very existence. At the same time, television – both BBC and commercial – is required by law to avoid editorialising, and to present a fair and balanced account of the news (see below). Newspapers have responded to this challenge by emphasising the difference between themselves and television; the broadsheets offer far more in-depth political analysis and comment, and the tabloids have become increasingly party political in both news and comment (Cook 1992).

Partisanship

The concentration of press power combined with its increasingly partisan nature has become a source of concern because, together, they undermine the pluralist ideal of a distribution of ownership and a wide variety of political sympathies. In 1945, the three national dailies that supported Labour had a readership of nearly 4.5 million, or 35 per cent of sales. The Conservatives had four papers, accounting for half daily sales, and the Liberals two, with 13 per cent. Since then the number and circulation of Labour and Liberal papers has declined: in 1992 the *Independent* was independent, the *Guardian* divided its support between the Liberal Democrats and Labour, and the remaining six major national dailies were staunchly Conservative. Not including the *Daily Star*, which was neutral/Conservative, Conservative papers accounted for almost two-thirds of total circulation (Butler and Butler 1986: 499). The national press is politically lopsided.

The rise of tabloid journalism

The sale of national dailies hit a peak in 1957 with nearly 17 million. The Sundays peaked a few years earlier, in 1951, with 30.6 million. Both have suffered a long and substantial decline since then. It did not take long for television to eat into the fixed amount of time of readers, or for commercial television to eat into limited funds for advertising. In 1960/61 alone, one national daily, three national Sundays, and a London evening paper ceased publication. Between 1959 and 1969, national daily sales fell by 1.3 million to 14.8 million, and national Sundays declined by a huge 2.5 million to 24.4 million. In the 1970s newspaper prices rose quite steeply and in the 1980s unemployment hit circulation – many people buy a paper to read on the way to work and to exchange with friends there. In the 1990s sales were hit hard a third time by rising newsprint costs. Circulation seems likely to fall again in the immediate future, and some papers are rumoured to be on the danger list.

The nature of the national newspaper market has also changed. As the figures in tables 1 and 2 show, the middle market has halved while the tabloid mass market almost trebled, and demand for quality broadsheets also strengthened, though it remains small. In other words, the national newspaper market seems to have polarised around a small but growing quality readership, and a vastly larger but declining popular readership. Of these two trends, the growth of the tabloids is, in some ways, the more significant politically.

Press standards have been subjected to criticism all over the world since the first newspapers were printed, but the British mass circulation tabloids seem to be the worst. It is not just a matter of inaccuracy or political partiality and bias, but of the editorial policy of mixing fact and opinion, and adding chequebook journalism, sensationalism, triviality, libel, and plain untruths to the mixture (Hollingsworth 1986; Snoddy 1992). In theory, various organisations have been set up to monitor press standards and maintain them. In practice these have been either toothless, or unwilling to sink their teeth into even the worst offenders. Neither the Press Council (recommended by the 1947 Royal Commission on the Press, but delayed until 1953), nor its reformed version (1963), nor the Press Complaints Commission (set up in 1991) has done much to prevent the slide (Calcutt 1993).

At the same time, there are no fewer than four quality national daily broadsheets (five, including the *Financial Times*), and four quality Sunday papers. Few other western nations are as well served. The disproportionate importance of the quality press lies in the fact that it is read by the educated members of the population with high levels of political participation – the political or 'chattering' classes. There has been a tendency for the population to divide between those with comparatively high levels of political interest, who rely on, and trust in, the quality press, and the tabloid readers, who are comparatively inactive in politics, do not place much confidence in their chosen paper, and who use the television as their main source of political information (Negrine 1994: 1–3).

The continuing importance of the press

The postwar press has maintained a fairly strong position, in spite of earlier predictions that it would be muscled out by the television age. Sales continue to fall from their peak in the 1950s, but most people still read a national paper and the press continues to carry political weight. It helps set the political agenda for the other media, and exercises influence over politicians and electors. For example, there is a tendency for television to take its cues from the morning papers' headlines, and political elites remain voracious consumers of newspapers. National papers seem to exercise a continuing influence on the political attitudes and behaviour of their readers, not least their voting behaviour. In the 1950s and 1960s, it was widely believed by social scientists that the media in general could do little more than reflect and reinforce the pre-existing political attitudes of citizens (Harrop 1987: 45–63). However, in the 1970s the idea gained ground that the media helped to frame the political agenda – that is, they influenced not what people thought, but what they thought about. More recently evidence has begun to accumulate to show that the national press does more than reinforce or set agendas, and that it has a significant influence on voting patterns and election outcomes (Dunleavy and Husbands 1985: 110–17; Miller 1991: 169–99; Newton 1992; Linton 1995: 14–15). Hence the *Sun*'s famous claim (which it later denied) that 'It was the Sun wot won' the 1992 election for the Conservatives. The research is still inconclusive, but, if correct, the bias of the national papers seems to have worrying implications for democracy.

Radio

Public service broadcasting

Radio broadcasting differs from the press in one essential respect: whereas it is possible in theory for anyone to set up a newspaper, magazine, journal, or newsletter (there are tens of thousands in Britain alone), radio broadcasting frequencies are limited, and therefore not open to all. For technological reasons radio broadcasting frequencies were more limited in the early days, but they are still regulated by international agreements (dividing frequencies between countries) and it is still necessary to reserve wavelengths for special purposes, such as the police, fire, ambulance, and air traffic control. Since broadcasting frequencies for radio – and later television – are strictly limited (known as 'spectrum scarcity') they are a form of public property, and should, it is argued, be controlled by public agencies and used for the public interest.

From this it was concluded that electronic broadcasting should follow the public service model, with the following features: a public monopoly, paid for by public money (the licence fee), controlled by a public body, the BBC (though not a political or a government one), and obliged to serve the national interest, with high-quality programmes that are available to all (Blumler 1992; McQuail 1993: 20–33, 55–9). From its early days, the BBC's responsibility was stated as being, in order of priority, to inform, educate, and entertain, and the entertainment was to be of a high cultural quality. The first director-general of the BBC, John (later Lord) Reith, was a powerful and effective advocate of this public service philosophy, and the tradition was carried on intact by BBC radio and television, at least until the mid-1950s, when commercial television first appeared on the scene.

The postwar pattern

The nature and value of the public service model are now controversial, but immediately after the war they were almost universally accepted. As the 'voice of the nation' during the war, BBC radio news had enormous esteem among its large audience (Barrat 1986: 72–4) and it resumed peacetime broadcasting in 1945 with two radio programmes, the Light Programme and the Home Service. The 1945 pattern did not last long, however. First, the daily broadcasting times of each station were gradually increased, and another station, the Third Programme, was added in 1946, although it was designed for a small audience. At its postwar peak of 1950, almost 12 million radio licences were issued. After that the figures are confused by the spread of television and the combination of radio and television licences into one.

Local and commercial radio

From the late 1950s the pace of change in radio increased for technical and political reasons. The technical reasons included a capacity to broadcast on a larger number of wavelengths (including VHF, first used by the BBC in 1955), which allowed the emergence of local radio stations, cheap and portable transistor radios, car radios, and Walkmans. The political reasons were mainly the election of Conservative governments in 1970, 1979, and 1983, which ended the BBC monopoly and introduced and extended independent (that is, commercial) radio.

BBC local radio was introduced in 1967 and the number of stations gradually increased, from the first in Sheffield, Merseyside, and Leicester, until there were over thirty stations by the 1990s. The Pilkington Committee of 1962 recommended a BBC monopoly of local radio, but shortly afterwards the pirate pop station Radio Caroline started broadcasting from international waters, in 1964. In response, the Marine and Broadcasting (Offences) Act of 1967 made it illegal to place advertising on pirate radio, so cutting off its supply of money, and in the same year the BBC opened its own pop radio station (Radio 1), so trying to cut off its supply of listeners. In effect the BBC co-opted pirate radio. This was not enough for the Conservative government elected in 1970, which authorised commercial local radio in 1971. The first stations began broadcasting in London two years later, and others followed in rapid succession until almost everyone now has a choice of at least two commercial stations. Since each broadcasts for more hours than the BBC's two stations in 1945, the total number of broadcast hours is immensely larger than it was. And since, by 1995, most households had at least two radios, and most cars had one, there are more stations, with more hours of programming, and more receivers to tune into them than ever before.

The limited political importance of radio

Important though it was as a source of news and information in the early postwar years, radio nevertheless had a restricted political influence. Its political coverage was limited by law and by convention such as the 'fourteen-day rule', which prevented broadcasts on a subject for fourteen days before it was due for debate in parliament. Parliamentary proceedings were not broadcast until 1978, and then only by radio. Coverage of elections and campaigns was limited. And the public service model established by the founder of the BBC, Lord Reith, kept radio (later television) within narrow confines of reporting the news, rather than analysing, questioning, or commenting. The use of a persistent, probing, and critical interviewing style, now found on some radio and television, did not emerge until the 1980s.

By the time laws and conventions had changed, the potential role of radio had been rudely usurped by all-conquering television. Although it is true that Radio 4 and BBC World News are excellent sources of political news and analysis, radio now ranks behind both newspapers and television as a source of information for the majority of citizens. Radio 4 has a substantial audience among the chattering classes, but since 1945 radio has generally sunk to the position of poor relation among the three main mass media of Britain, a position which it does not deserve in terms of the quality of its news and current affairs programmes.

Television

From status symbol to total saturation

The BBC resumed its postwar monopoly of television broadcasting in 1946, but only a few with televisions within forty miles of Alexandra Palace in London could watch. This amounted to an exclusive club of somewhat fewer than 25,000 people. Over the next fifty years television was to change more dramatically than any other branch of the media, and with far greater impact on public affairs. First, BBC Television spread north from London when transmitters were opened in Birmingham (1949), Yorkshire (1951) and Scotland (1952). In 1947, 15,000 households had (black and white) television licences: 15 million were issued in 1968. By 1960 practically all households in Britain could receive television, and by the mid-1980s household saturation with colour television was virtually complete. Today, almost 60 per cent of households have at least two televisions.

In 1946, the BBC broadcast about thirty hours of programmes in a good week. By the mid-1990s, the four terrestrial channels poured out almost 500 hours of television a week between the early morning and the small hours. From being little more than an exotic drawing-room status symbol in 1946, watching television had become the nation's main activity, after working and sleeping.

From 1946 the BBC gradually extended its broadcasting hours and its political coverage. The first (silent) newsreel was shown in 1948, and in 1950 there was the first news and current affairs programme (*In the News*), and the first television coverage of general election results (Even 1986: 294–305). The first televised prime ministerial broadcast was made in 1956, when Anthony Eden spoke to the nation about the Suez War. Election campaign coverage started in 1959. By then television news and current affairs programmes were a standard part of political life, more important than radio and, in some ways, than the papers. The House of Lords was televised in 1985, followed by the Commons in 1989. By 1992 television was devoting an estimated 200 hours a week, every week, to the general election campaign, and many were bored by it (Negrine 1994: 166).

Commercial television breaks the mould

The most important change, though, was the introduction of commercial television. The Beveridge Committee (1951) had argued for a state monopoly of television, like that of radio, but the Television Act 1954 authorised commercial television, which first broadcast in 1955 with about fifty hours a week of programming. The quality of programmes was still subject to regulation (no programmes unsuitable for children before the late evening) but after a shaky start commercial television was a raging success. Audiences grew rapidly, children started singing catchy advertising jingles, and by 1959 ITV had two-thirds of the television audience.

In retrospect we can see that the 1954 Act was the first of a whole sequence of media changes. It ended the BBC's monopoly and paved the way for commercial radio in the 1960s. It generated competition between commercial television channels and between them and the BBC. The BBC gained its second channel (BBC2) in 1964 – it first broadcast in colour in 1967 – and a second commercial channel (Channel 4) came on air in 1982. Although BBC2 was initially experimental, and Channel 4 still caters for minority groups and tastes, the effect of competition for audiences was inevitably to push programming down market. It also obliged channels to broadcast for longer hours, in an attempt to keep their market share, so requiring more imported programmes. A large proportion of the extra hours comprises American imports. According to Tunstall (1983) the mass media are American, and this has a strong effect on British culture and society.

Multimedia links

Though the 1954 Act succeeded in breaking the BBC monopoly it did not prevent the formation of oligopolies and cartels in the media business generally. Like the newspaper business, commercial television soon settled down under the control of a few main companies. Rather than competing for network programme material, they agreed to carve up the available material between them – the owner of Scottish TV, Roy (later Lord) Thomson, called it a 'licence to print money' (see Seymour-Ure 1991: 88). Since much of the initial investment came from publishing interests, some of this cash flowed back into the newspaper industry, and later into commercial radio.

The business and financial links between commercial television, commercial radio, the press, and other business activities are remarkably complex. There were statutory regulations against overlapping ownership and control, but these have been gradually relaxed, or simply not applied. Nevertheless, the overlapping and interlocking of corporate interests, partially unleashed by the 1954 Act, have helped to increase the 'concentration, conglomeration, and internationalization' of media interests. These links reduce the pluralist diversity of all three media.

The political impact of television

The impact of commercial television was enormous from the start (Smith 1995: 80–8), but it did not overturn the public service model of Lord Reith's BBC so far as politics was concerned. On the contrary, television news was (and still is) required to maintain impartiality and balance, to avoid editorialising, and to screen no political commercials. Its coverage of election campaigns is strictly regulated, as are party election broadcasts (Munro 1986: 294–305). In their turn, both BBC and ITV news are highly regarded by the general public, the great majority believing them reliable, accurate, and trustworthy (Kellner and Worcester 1983: 58; Negrine 1994: 3). In this way British television (and radio) has maintained much of the public service model so far as politics is concerned, and has managed to avoid some of the worst excesses of exclusive reliance upon commercial broadcasting.

In addition, the BBC has managed to keep a surprisingly large share of the mass television audience, perhaps by following commercial standards (backdoor commercialisation) or even by setting the pace. But those who forecast its wholesale commercialisation, or else its demise, have been proved wrong. 'Auntie' BBC has withstood many of the pressures (certainly not all) and maintains a strong presence. It was helped by the Peacock Committee on broadcasting finance, which opposed widespread commercialisation and recommended rather modest changes to the status quo. Despite doubts raised when the BBC's charter came up for renewal in 1994, and after a series of attacks on the BBC by the Conservative Party and the government over its reporting of Northern Ireland, the Falklands War, and the American bombing of Libya, the BBC (currently) appears to be in a surprisingly healthy, if under-financed, condition.

Cable, satellite and the 'wired nation'

Perhaps the big earthquake in electronic broadcasting is still to come – the widely anticipated revolution of satellite and cable, and the much vaunted capacities of the interactive information superhighway. The full integration of cable, satellite, radio, television, videos, telephone (or videophones), telex, fax, and computers makes it possible to create the 'wired nation', in which almost any form or quantity of information (pictures and films, sounds and music, words and figures, or all together in multimedia combination) can be relayed instantaneously to appropriate receivers (Negrine 1994: 179–85).

Cable was first installed in Britain in 1972, when a small handful of communities were wired. Twenty years later the large capital costs of laying cable prevented it from spreading to more than 100,000 subscribers (almost 60 million are plugged into cable television in the USA) and seems unlikely to rival satellite broadcasting. Satellite television came later, but quickly outgrew cable after its basis had been prepared in the Cable and Broadcasting Act 1984. Murdoch's Sky Television was on air in 1989, followed by British Satellite Broadcasting (BSB), which quickly ran into financial problems and merged with Sky to form BSkyB in 1990. It now broadcasts sixteen channels through cable and from its Astra satellite to – it claims – about 3 million households, and is growing fast (Peak 1993: 103–9).

Two facets of cable and satellite developments are important. First, it is no coincidence that one of the largest multimedia, multinational conglomerates leads satellite television in Britain – namely Murdoch's News International. Second, because cable and satellite will produce a large number of television channels (a hundred or more), they will end spectrum scarcity. Therefore, it is said, the need for state regulation will also end. The Peacock Committee (Committee on the Financing of the BBC 1986) made the point strongly, and argued that when television channels multiply in the near future, so the market should take over from public service television.

At this point there will no doubt be intense ideological and economic pressure to throw the whole media system into the market. At the same time, the study of British developments since 1945 suggests severe problems with this view. First, it is likely to intensify the concentration of ownership and control of the mass media, which will further undermine the principle of pluralist diversity. Second, it will hasten the development of 'tabloid television'. Guided by the public service model, British television is widely admired in the western world; the market model has produced, at the other extreme, Fleet Street tabloids. Third, political news is not a market commodity like cars or soap powder, which consumers can compare and test through first-hand experience. Most citizens have no first-hand experience of politics, and have to take the news on trust; there is no market test for its reliability, accuracy, or impartiality, only the standard of what makes money. If tabloid television makes money, it is likely to spread, and also to reduce the level of political knowledge, interest, and awareness of citizens. In this way it poses a threat to democracy.

Finally, recent developments in satellite television and the Internet have brought the problem of pornography and violence to public attention. Whereas the market model might argue that this is simply supplying a demand – what the market is supposed to do – many of those who favour the market believe strongly in the state regulation of pornography. If past experience is anything to go by, self-regulation of the media is unlikely to work, and yet satellite broadcasting and the Internet are beyond the powers of the national state. The issue of regulation and censorship of the market media is likely to be a difficult and politically controversial one.

The messenger boy joins the board of directors

In the general election of 1945, the Conservative Party had no official party manifesto. Instead, the prime minister, Sir Winston Churchill, presented his personal manifesto to the nation. There was no television, and Churchill and other politicians communicated with electors mainly by means of newspapers and public meetings. Newspapers were slim, relatively expensive, and their coverage of politics confined to rather few column inches; their coverage of the election campaign was fairly cursory by modern standards, and their analysis and commentary on the progress of the election campaign almost non-existent. At the same time, journalists' standards were comparatively high, even in the tabloids.

Although about 10 million households had a 'wireless', with its two national stations, broadcasting hours were strictly limited and there was little coverage of the election campaign, apart from party election broadcasts. Radio reporting of parliamentary affairs was tightly restricted by the fourteen-day rule, and apart from the formal news, there was not a lot in the way of current affairs or discussion programmes. If politicians were interviewed at all, they were subject to gentle and polite questioning (Butler 1986).

The situation was totally transformed by 1995. Virtually every household in Britain had at least one colour television and in addition to four main television channels there were a variety of satellite and cable television stations. There were five main BBC radio stations, thirty-two local BBC radio stations, and most people had a choice of commercial radio stations. Most radio and television stations broadcast for most of the day, some for twenty-four hours. There were about the same number of newspapers available selling about the same total number of copies, but they were much larger than in 1945, the broadsheets carried much more news and commentary, and the tabloids were far more party political.

Collectively these poured out thousands of column inches and thousands of hours on politics, especially during election campaigns. On average we now spend more than twenty-five hours a week watching television, and audiences for the main evening news programmes approach 10 million. Almost everything the country's leading politicians did and said was observed and commented on by the media. What they wore and how they appeared were scrutinised. Consequently, the parties and their leaders thought long and hard about their campaign strategy. They planned what to say and how to say it meticulously, and spent many millions of pounds on stage-managing and presenting themselves to the public.

This short account should not close without trying to convey the fact that the journey of the media from 1945 to 1995 was surrounded by heated political controversy and widespread interest at almost every turn: growing fears about concentration of press ownership; bitter opposition to commercial television; controversy about pirate radio; the contentious decision to broadcast parliament; the storms surrounding television franchise sales (Franklin 1994: 66–8). At the same time, flamboyant, powerful, and controversial media moguls have appeared – Lord Reith, Lord Beaverbrook, Robert Maxwell, 'Tiny' Rowland, Lord Grade, Cecil King, Rupert Murdoch, Conrad Black, to name a few at random. The pace of change in the media has been fast, and discussion about them has been furious. In the near future many issues will come to a head with commercialisation and the construction of the wired nation – the public service and the market models, press freedom and regulation, pornography and violence, extremist politics, control of media technology and content, the power of the media, and political advertising and government propaganda. As a technological revolution makes so much more possible, and with so much money, sex and power at stake, it is a safe bet that changes will be faster and discussion more furious in the next decade or two.

Appendix. The media and British politics, 1945–95: chronology of events

Year	Medium	Event
1945	Radio	BBC Home Service resumes. Light Programme replaces forces programme
1946	TV	BBC TV resumes
	Radio	BBC Third Programme introduced
1947	Press	Royal Commission on the Press (Ross) established
1948	TV	First TV newsreel (silent)
1949	Press	Royal Commission on the Press (Ross Commission) recommends control of performance, management and ownership of the press
	TV	New BBC transmitter at Sutton Coldfield opened
1950	TV	First TV coverage of general election results; first political TV programme (*In the News*) starts
1951	TV	New BBC transmitter at Holme Moss opens; Beveridge Committee on Broadcasting recommends that TV should follow the public service model of radio
1952	TV	BBC opens transmitter at Kirk O'Shotts
	Press	*Daily Graphic* bought by Associated Newspapers (Harmsworth)
1953	TV	First edition of *Panorama* on BBC
	Press	Press Council starts; *Daily Sketch* (formally *Daily Graphic*) relaunched by Associated Newspapers; the *Recorder* floated
1954	TV	Television Act establishes Independent Television Authority
	Press	Lord Beaverbrook passes control of Beaverbrook Newspapers Ltd (*Daily Express*, London *Evening Standard*) to Beaverbrook Press; demise of the *Recorder*
1955	Radio	BBC VHF transmission begins
	TV	First independent TV programmes
	Press	Wartime newsprint control ends; demise of *Sunday Chronicle*
1956	TV	Eden makes first TV prime ministerial broadcast
1957	TV	First edition of *Tonight* on BBC
	Press	Pearson group buys *Financial Times*
1958	TV	Value of TV advertising surpasses that of press
1959	TV	First TV election campaign coverage
	Press	Allied Newspapers (Thomson) buys *Sunday Times, Sunday Graphic*, and *Sunday News*; the *Guardian* drops 'Manchester' from title and prints in London

1960	Press	Mirror Group buys *Daily Herald* from TUC/Oldhams and changes name to *Sun*; *News Chronicle* merges with *Daily Mail*; *London Evening News* and the *Star* merged; *New Daily* floated; *Empire News* and *Sunday Graphic* close
1961	Press	*Sunday Times* colour magazine starts; Oldhams Press amalgamated with IPC, which also absorbs *Sunday Pictorial*; *Sunday Telegraph* launched; *Sunday Express* absorbs *Sunday Dispatch*
1962	TV	Pilkington report recommends second BBC channel; Advertising Standards Authority established; first live transmission, by Telstar Satellite
	Press	Royal Commission on the Press; *Sunday Citizen* incorporated with *Reynold's News*
1963	Press	First woman joins Press Council; IPC launches *Sunday Mirror* (formally *Sunday Pictorial*)
1964	TV	First BBC2 broadcasts
	Radio	Radio Caroline launched
	Press	*Daily Herald* relaunched as the *Sun*
1966	Press	*The Times* puts news on front page; Monopolies Commission approves common ownership of *The Times* and *Sunday Times* by Thomson organisation; *New Daily* closes; *Daily Worker* changes name to *Daily Star*
1967	TV	BBC2 broadcasts in colour
	Radio	BBC launches Radio 1 and renames Radio 2 (formally Light Programme) and Radio 3; first BBC local radio broadcasts
	Press	Times Newspapers formed to run *The Times* and *Sunday Times*; *Reynold's News* closed
1969	TV	BBC1 broadcasts in colour and on 625 and 405 lines
	Press	News International (Murdoch) buys *Sun* from Mirror Group, and acquires *News of the World*
1970	Press	Reed International acquires *Daily Mirror*, *Sunday Mirror*, and *People*
1971	Radio	Independent local radio authorised (starts 1973)
	Press	*Daily Sketch* merges with *Daily Mail* (both owned by Lord Rothermere)
1972	TV	Cable TV established in five English locations
1974	Radio	First election radio phone-in
	Press	Report of the Royal Commission on the Press (McGregor)
1975	Radio	Trial radio broadcasts of the House of Commons
1976	Press	*Observer* acquired by Atlantic Richfield Oil Co.
1977	TV	Annan report sets scene for Channel 4
	Press	*Daily Express*, *Sunday Express*, and London *Evening Standard* acquired by Trafalgar House (Lord Matthews)
1978	Radio	Regular broadcasts from House of Commons
	Press	*Daily Star* launched in Manchester by Trafalgar House; publication of *The Times* halted by industrial dispute (November 1978 to November 1979)
1979	TV	Independent Broadcasting Authority Act gives responsibility for Channel 4 to IBA
1980	TV	Broadcasting Act establishes Broadcasting Complaints Commission

	Press	*Evening Standard* sold to Trafalgar House and merged with *Evening News*; Lonhro ('Tiny' Rowland) buys *Observer* from Atlantic Richfield Co.
1981	Press	News International (Murdoch) buys *The Times* and *Sunday Times*
1982	TV	First Channel 4 broadcasts
	Press	Associated Newspapers (Rothermere) launches *Mail on Sunday*
1983	TV	Breakfast TV on BBC and ITV
1984	TV	Cable and Broadcasting Act to establish Cable Authority and Satellite Broadcasting Board; BBC and ITV form 'Club of 21' to plan direct satellite services
	Press	Maxwell acquires *Daily Mirror, Sunday Mirror, People*
1985	TV	House of Lords televised. Satellite Broadcasting Board wound up after less than a year
	Press	United Newspapers (Lord Stevens) acquires *Daily Express, Sunday Express, Daily Star*
1986	TV	Peacock report on financing of broadcasting; British Satellite Broadcasting wins contract for direct satellite broadcasting – major shareholders include Anglia and Granada TV, Pearson
	Press	Eddie Shah launches *Today* amid much publicity then sells it to Lonrho ('Tiny' Rowland); *Independent* launched; Murdoch moves *The Times* to Wapping
1987	Press	London *Daily News* launched, briefly, by Maxwell's Mirror Group; *Today* and *Sunday Today* bought by Murdoch's News International, which closes *Sunday Today*; *Daily* and *Sunday Telegraph* bought by Conrad Black; launch of *News on Sunday*
1988	TV	Broadcasting Standards Council established to regulate standards of radio, TV, and video
	Press	Murdoch announces plans for Sky TV satellite broadcasting; Shah launches the *Post* (33 issues only are printed); *Independent on Sunday* launched
1988	TV	Sky TV broadcasts; Officials Secrets Act
1989	TV	House of Commons agrees to televise its proceedings
1990	TV	Television Broadcasting Act replaces IBA and Cable Authority with Independent Television Commission and Radio Authority; establishes new procedures for licensing and regulating commercial TV (franchises auctioned to the highest bidder), and establishes Channel 4 as an independent corporation; BSB begins satellite broadcasting, then merges with Murdoch's Sky TV to form BSkyB
	Press	*Independent on Sunday* and *Sunday Correspondent* launched
	Radio	BBC Radio 5 launched
1991	TV	BBC World Service begins terrestrial TV broadcasts; Independent Television Commission replaces IBA and Cable Authority
	Radio	Radio Authority established for independent radio
	Press	Newspaper Press Complaints Commission formed from former Press Council
1992	TV	Yorkshire and Tyne Tees TV merge

	Radio	Classic FM broadcasts
	Press	*Sunday Mirror, Daily Mirror, People* acquired by creditor banks from Maxwell Corp.
1993	TV	Channel 4 sells air time; government announces relaxation of TV ownership rules making multiple ownership possible
	Radio	Virgin 1215 launched
	Press	Guardian Evening News Groups acquires *Observer* from Lonrho
1994	Radio/TV	BBC charter renewed until 2006; Radio 5 Live replaces Radio 5
1995	Press	*Today* and *Morning Star* cease publication

References

Barrat, D. (1986), *Media Sociology*, London, Tavistock Publications.
Blumler, J. G. (1992), *Television and the Public Interest*, London, Sage.
Butler, D. (1986), The changing nature of British elections, in I. Crewe and M. Harrop (eds), *Political Communications: The General Election Campaign of 1983*, Cambridge, Cambridge University Press.
Butler, D. and Butler, G. (1986) *British Political Facts, 1900–1985*, London, Macmillan.
Calcutt, C. (1993), *Review of Press Self-Regulation*, cmnd 2135, London, Department of National Heritage.
Committee on Financing the BBC (Peacock Committee) (1986), *Report*, cmnd 9824, London, HMSO.
Cook, S. (1992), Tabloid Tory bias grows more blatant, *Guardian*, 30 March, 1.
Curran, J. and Seaton, J. (1985), *Power Without Responsibility*, London, Methuen.
Davis, R. (1995), Media: becoming an autonomous force, in P. J. Davies (ed.), *An American Quarter Century: US Politics from Vietnam to Clinton*, Manchester, Manchester University Press.
Dunleavy, P. and Husbands, C. T. (1985), *British Democracy at the Cross-roads*, London, Allen and Unwin.
Even, M. (1986), Television broadcasting of the post-war elections and the case of 1983, in I. Crewe and M. Harrop (eds), *Political Communications: The General Election Campaign of 1983*, Cambridge: Cambridge University Press.
Franklin, M. (1994), *Packaging Politics: Political Communication in Britain's Media Democracy*, London, Edward Arnold.
Harrop, M. (1987), Voters, in J. Seaton, and B. Pimlott (eds), *The Media in British Politics*, Aldershot, Avebury.
Hollingsworth, M. (1986), *The Press and Political Dissent*, London, Pluto Press.
Jenkins, S. (1986), *Market For Glory*, London, Faber and Faber.
Kellner, P. and Worcester, R. M. (1983), Electoral perceptions of media stance, in R. M. Worcester and M. Harrop (eds), *Political Communications: The General Election of 1979*, London, Allen and Unwin.
Linton, M. (1995), Sun-powered politics, *Guardian*, 30 October, 14–15.
McQuail, D. (1993), *Media Performance: Mass Communication and the Public Interest*, London, Sage.
Melvern, L. (1986), *The End of the Street*, London, Methuen.
Miller, W. L. (1991), *Media and Voters*, Oxford, Clarendon Press.

Munro, C. (1986), Legal controls on election broadcasting, in I. Crewe and M. Harrop (eds), *Political Communications: The General Election Campaign of 1983*, Cambridge, Cambridge University Press.

Negrine, R. (1994), *Politics and the Mass Media in Britain* (2nd edn), London, Routledge.

Newton, K. (1992), Do people read everything they believe in the papers? Newspapers and voters in the 1983 and 1987 elections, in I. Crewe *et al.* (eds), *British Elections and Parties Yearbook 1991*, Hemel Hempstead, Simon and Schuster.

Peak, S. (ed.) (1993), *1994: The Media Guide*, London, Fourth Estate.

Seymour-Ure, C. (1991) *The British Press and Broadcasting Since 1945*, Oxford, Oxford University Press.

Smith, A. (1995), *Television: An International History*, Oxford, Oxford University Press.

Snoddy, R. (1992), *The Good, the Bad, and the Unacceptable: The Hard News About the British Press*, London, Faber and Faber.

Tunstall, J. (1983), *The Media in Britain*, London, Constable.

Whitaker, B. (1987), Newspapers and the new technology, in J. Seaton and B. Pimlott (eds), *The Media in British Politics*, Aldershot, Avebury.

10

Pressure groups
Wyn Grant

Pressure groups are deeply rooted in British politics. Their activity can be traced back to the eighteenth century, and many groups that still exist were formed in the nineteenth century, ranging from the Association of British Chambers of Commerce to the Royal Society for the Prevention of Cruelty to Animals. As liberal individualism gave way to more corporate forms of organisation, exemplified by the joint stock company, the role of pressure groups in political life became more central and more generally accepted. 'In Britain at the turn of the century, there were signs of a general shift in the climate of opinion toward legitimizing functional groups, in particular the new organized producer groups of the modern industrial economy' (Beer 1969: 74).

What has happened over the past half century is not only that the number of groups has increased, and that they have become important in new areas of public policy such as the environment, but that their role in the political process has been increasingly questioned. This enhanced interest in pressure groups has been reflected in the attention that they have received from academics. As Gilmour has commented (1971: 339–40), 'Not long ago interest groups were ignored; now they are sometimes used to explain everything about the government of a country from its political structure to its constitutional tradition and ideals.'

If we consider the postwar Labour government in Britain, there is plenty of evidence of pressure group activity, but the study of it took place many years later, using archival and other sources (see, for example, Blank 1973; Middlemas 1986). There had been discussion of the role of pressure groups in Britain in the 1930s, stimulated by organisations such as the Institute of Public Administration and reflected in the writings of political commentators such as Richard Crossman (Jordan and Richardson 1987: 54–5). It is perhaps not surprising that there was little academic commentary on pressure groups in the late 1940s or early 1950s, as the academic study of politics in Britain was only then beginning to be organised in any systematic fashion. The late 1950s and early 1960s saw a flurry of studies, such as those by Eckstein (1960), Finer (1958), Potter (1961), and Stewart (1958). Despite the existence of earlier studies, 'the studies of the 1950s ... began from the assumption that Britain had little group influence' (Jordan and Richardson 1987: 56). The early studies showed that this was not the case, but it was some time before the map of pressure group activity was completed. For example, David Marsh and I started to study the Confederation of British Industry (CBI) at the beginning of the 1970s, when we discovered that there was no article or book on the subject that we could recommend to our students.

'Professor Robert McKenzie's article in 1958 recounted how a British information officer lecturing in America in 1954 had claimed there was a complete absence of pressure groups and lobbies in Britain' (Jordan and Richardson 1987: 56). Such ignorance was understandable because the sphere of pressure group activity half a century ago was, in Finer's (1958) term, an anonymous empire.

During the Labour governments of 1945–51, three broad types of pressure groups may be identified. First, there were the sectional pressure groups representing business and the professions. These organisations were headed by establishment figures who interacted easily with civil servants, often in their London clubs. In many cases, they had worked together during the war. Something of the flavour of the relationship of Sir Norman Kipping, the director-general of the Federation of British Industries, with officials is revealed by his record of a conversation with the permanent secretary at the War Office, who asked him to help with setting up a civilian organisation to maintain a base in the Suez Canal:

'Could you come over, Norman, right away?'
'Well, I suppose I could, George. What's it in aid of?'
'We need a bit of advice from someone on your side of life. We know you are all a lot of sharks, but we happen to know you, so be a good chap and come over.'
(Kipping 1969: 13)

A second important category was made up of organisations that were not part of the traditional establishment, but which it was thought important to have 'on board' in the decision-making process. This category mostly comprised the trade union movement. 'Between 1940 and 1945, the trade union movement achieved its fundamental aim of parity with the employers in the eyes of government' (Middlemas 1979: 300). This parity was based on the central importance of labour in a full-employment economy and was not dependent on the presence of a Labour government in office. Hence, when the Conservatives came into office in 1951 Walter Monckton's task as Minister of Labour was to maintain good relations with the unions, not to challenge or undermine their authority. Churchill gave Monckton 'a simple brief: to reassure the trade union movement that a Conservative government would not introduce penal sanctions in any industrial relations legislation, and to make sure that government was not disrupted' (Middlemas 1986: 257).

The third category of pressure groups was made up of 'cause' groups of a worthy, more or less respectable kind, kept in being through the dedication of small groups of earnest middle-class reformers. Three examples indicate the variety of such groups. The National Smoke Abatement Society (later National Society for Clean Air) had among its members both commercial interests, such as the manufacturers of smokeless fuels, and organisations and individuals concerned to promote cleaner air. The Society had a clear insider strategy that emphasised a moderate and factual realism. Its efforts were directed at 'informed' minority opinion rather than general public opinion (Sanderson 1974).

The Abortion Law Reform Association was founded by three women in 1936. One was the wife of a wealthy stockbroker and provided much of the finance for the organisation; a second had administrative skills developed in the suffragette movement and the Labour Party; while the third was described as 'a somewhat eccentric blue-stocking of Canadian origin' (Hindell and Simms 1974: 152). This was a period when, despite the grant of the suffrage to women, their participation in public life was still very limited. The membership of the organisation was 'mostly recruited from women's Labour groups, and the women's branches of the co-operative movement' (Hindell and Simms 1974: 152). The organisation thus drew on the small population of politically active women. Its membership remained small and its activities limited throughout the earlier part of the postwar period, until it was revitalised by the influx of a group of women in their early thirties in the early 1960s.

The Howard League for Penal Reform can be traced back to the Howard Association founded in 1866. It was very much an insider group, which developed a close working relationship with the Home Office. Many of its members were 'magistrates, probation officers, social workers, all solid middle class professionals who have direct contact with the penal system. Until recently at least two-thirds of the League's members lived in London and the south-east, and most of these lived in London itself' (Ryan 1978: 3). It was almost a prototype of the type of establishment cause group that flourished fifty years ago. It 'traditionally functioned as a small, well connected, London based elite with no democratic structures' (Ryan 1978: 86). In recent years, its status has been challenged by more radical groups who have argued that prisoners and former prisoners should speak for themselves rather than being represented by those with a professional interest in prisons.

It should not be supposed that the only pressure groups that existed fifty years were either sectional groups or cause groups pursuing insider strategies. A great worry of the 'respectable' cause groups was avoiding 'the crippling accusation of crankiness. In its early days [the National

Smoke Abatement Society] was often dismissed as an organization of eccentrics' (Sanderson 1974: 30). This type of stigma almost certainly attached to some animal rights organisations such as the League Against Cruel Sports fifty years ago.

The economic, political and social context in which pressure groups operate has changed substantially over the last fifty years. In the late 1940s most pressure groups were organised around one of the great hierarchical interests that structured society: business, labour, agriculture or the professions. The exceptions were a number of cause groups supported by reformist members of the middle class. Today, there is a tremendous diversity of pressure groups, reflecting a more fragmented society in which personal identity does not derive from membership of a social class or professional grouping, but from a much wider range of possible identities. After the war, the emphasis in domestic politics was on the politics of production: how could Britain improve its productivity to overcome its economic problems, and how should the fruits of greater output be shared out among capital and labour. The issues of consumption that arose were issues of collective consumption: how could the National Health Service be created, or how could educational provision be improved? Fifty years later society is much more individualised and supporting a particular pressure group can almost be a lifestyle choice. The growing potency of 'green consumerism' reflects a society in which the relatively affluent section of the population have available to them more individualised forms of what might have been collective expression at an earlier period.

Some of the issues that are at the centre of the pressure group agenda today hardly featured on the political agenda in the immediate postwar years. Pollution issues in Britain had been discussed since the nineteenth century, but largely in terms of the costs imposed on one economic actor by another, such as farmers whose land was made unusable by nearby chemical plants. In London in the 1950s one could smell the Thames from some distance away in the summer, while the air in winter was choked by smogs resulting from smoke from a combination of domestic fires and industrial plants. There was, however, little political agitation about these issues: they were regarded almost as natural phenomena which, like the weather, could be a serious nuisance, but were simply something to grumble about.

In terms of Maslow's 'hierarchy of needs' theory such an outlook was perfectly understandable. At the end of the war, the objectives of most people were to have a job (in plentiful supply), decent housing (in short supply) and to leave behind the constraints of rationing and other forms of austerity and regain the modest prosperity those in work had enjoyed in the 1930s. As people's basic needs are satisfied, they develop new priorities. It is no accident that environmental concerns have become particularly pronounced in affluent countries such as Germany. The story of the rise of environmental pressure groups in Britain is, however, quite a complex one, returned to below.

New definitions of 'rights' have affected a wide range of pressure group activity. Gender roles were much more rigid in British society fifty years ago, with a woman's most usual role being seen as that of homemaker. The feminist movement has been a broad social movement, rather than pressure group activity, which has perhaps had its greatest effect on the consciousness of women and, to some extent, the perceptions of men. Indeed, the principal sectional interest groups, such as the CBI, continue to be dominated by men to an even greater extent than is true of political parties. None of these groups has ever had a woman as its president or chief executive.

Fifty years ago disabled people were seen as worthy recipients of charity. In many practical respects, they were denied the status of full citizens. Disabled individuals no longer see themselves as worthy objects for charity or supplicants for government handouts. They would argue that adjustments have to be made in society so that they can live as full lives as possible. Groups representing people with disabilities have become increasingly militant in their tactics, as happened in Birmingham in the autumn of 1995 when disabled campaigners blocked main roads during the rush hour as well as stations with inadequate facilities for those with impaired mobility.

Animal welfare groups have been active in Britain since the nineteenth century, but the emphasis on animal rights is relatively recent. In part, it is related to the development of the women's movement, as it could be argued that values such as compassion and a unity of reason and emotion represent a challenge to traditional macho values and may lead to sustained opposition by women to cruelty to animals (Garner 1993: 97–8). Although women are generally strongly represented in animal rights organisations, there are clearly other factors that help to explain the growth in their support. Whatever the precise mix of explanations, the emphasis on animal rights as distinct from welfare has produced 'the key division within the animal protection movement; between those who consider that animal interests should take a subordinate, albeit important, position and those who recognise a higher moral status for animals' (Garner 1993: 49). This division has led to endemic conflicts within the animal protection movement.

The economic and social context in which pressure group activity takes place has changed over the last fifty years. In many respects, domestic political structures have, in contrast, changed relatively little. Although parliamentary parties are somewhat less cohesive than they used to be, and there has been an increase in lobbying activity at Westminster for this and other reasons, power in Britain remains concentrated in the executive. The autonomy of the British executive has, however, been influenced by membership of the European Union (EU). The EU represents a new and significant arena of pressure group activity, and is discussed under a separate heading below.

The rise and fall of tripartism

One of the most significant developments in pressure group activity in the postwar period has been the rise and fall of tripartism, or what is sometimes called corporatism. In reality, Britain never had corporatism in the sense that it existed in some smaller European countries, where the 'social partners' reached wide-ranging agreements with government on economic questions that organised labour and the employers had the capacity to implement. One of the problems with tripartism in Britain was that neither the CBI nor the Trades Union Congress (TUC) had much effective control over their members.

The close involvement of employers and organised labour in running the war economy had transformed their organisations into what Middlemas calls 'governing institutions'. 'To put it simply, what had been merely interest groups crossed the political threshold, and became part of the extended state: a position from which other groups, even if they held political power, were still excluded' (Middlemas 1979: 373). There were, of course, strict limits to this process. Under the postwar Labour government, the employers were unhappy about nationalisation, particularly once it extended beyond the often capital-starved public utilities to then profitable private industries such as steel. The 1948 wages bargain, however, involved the employers agreeing to limit profits and dividends while 'the traditional alliance and loyalties between the TUC and the Labour party, coupled with the magnitude of the crisis, overcame the General Council's objection that wage restraint seriously violated trade union interests' (Dorfman 1973: 72).

The lesson of the 1948–51 period is that one policy that boosts tripartism more than any other is a prices and incomes policy. It creates an imperative for government to seek the cooperation of business and labour. However, while the leaderships of the unions may endorse restraint, it is likely to meet increasing resistance from their members and militant action, as happened in the 'winter of discontent' of 1978/79. Similarly, cooperation with Labour governments produced strains within the CBI, leading to the resignation of some member firms on more than one occasion.

The real heyday of tripartism in Britain was between 1960 and 1979. It was ushered in by the 'Brighton revolution' of 1960, when concern about British economic performance led government and employers (who met together at Brighton) to signal a move in the direction of more indicative planning. The principal formal institution of tripartism, the National Economic Development Council, was established in 1962 and three separate employers' organisations merged to form the CBI in 1965 to facilitate a more effective dialogue with government.

In the 1970s tripartism was particularly prominent. The Heath government of 1970–74 quickly moved away from its declared intention to move in the direction of a more liberal economy, passing an interventionist Industry Act in 1972. Prices and incomes policies were also reintroduced, with the CBI seeking to demonstrate its effectiveness by instituting a voluntary price restraint policy. The attempt systematically to involve the employers and trade unions in the formation of economic policy might have been more successful if the Heath government's relations with the trade union movement had not been so soured by its industrial relations legislation.

The Labour government of 1974–79 continued on a tripartite path, even referring in the Queen's speech to its intention to cooperate in the management of economic policy with the CBI and the TUC. The TUC was offered a series of trade-offs for its cooperation. For example, in 1976 the chancellor offered a package of conditional tax relief which would be implemented if the TUC agreed to a pay guideline. The economy was, however, being buffeted by external forces, including a collapse in sterling:

> The stark facts in sum were that the trade-offs built into the social contract had yielded nothing better than a poor holding action. High prices, high unemployment, a poor balance of payments, a falling standard of living was the spectacle, only relieved by some evidence that the situation would have been considerably worse had it not been for the success of wage restraint. (Dorfman 1979: 129)

Disillusionment among employers and unions with the experience of tripartism, and its evident failure to cope with the problem of British relative economic decline, helped the Thatcher government to diagnose corporatism as the problem rather than the solution. Dismantling corporatist institutions and arrangements took some years, but the organised employers were sidelined, while the status given to the unions in the postwar settlement was taken away from them. Some erosion of corporatism was probably inevitable, even if the Thatcher government had not come to power. Tripartism was the product of an economic arrangement in which large-scale, labour-intensive manufacturing industry played the key role in the economy, and a political context in which the politics of production was dominant. Technological change undermined the economic centrality of labour-intensive industry, while society became more consumption oriented. The Thatcher government speeded up and intensified these processes, but it did not create them. Corporatism had no answers for a politics in which environmental issues played an increasingly central role.

Although 'New Labour' has declared that it will not return to the policies of the past, it is likely to be more interventionist in some areas of the economy than a Conservative government and in ways that would draw it into tripartite relationships. Fixing a minimum wage is expected to involve a commission that will include employer and union representatives. The social chapter of the Maastricht Treaty, which a Labour government would sign, requires consultation with management and labour on social policy proposals, and also includes a procedure for management and labour to implement EU directives. The strongest pressures towards tripartism may therefore come from the social partnership procedures of the EU than from the domestic policies of any Labour government.

Environmental pressure groups

A number of conservationist and wildlife groups were formed in the late-Victorian period. Examples include the Commons, Open Spaces and Footpaths Preservation Society; the Royal Society for the Protection of Birds (RSPB); and the National Trust. The interwar period saw the formation of a number of key groups including the Council for the Protection of Rural England and the Ramblers' Association. The latter organisation reflected the interest of the urban population in spending leisure time in the countryside. Many of the organisation's members were left of centre in outlook and in the 1930s it organised a number of mass trespasses on land closed to walkers, a technique to which it returned in the 1990s. The late 1950s and early 1960s saw more groups being formed, such as the Victorian Society and the Civic Trust. 'The membership statistics of groups, however, showed no dramatic increase until the early 1970s when most groups experienced rapid growth and there was a large crop of new groups' (Lowe and Goyder 1983: 17).

The new environmental pressure groups with wide-ranging agendas such as Friends of the Earth and Greenpeace experienced particularly striking increases in their memberships. Friends of the Earth went from just a 1,000 members in 1971 to 116,000 in England and Wales by 1992. Greenpeace saw its British list of supporters increased from 30,000 in 1981 to 411,000 in 1992. Some of the long-established groups also experienced a substantial increase in membership, with the RSPB reaching 850,000 members by 1992 (Grant 1995: 15).

How is one to explain this rapid expansion of support for environmental groups? It is evident that the members of environmental organisations are overwhelmingly middle class and, in particular, highly educated. This is not surprising in the case of local environmental organisations, whose real function may be to protect property values, but it also applies to more 'radical' groups. For example, data from the British Interest Groups Project show 'that the overwhelming majority of [members of Friends of the Earth] were in professional, managerial or senior administrative occupations' (Maloney and Jordan 1995: 1141). In terms of hierarchy of needs theory, these are individuals whose basic material needs have been satisfied. There is a considerable body of evidence that suggests an association between support for an environmental movement and 'postmaterialist' values. It is significant that the British Interest Groups Project data show that over half the membership of Friends of the Earth has a degree, with another 10 per cent in full-time education (Jordan *et al.* 1994: 524). Environmental pressure groups are appealing strongly to a segment of the population likely to have a better understanding of public policy issues and a more reflective attitude towards them.

The media, particularly television, have played an important role in stimulating interest in environmental issues. Immediately after the war, television was available to a restricted audience, while newspapers were subject to the rationing of newsprint. With the development of colour television, environmental issues had a strong appeal to producers, as they offered compelling visual images that could be relied on to produce a response among viewers. 'The media's coverage of the Canadian baby seal clubbing in the 1970s ... had a phenomenal impact resulting in huge public outrage and eventually the banning of seal products into America and the European Community' (Garner 1993: 65). There is a risk, however, that environmental organisations may become too preoccupied with media coverage as an end in itself rather than as part of an integrated strategy intended to change public policy.

> For example, watching a handful of heroic Greenpeace 'rainbow warriors' ... on television, the audience may think that effective action has already taken place.... Coping with the many persistent environmental problems ... requires a steadier engagement at the international level, and changes in personal behaviour, instead of merely spectacular, predominantly symbolic, actions which may simply soothe the broader public. (Rucht 1993: 93)

The factors outlined help to explain the growth in the numbers of people involved in the environmental movement in the 1970s and the 1980s. The 1990s is, however, an era of greater job insecurity for the middle-class professionals who have formed the backbone of the environmental movement. Suddenly, many of them have had to cope with redundancy or being 'contracted out' and their own personal economic survival has become more salient. Whether existing levels of membership will continue to increase, or even be maintained, is open to question:

> In the past decades there have been two conflicting perspectives on the growth of environmental support. On the one hand it is seen as ever expanding and rippling through the population.... There is an alternative view that sees environmentalism as a 'sunshine issue' that emerges only when economic improvement permits this 'luxury'. (Maloney and Jordan 1995: 1150–1)

Membership of Friends of the Earth appears to have peaked in 1991, while Greenpeace has had to lay off staff because of falling income. It is useful to make a distinction between the core of dedicated environmental activists and the intermittent supporters who send in a donation when aroused by a particular issue. Maloney and Jordan comment, 'There may be an activist/lifestyle environmentalism for which the [new social movement] imagery is appropriate, but the mass scale [Friends of the Earth] is nearer something that can be termed a pressure business than a new social movement' (1995: 1152). Marketing the organisation in order to sustain its financial base therefore becomes a key activity, with newspaper advertisements being placed whenever there is an environmental disaster.

The environmental movement brings sharply into focus the difficult choice that a pressure group has to make between an insider and an outsider strategy. Insider groups seek to exert influence on the executive branch of government in particular, supplemented where necessary by pressure in parliament. They rely on the expertise of their members and staff to put forward a reasoned and persuasive case for changes in public policy. The trust they win from decision makers involves them in the policy-making process at an early stage. Outsider groups are reluctant to compromise themselves by entering into a policy debate whose basic premises they reject. They rely on various forms of direct action to draw attention to their demands and to mobilise public support, leading to pressure on decision makers to give way.

A number of environmental groups have benefited from an insider strategy. When the Wildlife and Countryside Bill was introduced in the late 1970s, 'the RSPB – the only conservation group which was consulted before the proposals were aired in public – achieved a great many of its aims at the initial stages and did not need to fight a rearguard action in parliament' (Garner 1993: 193). The RSPB continues to work by seeking to define its own policies carefully, on the basis of research and producing detailed policy papers. In 1995 it launched a new series of papers on arable policy, which, it was hoped, would 'provide the starting point for informed discussion' (Royal Society for the Protection of Birds 1995: 2).

Friends of the Earth has also moved in the direction of suggesting constructive and feasible policy solutions rather than staging demonstrations designed to draw attention to the shortcomings of existing policies. Indeed, most environmental groups aspire to achieve insider status and many have attained it. The most prominent exception is Greenpeace. Its success in persuading Shell not to dump the Brent Spar oil platform at sea might suggest that direct action may still achieve results that could not have been brought about in any other way. However, there have been recurrent internal tensions within Greenpeace on the continued appropriateness of an outsider strategy. If it abandons an outsider strategy, Greenpeace runs the risk of being outflanked by more radical groups. Some former supporters formed a British branch of the US environmental organisation Earth First!, which used the slogan 'No Compromise in Defence of Mother Earth' to justify the sabotage of buildings and machinery used in road building projects. 'These localised, single issue movements – notably road protesters and the animal rights groups unconstrained by bureaucratic conventions, have tended to make the green establishment look staid and out of date' (O'Neill 1995: 82).

The Brent Spar episode initially gave a new boost to Greenpeace and quietened some of the tensions in the organisation between 'lounge suits' and 'wet suits'. However, for some scientists the episode 'has again exposed the shallowness of Greenpeace on scientific issues' (*The Economist*, 15 July 1995: 91). There were signs of increasing concern in the media about the extent to which they were manipulated by Greenpeace. In September 1995 Greenpeace admitted that it had given out incorrect information about the quantity of oil in the Brent Spar because of a sampling mistake. The BBC commented:

> We suppose to a certain extent we illustrated at [the Edinburgh TV festival] that there was an attempt to manipulate a situation by Greenpeace. They've now admitted to a mistake which demonstrates how important it is for the media to test the veracity of what any organisation declares or states. (*Financial Times*, 6 September 1995)

The difficulty of assessing whether an insider strategy is effective or not is illustrated by the case of the roads lobby. By 1995, it was clear that the Major government was cutting back on its roads programme to such an extent as to alarm the CBI, which complained that Britain's infrastructure was being undermined. At least three explanations of this policy shift are possible. One is that increasing public opposition to new road building forced the government to reconsider its policy, particularly as the delays being imposed by anti-roads activists were forcing up the cost of road building. A second explanation is that opinion within the Department of Transport on the desirability of road building has changed. Particularly influential was the 1994 report from the Standing Advisory Committee on Trunk Roads, which argued that new or improved trunk roads failed to reduce congestion because they generated more traffic (Page and Robinson 1995). A third explanation is that with a political imperative to find budget cuts to fund tax reductions, the Treasury settled on roads as a popular target.

The first model implies a considerable role for pressure groups both in helping to mould public opinion and in impeding the implementation of policy. If it is correct, it suggests that outsider pressure groups can be highly effective. The second model suggests a more elitist form of policy making in which the key actors are civil servants and their expert advisers, but in which there might be some scope for input by insider groups. The third model implies a politically directed form of decision making in which external pressures of any kind are of secondary importance. These different explanations are not mutually exclusive, and no doubt elements of all three help to explain the shift in policy. An outsider group using direct action in an attempt to halt road building could claim that its activities have helped to create a climate in which road building is less popular, while a more sceptical observer might argue that no road has been stopped once building work has started. Assessing effectiveness is one of the most difficult aspects of pressure group studies, making it possible for the debate about the relative merits of insider and outsider strategies to continue without ever being settled.

The growth of European representation

One of the biggest changes in the operating environment of pressure groups since the war has been British membership of what has become the EU. Any effective pressure group now has to operate on two levels: the domestic and the European. Any group that aspires to insider status is likely to belong to a European federation of pressure groups in its area of interest. These pressure groups vary in their effectiveness; in a few industrial sectors also, such as motor vehicles, direct membership associations have been formed at the European level.

The interpretation of the impact of EU membership on pressure group activity in Britain has produced two schools of thought. Both are agreed that any credible sectional group, and some cause groups, have to be active at the European level and that this has led to changes in the internal organisation of groups and placed more demands on their resources. Indeed, well resourced groups such as business organisations have something of an advantage at the European level compared with less well resourced groups such as those concerned with the environment or consumer affairs.

One school of thought argues that, particularly since the Single European Act and the Maastricht Treaty, the importance of the EU for pressure groups has increased considerably. The treaties have widened and deepened the functions of the EU and there has been greater use of qualified majority voting. Hence, a national group can no longer place too much reliance on its national government protecting its position at the European level by refusing to agree to a particular measure. Greenwood *et al.* argue (1992: 23–4), in the introduction to a series of case studies of European-level representation, that:

> The importance of the national route in fact appears to have been somewhat overstated.... The evidence of this book suggests that there is an increasing confidence and familiarity with the European level and that the 'Brussels strategy' (that is, working through European organizations or approaching EC agencies directly or through appointed agents) is increasingly being taken.

The alternative view, to which I adhere, argues that many pressure groups are ineffective at the European level. As the EU has admitted more members, it has been difficult to maintain unity within federations of federations. One must be cautious of generalising from the experience of those associations that are highly effective operating in relatively concentrated industries such as chemicals or motor vehicles. More fragmented or newer industries face considerable organising difficulties. This point is well brought out in a study of the courier industry by Campbell, who argues (1994: 144–5) that their experience offers 'an example of the difficulties faced by an entrepreneurial industry in trying to maintain basic policy changes at Union level.' He notes:

> Putting forth a case for changing policy in the European Union is extremely difficult, costly and frustrating for an entrepreneurial group. Much of the cost arises from the fact that a case for change must be presented at both Union and Member State levels. (Campbell 1994: 145)

Although greater use has been made of qualified majority voting, only forty of 283 legislative acts passed by the various councils of ministers between December 1993 and March 1995 involved votes. In other words, bargaining in an attempt to reach a consensus remains the norm, with many decisions being postponed until agreement can be achieved. Of course, in the bargaining process, a position advocated by a particular pressure group may be sacrificed in the interests of reaching the best possible overall agreement from a national perspective. That is why any serious sectional pressure group has always needed to take an interest in the European level. In the case of the Common Agricultural Policy (CAP), which is the EU policy that has been operational for longest, 'What a Brussels-centric perspective on CAP policymaking neglects to consider is that the national level represents both the first line and the last line of defence for agricultural interests' (Keeler 1996). Policies have to be implemented at the national level and there is considerable scope for 'slippage' in programmes to suit national interests. Nor should it be assumed that more decision-making authority will necessarily be transferred to the EU level. In the CAP, the trend is towards more decentralisation of decisions, to national level.

Nevertheless, important decisions are being taken at the EU level. During the years of Conservative government, environmental groups and trade unions have seen EU institutions as better disposed to their concerns than national ones. Effective group operation at the European level relies on the ability to influence policy at a very early stage, when the first drafts are being prepared by the directorates-general of the Commission. A pressure group needs to know when a new measure is being considered, who is drafting it, and when it is likely to be forwarded to the council of ministers for a decision. When a Commission official is seeking to draft a new proposal, he or she may welcome expert advice from a pressure group, provided that it is reasonably objective. Some estimates suggest that there is one lobbyist for each Commission official, and most of these lobbyists are representing business interests, with regional and local government being the next best organised category. Although environmental groups have been given financial assistance by the Commission, they are not as well entrenched in the policy-making process.

Groups that do not enjoy full insider status in the Commission may seek to exert pressure through the European parliament. In seeking to stop cosmetics testing on animals, the British Union for the Abolition of Vivisection (BUAV) 'knew that it had little chance of successfully lobbying the most influential institutions directly, particularly as the (opposing) views of industry were already well represented at that level' (Fisher 1994: 233). The BUAV therefore worked through the European parliament. Although the parliament has greater opportunities to exert influence than was once the case, the council of ministers remains the real legislative body. Fisher concludes that it is easier in the EU to resist change than to promote it, and in order to be successful, 'pressure groups will need to establish effective structures which can deliver strong national pressure in addition to that targeted to Brussels and Strasbourg' (Fisher 1994: 239). The EU is a new and important arena of action for pressure groups, but it has not supplanted the national level.

Conclusions

There has been substantial economic change and a transformation in everyday life over the last fifty years. What then becomes striking is how little the political process has changed in comparison. The British political system in 1995 recognisably has the same distinctive features as in 1945: a unitary state with a strong executive based on a permanent civil service; a first-past-the-post electoral system; a relatively disciplined party system with one of two parties likely to form the government; no written constitution; an unelected second chamber. There have been some changes: the judiciary has become more activist; political party discipline has been eroded, and minor parties are more strongly represented in the Commons; and the traditional civil service is increasingly under threat. It could be, of course, that as the end of the century approaches, the British polity is on the verge of major constitutional changes.

One area in which there has been some change in politics since 1945 is the rise in prominence of pressure groups. There are more of them; they have more members; and more attention is paid to them in the media. Whether they are any more effective than the groups that worked mostly behind the scenes in the immediate postwar period is open to question. It may still be easier for groups to stop things happening, or at least to modify them to protect their members, than for them actually to achieve positive goals that lead to real change.

The growth of pressure group membership has been accompanied by a decline in party membership (albeit recently reversed in the case of the Labour Party); this may reflect a general discontent with the relevance of existing political structures. They may be perceived as too inward looking, too resistant to change, and insufficiently concerned with, or able to respond to, issues that concern electors. For example, it seems impossible to have any balanced and rational discussion about how one copes with the extensive use of recreational drugs by young people. Against that, there is a concern that some pressure group activity may encourage a kind of superficial lifestyle politics in which one can identify with a cause without having to think too deeply about how one might seek to resolve complex policy problems.

Concern has been expressed first about tripartism, and more recently about single-issue pressure groups, that they represent a threat to democracy. If tripartism had actually worked, one might have had to worry about how it related to representative forms of government based on an elected legislature. Single-issue pressure groups are open to the criticism that they do not have to concern themselves about the trade-offs between different policies that politicians have to consider. In many ways, however, the existence of such groups is a sign that democracy at the grass-roots level is still alive and well. Their prominence in the latter years of the Major government might be seen as a sign of the weakness of the government itself and its tendency to cave into pressure from any direction (for example, objections to the privatisation of the port of Dover by the Queen Mother and Dame Vera Lynn).

Pressure groups are now a highly established and visible part of the British political landscape. As interests and belief systems become more fragmented, their prominence in the political process is likely to grow rather than decrease. There is a sense in which pressure groups enjoy influence without responsibility. They can press for tax breaks or subsidies for their own client group without having to consider the costs for others. Pressure groups are important sources of expert advice and new ideas, but a political process in which they exerted disproportionate influence could be characterised by incoherent policies that leave everyone feeling they had had a poor deal. If we are going to consider constitutional reforms such as proportional representation or devolution, we should also think more systematically about how pressure groups fit into a twenty-first-century democracy.

References

Beer, S. H. (1969), *Modern British Politics*, London, Faber and Faber.

Blank, S. (1973), *Industry and Government in Britain: The Federation of British Industries in Politics*, Farnborough, Saxon House.

Campbell, J. I., Jr (1994), Couriers and the European postal monopolies, in R. H. Pedler and M. P. M. C. Van Schendelen (eds), *Lobbying the European Union*, Aldershot, Dartmouth Publishing.

Dorfman, G. (1973), *Wage Politics in Britain 1945–1967*, Ames, Iowa State University Press.

Dorfman, G. (1979), *Government versus Trade Unionism in British Politics since 1968*, London, Macmillan.

Eckstein, H. (1960), *Pressure Group Politics: The Case of the BMA*, Stanford, Stanford University Press.

Finer, S. (1958), *Anonymous Empire*, London, Pall Mall.

Fisher, C. (1994), The lobby to stop testing cosmetics on animals, in R. H. Pedler and M. P. C. M. Van Schendelen (eds), *Lobbying the European Union*, Aldershot, Dartmouth Publishing.

Garner, R. (1993), *Animals, Politics and Morality*, Manchester, Manchester University Press.

Gilmour, I. (1971), *The Body Politic*, London, Hutchinson.

Grant, W. (1995), *Pressure Groups, Politics and Democracy in Britain*, Hemel Hempstead, Harvester Wheatsheaf.

Greenwood, J., *et al.* (1992), Introduction: organized interests and the transnational dimension, in J. Greenwood *et al.* (eds), *Organized Interests and the European Community*, London, Sage.

Hennessy, P. (1993), *Never Again*, London, Virgin.

Hindell, K. and Simms, R. (1974), How the abortion lobby worked, in R. Kimber and J. J. Richardson (eds), *Pressure Groups in Britain*, London, Dent.

Jordan, A. G. and Richardson, J. J. (1987), *Government and Pressure Groups in Britain*, Oxford, Clarendon Press.

Jordan, G., Maloney, W. and McLaughlin, A. (1994), Collective action and the public interest problem: drawing a line under Olson?, in P. Dunleavy and J. Stanyer (eds), *Contemporary Political Studies 1994*, vol. 2, Belfast, Political Studies Association.

Keeler, J. T. S. (1996), Agricultural power in the European Community, *Comparative Politics*, 28, 127–49.

Kipping, Sir N. (1969), *The Suez Contractors*, Havant, Kenneth Mason.

Lowe, P. and Goyder, J. (1983), *Environmental Groups in Politics*, London, Allen and Unwin.

Maloney, W. and Jordan, G. (1995), Joining public interest groups: membership profiles of Amnesty International and Friends of the Earth, in J. Lovenduski and J. Stanyer (eds), *Contemporary Political Studies 1995*, vol. 3, Belfast, Political Studies Association.

Middlemas, K. (1979), *Politics in Industrial Society*, London, André Deutsch.

Middlemas, K. (1986), *Power, Competition and the State, Vol. 1: Britain in Search of Balance 1940–61*, London, Macmillan.

O'Neill, M. (1995), How Shell poured oil on the troubled waters of Greenpeace, *European Brief*, 2:8, 82–4.

Page, E. and Robinson, N. (1995), *Future Generations, Ethics and Transport Policy*, working paper no. 122, Department of Politics and International Studies, University of Warwick, Coventry.

Potter, A. (1961), *Organised Groups in British National Politics*, London, Faber.

Royal Society for the Protection of Birds (1995), *A Review of the 1992 CAP Arable Reforms*, Sandy, Royal Society for the Protection of Birds.

Rucht, D. (1993) 'Think globally, act locally?' Needs, forms and problems of cross-national cooperation among environmental groups, in J. D. Liefferink, P. Lowe and A. Mol (eds), *European Integration and Environmental Policy*, London, Belhaven.

Ryan, M. (1978), *The Acceptable Pressure Group*, Farnborough, Saxon House.

Sanderson, J. B. (1974), The National Smoke Abatement Society and the Clean Air Act (1956), in R. Kimber and J. J. Richardson (eds), *Campaigning for the Environment*, London, Routledge and Kegan Paul.

Stewart, J. D. (1958), *British Pressure Groups*, Oxford, Clarendon Press.

11

The disunited kingdom: the territorial dimension of British politics

Roger Levy

As the twentieth century draws to a close, few scholars would deny the significance of territorial issues in postwar British politics. In his authoritative study, Richard Rose noted a bibliography of over 2,000 items 'of relevance to understanding the United Kingdom' (Rose 1982), a figure which must at least have doubled by now with the ongoing cycle of events – both tragic and hopeful – in Northern Ireland, the continuing demands for constitutional reform in Scotland and Wales, the seemingly permanent revolution in local government and doubts over the identity and integrity of the British state generally. In coining the term 'Ukania', Tom Nairn (1988) has found an argot for a multinational state in a predicament somewhere between banana monarchy and Marx Brothers farce.

Yet it was not always so. Until the end of the 1960s, little was heard about the territorial dimension. As documented in the famous 'civic culture' study, political institutions in Britain were a model of stability and predictability, enjoying an enviable level of public confidence (Almond and Verba 1963). Local government coexisted fairly comfortably with central government in what has been termed the 'dual polity' (Rose 1982; Bulpitt 1983: 161), British voters supported the two British parties in overwhelming numbers and according to stable patterns, and manifestations of political dissent in the 'Celtic fringe' (including 'the troubles' in Northern Ireland) were only just making an appearance.

Of course, crises and conflicts within the political system are not exclusively related to territorial issues, but it is the purpose of this chapter to focus on these only. Thus, our first task is to define the parameters of the territorial dimension of British politics with greater precision. Having done that, we will examine each aspect in more depth.

Defining the territorial dimension

Compared with old favourite subjects of study like voting behaviour, the cabinet or even local government, the territorial dimension has a distinctly nebulous quality, both empirically and conceptually. The literature reflects this and while the division is nowhere near as neat in practice, four main trends may be identified.

In the first category are general academic studies. Rose's study of the 'territorial dimension in government', for example, takes a very broad view in which every aspect of the system of government is included: 'to understand the United Kingdom as a whole, we must understand how its diverse territorial parts – England, Scotland, Wales and Northern Ireland – are governed. To understand the parts, we must also understand the government of the whole' (Rose 1982: 2–3). Only slightly less expansive is Bulpitt's designation of territorial politics as 'centre–periphery relations' or 'the structure of central–local relations' (Bulpitt 1983: 1, 6), which can include any type of political interaction between the centre and periphery. At the other extreme – and at all points in between – is a vast number of empirical studies of particular nationalist parties, specific patterns of political behaviour, individual territorial ministries and policies, all aspects of central–local relations, subnational government generally, the overall governance of particular geographical areas, and so on. Other studies, of which the most well known perhaps are those by Michael Hechter (1975) and Tom Nairn (1977), have focused on the process of incorporation of the Celtic 'fringes' into the British state which, they argue, supports certain theories of state building and 'explains' the current pattern of core–periphery relations. Finally, there are studies that are overtly speculative and polemical in nature (Mackintosh 1968; Banks 1971; Bogdanor 1979; Edwards 1989), which build arguments for or against particular forms of constitutional change for regional and national governance.

Within this vast literature, we can identify five principal sites (some behavioural, some institutional) for the analysis of territorial politics.

- Patterns of political behaviour that are peculiar to particular regions and places. This could include the behaviour of voters, parties (be they national or local), interest groups, executive decision makers, bureaucrats and managers.
- Political beliefs and values that are specific to particular regions and places (i.e. the existence or otherwise of distinctive geographically based political cultures).
- The institutional structures that exist for the exercise of government in the regions that have distinct local characteristics. These include elected local authorities, regionally/locally specific quangos, and territorial ministries.
- The systems of management that regulate relationships between these institutions and government agencies, at the centre.
- Sets of issues that animate political life in the Britain. These include debates about the geographical distribution of inequalities (be they

social, economic or political) and the remedies for them, the nature of political identity, and criteria for the design of the most efficient and representative systems of government in the regions and nations of Britain.

The fragmentation of political behaviour and political beliefs

Until the rise of the nationalist vote in Scotland and Wales in the late 1960s, British voting behaviour – excluding Northern Ireland – approximated closely to a functionally based model. While Pulzer's famous dictum that 'class is the basis of British party politics; all else is embellishment and detail' (Pulzer 1972: 102) was always compromised by the working-class Tory vote, middle-class Labour supporters and Northern Irish voters generally, it has long since been overshadowed by social change and the political dealignment identified by Crewe and his colleagues (Crewe *et al.*, 1977) (see chapter 7).

The fragmentation of the class structure, the weakening of partisanship, the rise in home ownership, increasing general levels of affluence and a decline in confidence in government have all been held responsible for a more volatile and issue-oriented electorate (Rose and McAllister 1986). One result has been an increasing regional variation in the vote for the two major parties since 1945 (see table 1). (The points raised by Denver in chapter 7 concerning regional voting patterns are reconsidered here in the context of party representation and policy implications for Scotland and Wales.)

The main trends are a sharp decline in the Labour vote in all parts of the south, with a lesser but significant decline in the Midlands and a more stable picture in the north, Scotland and Wales. The Conservative vote has remained steady or increased in most of the south and the Midlands, and remained steady elsewhere except in Scotland, where it has declined precipitously. Thus, at the 1955 general election, the Conservatives secured 50.1 per cent of the popular vote in Scotland compared with only 24 per cent in 1987.

The data illustrate the increasing difficulty of the major parties in claiming to be truly 'national'. Disregarding the special case of Northern Ireland and the nationalist vote in Scotland and Wales, the Conservatives have always had a problem in Wales, and have declined to even lower levels in Scotland. Labour, on the other hand, was mildly underperforming only in the south-west in 1945, but by the 1980s was chronically underperforming in all parts of the south, including much of London.

The actual effects of this regional fragmentation are more dramatic. In the context of the first-past-the-post electoral system, regional variations in vote produce even more pronounced concentrations of parliamentary

Table 1 Percentage share of the vote for Conservative and Labour by region, 1945–92

	1945	1950	1951	1955	1959	1964	1966	1970	Feb. 1974	Oct. 1974	1979	1983	1987	1992
Britain														
Con.	39.8	43.5	48	49.7	49.4	43.3	41.9	43.0	37.8	35.8	43.9	42.4	42.3	41.9
Labour	48.3	46.1	48.8	46.4	43.8	44.1	47.4	43.0	37.1	39.2	37.0	27.6	30.8	34.4
England														
Con.	40.0	41.1	49.2	50.6	50.2	44.1	42.8	48.4	40.2	38.9	47.2	46.0	46.2	45.5
Labour	48.0	46.2	48.8	46.9	43.6	43.5	47.9	43.3	37.6	40.1	36.7	27.0	29.5	33.9
London														
Con.	38.0	43.2	47.5	49	49.1	42.2	40.7	46.9	37.2	37.4	46	43.9	46.1	45.3
Labour	53.0	47.2	50.5	48.3	43.9	45.3	49.9	45.3	42.6	43.8	39.6	29.8	31.9	37.1
South/east (excluding London)														
Con.	47.0	49.2	55.4	56.0	54.5	47.4	47.4	53.9	44.8	45.0	54.3	54.1	54.9	54.0
Labour	42.0	48.2	41.6	39.9	35.4	35.0	38.8	35.2	28.1	31.4	27.5	16.1	17.6	21.9
South-west														
Con.	48.0	48.4	54.2	53.3	50.2	45.6	45.7	51.1	43.2	43.1	51.3	51.4	50.6	47.6
Labour	31.0	32.7	35.5	32.5	27.5	26.6	31.3	34.3	26.8	29.1	24.8	14.7	15.9	19.2
Midlands														
Con.	37.0	41.0	45.8	48.2	49.2	44.8	43.2	49.2	40.1	37.7	46.9	46.9	46.8	45.6
Labour	55.0	50.9	52.9	50.4	47.2	46.4	51.5	46.4	42.5	43.6	39.9	30.7	31.9	37.2

North														
Con.	38.0	41.8	46.8	48.1	47.3	40.8	38.8	43.4	36.6	34.2	40.8	38.4	36.6	36.9
Labour	52.0	49.6	51.6	50.2	48.9	49.5	54.3	49.0	44.3	46.5	44.5	36.7	42.1	46.0
Scotland														
Con.	43.0	46.2	49.6	50.1	47.6	40.6	37.6	38.5	32.9	24.7	31.4	28.4	24.0	25.7
Labour	48.0	46.2	47.9	46.7	46.7	48.7	49.9	44.5	36.6	36.3	41.5	35.1	42.4	39.0
Wales														
Con.	24.0	28.3	33.1	33.5	33.8	29.4	27.9	27.7	25.9	23.9	32.2	31.0	29.5	28.6
Labour	59.0	58.1	60.5	57.6	56.4	57.8	60.7	51.6	46.8	49.5	48.6	37.5	45.1	49.5
Northern Ireland														
Unionist	57.0	62.8	59.4	68.5	77.2	63.0	61.8	54.2	64.2	62.0	59.0	57.1	54.8	50.3
Nationalist	18.8	15.8	20.0	23.5	14.5	18.2	18.6	22.0	25.0	26.2	28.2	33.2	35.2	36.5

Sources: D. Butler and D. Kavanagh (1992, 1988, 1984, 1980, 1975, 1974), *The British General Election...*, London, Macmillan; D. Butler and M. Pinto-Duschinsky (1971), *The British General Election of 1970*, London, Macmillan; D. Butler and A. King (1966), *The British General Election of 1966*, London, Macmillan; D. Butler and A. King (1965), *The British General Election of 1964*, London, Macmillan; D. Butler and R. Rose (1960), *The British General Election of 1959*, London, Frank Cass; D. Butler (1955), *The British General Election of 1955*, London, Macmillan; D. Butler (1952), *The British General Election of 1951*, London, Macmillan; H. Nicholas (1951), *The British General Election of 1950*, London, Macmillan; R. McCallum and A. Rendman (1947), *The British General Election of 1945*, London, Oxford University Press; A. King, et al. (1993), *Britain at the Polls 1992*, Chatham, Chatham House.

seats. Thus, between 1955 and 1992 there was a growing divergence in the pattern of party control between the north and the south of Britain while the overall share of the seats held by Labour and Conservative parties remained roughly the same (Butler 1995: 67). In recent elections, for example, the number of Labour-held seats in the south outside London has been in low single figures, while the Conservatives held only ten out of seventy-two Scottish seats in 1995.

As can be seen from tables 2 and 3, the 'north–south' political divide is reflected in socio-economic terms by historically higher rates of unemployment and lower levels of per capita income. Throughout the postwar period, high levels of out-migration to the south and the Midlands from the north, Scotland, Wales and Northern Ireland have been caused by conditions in the latter areas. In the context of full employment in the south, migration also represented a solution for some; however, the general rise in unemployment levels has made this an increasingly scarce option. With higher unemployment and lower per capita income (the latter partly the consequence of the former, but also a result of lower wage rates), dependency on public expenditure is consequently greater in Scotland, Wales and Northern Ireland. This is probably the case in the north of England too, but official statistics for public expenditure do not provide a regional breakdown within England.

Typified by declining heavy industrial and primary production, the densely populated areas of the north of England, Scotland, Wales and Northern Ireland failed to match levels of affluence and the growth in the service sector achieved in the south during the postwar boom (from 1945 to 1970 approximately). However, there was a broad consensus between the major parties on the need for an active state role in the economy and the further development of welfare policies, and thus regional differences in party support were minimised. After 1970, this consensus started to break down and the social changes referred to earlier began more clearly to affect political behaviour. Thus, Labour became increasingly identified as the party of state intervention, universal welfare provision, traditionally organised trade unionism, council tenants and high taxation, while the Conservatives remodelled themselves in an overtly free-enterprise mould, extolling the virtues of home ownership, low taxation, privatisation of state enterprises and means testing welfare ever more vigorously.

Although attitudes to many aspects of public policy are similar across Britain, evidence from the fifth and ninth British Social Attitudes surveys (Jowell *et al.* 1988; Jowell 1992) does suggest that voters in the north, Scotland and Wales are more collectivist in their political orientations, even when other factors (such as age and occupation) are controlled for. The 1988 survey thus concluded that 'region now accompanies class as a basis of voting behaviour and as an influence upon social attitudes' (Jowell *et al.* 1988: 142), with the strongest regional effects in Wales and Scotland.

Table 2 Selected economic/social indicators by region

	Registered unemployed (%)					Home ownership (%)[a]			Gross domestic product per capita (Britain = 100)[a]		
	1950	1960	1970	1980	1990	1971	1981	1991	1971	1980	1991
Britain	1.5	1.6	2.5	7.3	5.8	51	57	66	100	100	100
England	1.35	2.2	2.6	6.8	5.3	53	58	69	102.3	102.0	101.9
North	2.6	2.9	4.6	10.9	8.9	42	48	61	87.1	92.7	89.6
Yorkshire/Humberside	–	–	2.8	7.8	6.8	50	57	67	92.7	92.7	91.8
East Midlands	0.7	1.1	2.2	6.4	5.1	53	60	71	95.6	97.4	96.8
East Anglia	–	–	2.1	5.7	3.7	53	59	71	94.6	94.4	100.1
South and east (inc. London)	1.1	1.0	1.6	4.8	4.0	53	59	70	113.8	115.1	117.3
South-west	1.4	1.9	2.8	6.7	4.4	59	64	74	94.0	94.9	94.5
West Midlands	0.6	2.7	1.9	7.8	6.0	52	58	68	102.9	94.7	92.5
North-west	1.7	3.6	2.7	9.3	7.7	55	60	69	96.3	95.0	90.2
Wales	4.0	6.7	3.8	10.3	6.7	56	63	72	88.0	87.3	85.0
Scotland	3.0	–	4.2	10.0	8.2	31	36	53	93.3	96.0	96.6
Northern Ireland	6.5	–	6.8	13.7	13.0	47	54	66	75.4	74.9	81.5

[a]Regional figures before 1971 are not available.
Sources: Regional Trends. 1971, 1982, 1992. London. HMSO: The Economist Pocket Britain in Figures (1993), London, Economist Publications.

Table 3 Identifiable public/general government expenditure per head in England, Scotland, Wales and Northern Ireland, 1960–90 (England = 100)

	1963/64	*1969/70*	*1981*	*1990/91*
England	100	100	100	100
Scotland	118	131	126.6	123.5
Wales	116	116	131	114.6
Northern Ireland	103	118	145	148.5

Sources: *Regional Trends*, 1986, London, HMSO; Royal Commission on the Constitution (1973), *Report*, cmnd 5460, London, HMSO; *Scottish Abstract of Statistics*, *1993*, Edinburgh, Scottish Office.

The changes in Conservative policies are most closely identified with the Thatcher leadership (from 1975 onwards), although the intellectual ground was already being prepared during the Heath government of 1970–74. Indeed, while the 1979 election is generally regarded as a turning point as far as Conservatism is concerned, the pattern of sharp Conservative decline in the north and Scotland was evident in 1974. This is equally true of Labour's precipitate decline beyond any salvageable position in the south. It would appear that the events and social changes over 1970–74 were critical in fixing the regional political divide, and nothing that the two major parties did between the mid-1970s and the early 1990s altered this trend.

Thus it would be a mistake to see the north–south divide as simply a reaction to nascent or fully blown 'Thatcherism'. The 1970–74 Heath government ended in confrontation with the miners, a strongly unionised workforce of a nationalised industry based predominantly in the north, Wales and Scotland. The first task of the incoming minority Labour government was to make a deal with them while relying on the minor parties in parliament (including the Welsh and Scottish nationalists) for support. Not least because of what Jim Sillars, the former Labour, then Scottish Labour, then Scottish National Party MP called Labour's 'abiding fear of nationalism', the 1974–79 Labour government pursued an active policy of economic intervention particularly favouring the north, Scotland, Wales and Northern Ireland (e.g. state support for the shipbuilding, aircraft and steel industries, the placing of the Britoil headquarters in Glasgow, the De Lorean car plant in Northern Ireland, the GEAR project in Glasgow, and the creation of the Scottish and Welsh development agencies), and introduced legislation for measures of devolved government for Scotland and Wales. The latter occupied virtually the whole parliament and eventually brought the government down. Far from Labour rethinking its policy in this area after 1979, it became ever-more nationalistic in Scotland (and in Wales to a lesser extent) during the Thatcher years (see Geekie and Levy 1989).

The numerous studies of 'Thatcherism' have dwelt extensively on the privatising/property-owning/anti-collectivist aspects of the phenomenon, and its ostensibly 'English' (read southern English) characteristics. Given the greater role of the public sector outside the south of England up to the 1970s (via nationalised industries such as coal, steel and shipbuilding, and welfare payments resulting from higher rates of unemployment), it is not surprising that the Thatcher agenda of rolling back the state was deeply unpopular in the north, Scotland and Wales. The settling of accounts with the miners during the 1984–85 strike and the subsequent promise to privatise the coal industry epitomised the overall approach dramatically. Policies aimed at weakening the unions, raising council house rentals (via the successive reforms of local government finance), and privatising state assets were bound to have an uneven regional effect politically. Thus, despite Thatcher's attempts to convince the Scots that Thatcherism actually originated in Scotland, she and it remained uniquely unpopular north of the border. Unlike her predecessor Edward Heath, she was also implacably opposed to any measure of self-government for Scotland and Wales.

Nationalist voting in Scotland and Wales – and the unique patterns of political allegiance in Northern Ireland – can be seen as part of the 'regional effect'. Support for the Scottish and Welsh nationalists remained at insignificant levels until 1966, but in the general election of that year, the Scottish National Party (SNP) secured 5 per cent of the Scottish vote, while Plaid Cymru (PC) gained 4.3 per cent of the Welsh vote and won its first parliamentary seat at the Camarthen by-election in July of that year. This was followed by a string of good by-election and local election performances by both parties (the most spectacular of which was the SNP victory at Hamilton in 1967), and culminated in a share of the vote of over 11 per cent for the nationalists in 1970. Since then, their vote has fluctuated considerably (with a high of over 30 per cent for the SNP in October 1974), but from a much higher base (table 4).

The explanations for the rise (and fall) in the nationalist vote are, predictably, varied. At the macro level, there are models relating the rise of nationalist voting to broad social and economic forces. One of the most well known is Hechter's (1975) seminal work applying the internal colonial

Table 4 Percentage share of the vote in Scotland and Wales for the SNP and PC, general elections 1970–92

	1970	Feb. 1974	Oct. 1974	1979	1983	1987	1992
SNP	11.4	21.9	30.4	17.3	11.8	14.0	21.3
PC	11.5	10.7	10.8	8.1	8.0	7.3	8.8

Sources: R. Levy (1995), Finding a place in the world-economy – party strategy and party vote: the regionalization of SNP and Plaid Cymru support, 1979–92, *Political Geography*, 14:3, 295–308.

model to the incorporation of the 'Celtic fringe' into Britain. It argues that regional differences in political behaviour are a result of the exploitation of the periphery by the core, and pre-existing cultural differences became crystallised as economic inequalities were grafted on during the modernisation process (Hechter 1975: 10–16). This ultimately resulted in a low Conservative vote in the peripheries and support for home rule.

As many critics have pointed out, the data for Scotland and Wales provide only limited support for this thesis, and indeed Hechter modified it significantly himself (Hechter and Levi 1979). There is an alternative model that suggests that support for nationalism grows as modernisation accelerates in the peripheries. As they become more like the 'core' region economically and socially, there is a 'revolution of rising expectations' that cannot be satisfied by the 'traditional' parties (Birch 1978; Smith 1979; Mughan and McAllister 1981). A corollary of this argument is that policy failure at the centre (or government overload) was a major factor in precipitating the nationalist revolt in the peripheries of Britain.

Studies of nationalist voting and voters suggest a very complex reality, although the broad 'cultural' basis of Scottish and Welsh nationalisms are clear. Reliable survey evidence stretching back at least to the 1960s shows that large proportions of those living in Scotland and Wales identify themselves as Scots or Welsh first rather than British (more so in the case of Scots), with the vast majority identifying themselves as Scots or Welsh and British simultaneously. Whatever this identity may mean to particular individuals, it is generally present among them and thus open to political suggestion. If the dealignment thesis is correct, then ex-Labour and ex-Conservative partisans in Scotland and Wales may orient themselves towards political feelings based on national identity rather than other forms (such as Liberal/Liberal Democrat voting in England).

In the case of Wales, patterns of nationalist support are relatively unambiguous. Whatever the initial impulse, Balsom (1979, 1985) has shown that the PC vote is strongly concentrated in the Welsh-speaking areas of the north and west, and has made little substantive progress elsewhere. This picture has been borne out by more recent studies (Levy 1995). Despite attempts to broaden the policy agenda (to become rather more like the SNP), PC continues to be identified as a one-issue party by English-speaking voters in Wales. This is both a strength and a weakness, in that the party has acquired a secure electoral base, but one that is very difficult to extend or build a coalition on to. Even the addition of an overtly socialist orientation since the early 1980s has not produced electoral dividends in south Wales, although this may be partly the result of Labour pre-empting PC by becoming less hostile to some limited form of self-government.

The SNP's rise has produced a much greater diversity of explanation. Initial studies focusing on the 'protest vote' model (McLean 1970; Kellas 1973) suggested that the SNP drew most of its support from new voters and previously non-voters, and those with little existing loyalty to the major parties. As the nationalist vote persisted and then strengthened, it was suggested that SNP voting represented the development of a new political allegiance based on ethnic identification (Hanby 1976; Brand 1978), while other explanations focused on the increased salience of the nationalist agenda to voters. The issue-driven model of SNP voting (Miller *et al.* 1980; Miller 1981) suggested that there was a close fit between the party's policies on self-government and North Sea ('Scottish') oil and voter attitudes, which drove support up in the 1970s. As voters became more sceptical about self-government and less nationalistic about oil, so SNP support fell. While the party's fortunes rose and fell in line with voter attitudes on oil and self-government in the 1970s and '80s (although the link was never simple), cause and effect remain an open question. At present, support for full self-government runs consistently ahead of support for the SNP, but in the 1970s the reverse was true.

Until the end of the 1970s the SNP electorate was much like that of the Scottish Liberal Party in that it was drawn evenly from a wide social spectrum. Latterly it has been variously suggested that nationalist voters are more attracted to postindustrial values than others (Studlar and McAllister 1988), or that the social base of the nationalist vote is shifting towards that of the Labour Party (Newman 1992), two trends that do not fit easily together. Reviewing the distribution of the nationalist vote since 1979 shows that the SNP achieved a higher aggregate gain in traditional Labour areas than elsewhere, and that its support is now more evenly distributed than it used to be (Levy 1995). The decision of the party to direct itself consciously towards the Labour vote since the mid-1980s would thus appear to have paid off in a way that has eluded PC.

The role the nationalist parties themselves have played in changing public attitudes is an open question. Both the SNP and PC have changed and developed their policies over the years, and have transformed themselves from nebulous movements into normal political parties, or at least 'movement parties' (McAllister 1979; Brand 1992). This is most evident in their organisational growth and adoption of policy programmes that go beyond the simple call for full independence (SNP) or self-determination (PC). They have become effective campaigning machines able to mobilise significant resources at election times, thus providing a credible political 'home' for nationalist voters new or old. It is also fair to say that both parties can currently be described as broadly 'socialist' in orientation (Levy 1994, 1995), arguably a rational strategy in the context of the high Labour vote in Scotland and Wales.

Traditionally, PC has concentrated on the defence and promotion of the Welsh language and, despite its efforts to diversify its policies, is still principally associated with that issue. Thus, although PC invented the 'independence in Europe' slogan, that policy is much more closely associated with the SNP. The SNP has also developed policies on everything, and very successfully in the case of the 'It's Scotland's Oil' campaign of the early 1970s. Where it has had and continues to have difficulty is on the question of support for devolution, which party die-hards are opposed to fundamentally. This has split the party on more than one occasion (Levy 1990).

Political behaviour and belief in Northern Ireland have never conformed in either form or content to that found elsewhere in the UK. In the situation of severe civil disorder that pertained after 1969 and until very recently, it was insufficient merely to look at voting and party behaviour as the only meaningful expressions of political behaviour. If the UK as a whole is becoming less united, Northern Ireland has always been its least united part.

The bases of political allegiance in Northern Ireland are fundamentally different from those on British mainland, for three reasons. First, religious affiliation rather than class or occupation has been the overwhelming factor affecting voter choice (Aughey 1995). Second, the electorate is crudely divided between those who identify themselves as British and wish to remain so, and those who identify themselves as Irish and wish to be part of a different state altogether (the Irish Republic) (Whyte 1990). Third, the main British parties have not really had a significant presence there, although both have tried (in the form of the old Northern Ireland Labour Party and the more recent attempts by the Conservatives to put up candidates at elections).

None of this mattered until the outbreak of 'the troubles' in 1969. Between 1945 and the advent of the civil rights movement in the late 1960s a phoney normality pervaded, in which Ulster simply vanished from the British political radar screen. There were only a few parliamentary seats at stake anyway (twelve until 1983), of which ten invariably returned a Unionist MP; the Unionists were a de facto part of the Conservative parliamentary party, and the internal affairs of Northern Ireland were run by the elected government at Stormont, which was always Unionist.

Even the slightest acquaintance with the history of the island of Ireland reveals this period as an exceptional situation that could not last, built as it was on the economic and political subordination of the Catholic minority by the Protestant majority. If Hechter's model applies anywhere in the British Isles, then it is in regard to Ireland as a whole until partition in 1920, and latterly within Northern Ireland. Thus, the relative intercommunal peace of the 1940s and 1950s, disturbed only by some very minor activity on the part of the Irish Republican Army (IRA), was an aberration.

With the growth of the civil rights movement in the Catholic community and the predictably hostile response to acts of civil disobedience by the infamous 'B specials' of the Royal Ulster Constabulary, the violent pattern of Irish politics typical of earlier periods returned to the streets. While extra-parliamentary political action is not uncommon on the British mainland, the type and degree present in Northern Ireland after 1969 was of a completely different order of magnitude. Until the IRA cease-fire of August 1994, over 3,000 people had died in the province and on the mainland as a result of 'the troubles', whole communities had been 'ethnically cleansed' from areas of Belfast in the early years, and property damage had totalled billions of pounds on both sides of the Irish Sea (for a comprehensive account of the whole period, see Bowyer Bell 1993).

From the present point of view (we will return to the institutional aspects of the question later), 'the troubles' have had four main consequences. Perhaps most significantly, they have shattered the Unionist camp into factions, none of whom trust the Conservative Party or are trusted as allies by the Conservatives. It should be added that the initial onset of the troubles in 1969–70 also split the republican movement between 'official' and 'provisional' wings of the IRA, and put clear water between the constitutional republicans (the Social Democratic and Labour Party, SDLP) and the military factions. Like the constitutional parties, the paramilitary organisations on both sides of the confessional divide factionalised during the 1970s and 1980s, in their cases with murderous results in the ensuing struggle for supremacy. Second, the IRA's mainland bombing campaign and the imposition of direct rule from Westminster from 1972 made Northern Ireland a major domestic problem for governments of both parties. Third, with more 'balanced' parliaments (especially 1974–79 and after 1992) and the increase in the number of Northern Ireland MPs from twelve to seventeen, unionist and nationalist MPs have gained more potential power at Westminster. Thus, although Labour and Conservative governments have basically pursued a bipartisan policy on Northern Ireland, they have sought support in government from one side or the other to stay in office (famously over the devolution legislation in 1978–79 and the Maastricht Treaty ratification in 1993–94). Finally, through reforms affected by the boundary commissioners and movements of population, the vote going to the nationalist parties (the SDLP and Sinn Fein) has increased, although the number of seats held is still low because of the electoral system.

In summary, the spatial distribution of political diversity in Britain has become decidedly more uneven since 1945. This is most obvious in the case of the rise in support for nationalist parties in Scotland and Wales, and is reflected in a secular rise in the apparent desire for more self-government and in levels of national self-identification. Within Britain generally, both Conservative and Labour support has shown a tendency to concentrate geographically, which appears to be related to greater issue salience and increased social differentiation within the electorate. As the parties differentiated themselves from each other at the policy level, so their electorates increasingly separated geographically. Despite the very special circumstances in Northern Ireland, it too has experienced a shift in voter loyalties and a fragmentation of the party system.

The system of territorial management, 1945–95

Constitutionally, Britain is a unitary state. This means that sub-central government – local authorities, the territorial ministries, ministry field agencies and quangos – is either subordinate to or a part of central government. With hundreds of elected local authorities, an equally numerous regiment of appointed quangos, National Health Service trusts, authorities and boards and three powerful territorial ministries, the system of territorial management is both comprehensive and complex. Much of it is designed to ensure that the writ of central government runs uniformly throughout Britain – in the terminology, these organisations are 'agents' of central government, delivering policies and services – thus serving to maintain and strengthen the integration of the polity.

There is an alternative view, however. As Rhodes (1988: 3) remarks, 'Behind the easy maxims of the unitary state lie some uncomfortable truths. Central policies fail and are subverted by sub-central government which develops policies unknown or unwelcome to the centre'. Such a charge would be most readily associated with elected local authorities, which, precisely because of their elected status, can lay claim to a local mandate. In addition, they have administrative, informational and (limited) financial resources that can assist in the achievement of locally set priorities.

Over the years, there have been a number of well publicised confrontations between central and local government, of which the Clay Cross council rents policy (1971), the Tameside selective schools issue (1975), the Greater London Council's 'fares fair' policy (1984) and the Liverpool Militant council budget (1985) are only some of the most well known examples. The idea that local authorities have successfully subverted central government policies since 1945, however, depends on how subversive behaviour is defined. Most would agree that the definition has changed over the years. What may have been acceptable differences in levels of local taxation and standards of service in the 1950s and 1960s, for example, may have been seen as subversive in the 1980s. Differing standards of service in or expenditure on education, personal social services, roads or refuse collection are not in themselves subversive of central government.

The 'dual polity' model put forward by Rose (1982) and Bulpitt (1983) helps make sense of this changing relationship. This argues that central and local government have run independently of each other for most of the century. Despite the centralising forces at work in the 1940s brought about by the war economy, the development of the welfare state and nationalisation of basic industries, local differences prevailed. Central and local administrations had their defined spheres of control, collaborating when and where necessary irrespective of differences in party control at the centre and in the localities.

From the 1960s onwards, this model was increasingly challenged by policy initiatives from the centre, the need to reform a very outdated structure of local government, nationalism in Scotland and Wales and the increasing politicisation of local authorities. With the high tide of national and regional economic planning in the 1960s, central government was intervening in local economic development to an unprecedented degree via new town authorities, special development areas and latterly regional economic planning boards and councils (Mackintosh 1968). In addition, the Scottish Office (SO) and Northern Ireland Departments (NIDs), later Northern Ireland Office (NIO, from 1972), were taking on more responsibilities, with the Welsh Office (WO) created in 1964 to perform a similar (if more limited) role.

Simultaneously, the royal commissions on local government in England, Wales and Scotland concluded that existing authorities were too small, too weak, poorly managed, insufficiently democratic and inadequately financed. Bigger, more powerful, better-managed and better-financed authorities were needed in their place (Royal Commission on Local Government in England 1969; Royal Commission on Local Government in Scotland 1969). The Local Government Acts of 1972 (for England and Wales) and 1973 (for Scotland) created a new streamlined system broadly based on a two-tier model, with a reformed system of management. There was no change in the financing of local government, however, which the Wheatley Commission (on Scottish local government) had considered essential for the new bigger authorities to carry out their tasks adequately and be accountable to local communities.

So, at the same time as central government was intervening increasingly in the territorial management of economic policy, it was creating new, powerful elected local authorities – which were more party politicised than the authorities they replaced – without an adequate financial base of their own. When the Labour local government minister, Anthony Crosland, announced in 1977 (three years after reorganisation) that 'the party is over' as far as local government spending was concerned, it was just a matter of time before an irresistible force met with an immovable object. It fell to the Thatcher governments to sow and reap the full whirlwind of an increasingly adversarial system of central–local relations. Between 1979 and 1987, some forty acts dealing with local government were passed, the thrust of which were to assert greater control over local government and local spending in particular (Stewart and Stoker 1989). This resulted in a series of confrontations between Labour-controlled local authorities and central government on spending during the 1980s (see Midwinter 1984, on the Scottish case). The apotheosis of the struggle over territorial financial management was the imposition of the poll tax (community charge) on an unwilling local government system in 1988. On this issue, it was those supporting rather than those opposing the government who were isolated (such Conservative enclaves as Westminster and Wandsworth).

In the words of the Audit Commission, local government was 'in the throes of a revolution' (1988: 1), which went well beyond the issue of finance. The old 'dual polity' had been swept away. According to Travers (1989: 13) the government wanted to change the culture of local government from one of service provision to 'a kind of publicly run holding company for local services'. In addition to divesting local government of much of its housing stock and (some) schools and colleges, the Conservatives reshaped and reformed the internal management (mainly via compulsory competitive tendering of services) and external structure of local government. The latter process started with the abolition of the metropolitan counties and the Greater London Council in 1986 and ended with the overhaul of Scottish and English local government in 1996. In tandem with the deconstruction and fragmentation of local government, the government has created a parallel universe of local quangos (e.g. training and local enterprise councils, urban regeneration 'task forces', development corporations, housing trusts, etc.), under the direct patronage of central and territorial ministries. Thus, the system of territorial management has been transformed by weakening elected local government and strengthening central control.

As the territorial ministries are often depicted as 'mini-governments' with their own secretary of state, team of ministers and multifunctional departmental structure scrutinised by specialist select committees in parliament, to what extent have they diverged from the centre's policies? And, as Midwinter *et al.* (1991) ask, are there distinct policy networks focused on the SO, WO and NIO that are able to make policies rather than simply adapting those coming from Whitehall? In one view, their very existence is a recognition of the political and cultural divergence of the Celtic fringe from the 'core' which it is the job of these ministries to accommodate and integrate simultaneously. Others see the growth of the SO, WO and NIO as a consequence of the expansion of the state to the point where administrative decentralisation simply became a necessity, while others argue that the territorial ministries were created as a direct response to nationalist pressure.

While each case is rather different, the establishment of the territorial ministries can generally be related to political imperatives of the time. This is true both of the WO (promised in the Labour manifesto of 1964) and the NIO (made necessary by the imposition of direct rule in 1972). There is certainly evidence that the territorial ministries have different styles of policy implementation (Ross 1981) and do on occasion pursue different policies (e.g. over licensing laws, juvenile justice and opted-out schools in Scotland). It is generally the case that divergence is greater where there is a separate legal base for it (as in Scotland and Northern Ireland), although the economic 'dirigisme' of the WO under secretary of state Peter Walker in the mid-1980s is often cited as an example of a territorial ministry successfully pursuing a separate path in a major policy area without this. Despite its relative newness, there is evidence that the WO was 'spreading its wings' in other areas of policy too in the 1980s (Rhodes 1988: 149).

In Keating and Midwinter's (1981) view, the SO's action is always conditioned by the balance of issues animating central government. Within this, Parry (1981) distinguishes between three types of policies in attempting to assess the influence of the SO in policy making, and dubs those relating to health, education, housing, social work and planning as the 'Scottish autonomous field'. Other areas of strong influence include agriculture, fisheries, the criminal justice system and industrial strategy. This assessment is basically supported by Midwinter *et al.* in their later study, who also note 'a marked increase in policy experiment' by the SO during the 1980s (1991: 82). This can be contrasted with Mackintosh's assessment of the SO in the 1950s and 1960s, which ascribed little autonomy or indeed sufficient capability and resources to it at that time. Although it had a great range of responsibilities in theory, in practice it did little more than administer. For example, although it had been responsible since 1945 for producing an annual white paper on industry and employment, there were no economists or economic planning group at the SO before 1962 (Mackintosh 1968: 110–33).

The NIO is an altogether different case. Not only is it the most developed territorial ministry organisationally and functionally, but it is also staffed by a separate (Northern Ireland) civil service (the NICS) and has its own 'treasury'. Paradoxically, it is also the newest as it was created after the imposition of direct rule from Westminster in 1972. Before that, the administrative arm of the NIO, the NIDs, were part of the separate elected government in the province based at Stormont. As such, they followed the priorities set for them by successive Unionist governments since 1921, which at the very least had done nothing to counteract the economic and social disadvantages suffered by the minority community. Indeed, the deliberate gerrymandering of electoral boundaries showed, if any evidence were needed, that the Unionist state actively maintained patterns of discrimination. With the imposition of direct rule in 1972, there was a concerted attempt to 'depoliticise' public administration in the province (Connolly 1990). In order to achieve this, there has been a greater use of non-elected public bodies (such as the Northern Ireland Housing Executive (NIHE)) at the expense of elected local authorities. This has not been wholly successful according to some observers. For example, it is argued that the NIHE 'has been overwhelmed by the politico-religious influences on it' (Birrell and Murie 1980: 217).

The figures for identifiable public expenditure per head (see table 3) suggest that the peripheries have been relatively favoured, although nationalists do not see it that way. The so-called Barnett formula for allocating public funds to Scotland and Wales has protected spending there, and this can be seen as reflecting a genuine difference in need and priority, a necessary bribe to keep the union together or the result of effective pressure from peripheral interests on the centre. The evidence does suggest that the territorial ministries behave autonomously on occasions, and are subject to the influence of local policy networks. Insofar as they provide a focus and a structure for such networks, they may act as an instrument of differentiation, much like the Canadian provincial governments have, according to many observers there. It is interesting that the Welsh nationalist Dafydd Elis Thomas observed that the WO had developed its own dynamic to become part of the 'actually existing government of Wales' (Elis Thomas 1991: 65). Even if it had not been intended to be a focus of national debate, it had assumed that mantle.

Can these observations be applied to the regions of England? Are there administrative foci bringing together local and central agencies to create identifiable regional 'centres'? The only instances where this might be applicable are in some well publicised government interventions over the heads of local authorities, as in the case of the Merseyside task force of the early 1980s, headed up nominally by Michael Heseltine, who was unofficially dubbed as the 'minister for Merseyside' as a consequence (Rhodes 1988: 354–6). The infrastructure of government in the English regions tends to be fragmented precisely because functions carried out by the territorial ministries in the Celtic fringe are divided between numerous departments in England.

However, the creation of new local quangos in combination with the regional government directorates by the centre might provide a basis for regional government in the future. These agencies are not based on the same foundations of cultural identity, legal particularity or geographical coherence as is the case with the territorial ministries, but they do wield substantial financial resources and provide an organisational focus for regional interests (see the *Guardian*, 19 January 1995). As in the case of the territorial ministries, the real issue is how such regional institutions of government are accountable to citizens.

Devolution, home rule and regionalism, 1945–95

As Philip Cowley in chapter 6 terms it, the history of devolution in Britain since 1945 is of 'nearly reform'. Well, not quite. The only substantive change since 1945, ironically, has been the suspension (in 1972) and then abolition (1973) of the one example of devolved government in Britain – namely, the directly elected parliament and government of Northern Ireland. Equally ironically, Stormont was the model that the Royal Commission on the Constitution (Kilbrandon Commission, 1968–73) drew most heavily upon for its proposals for Scotland and Wales in its report (1973); by the time these were made Stormont had already disappeared.

Given that the incoming Labour government of 1974 drew heavily on Kilbrandon for its own plan, it is important to understand what the Stormont model represented. As Bogdanor (1979) argues, the relationship between Stormont and Westminster was essentially a federal one. Westminster did not intervene in matters falling under Stormont's legislative jurisdiction, nor did it invoke constitutional safeguards to protect the minority community. Under the Government of Ireland Act 1949, the Stormont parliament gained the sole right to decide whether Northern Ireland should continue to be part of the UK, and it was generally perceived within the Stormont government that a federal relationship prevailed between London and Belfast. Applying these principles and practices to a Scottish parliament envisaged by the 1978 Scotland Act would have meant a de facto extension of federalism within Britain.

However, it was the improvement of accountability generally that was felt to be the crucial issue by both Mackintosh in 1968 and the Royal Commission. Yet there is a qualitative difference between devolution for Scotland, Wales or Northern Ireland, and devolution for the English regions. As there are significant minorities demanding outright independence in Scotland, Wales and Northern Ireland, changes in governance there potentially affect the integrity of the state itself. In contrast, in no part of England are there demands for separation, nor have there been since 1945. When the Royal Commission looked at this issue in the late 1960s, it found practically no support for a federal system in England, although there was support for some form of regional assembly structure (to coordinate and advise local authorities in an area). Unlike Scotland and Wales (not to mention Northern Ireland), there was very little evidence of distinct regional identities within England.

Proposals for devolution have always been a response to nationalism in the peripheries (Dalyell 1977), and the Stormont regime of 1921–72 was no exception. It is important here to distinguish between nationalism as a general political sentiment and nationalism as a defined political movement or party. As we have already discussed, nationalism as a movement in Scotland and Wales has ebbed and flowed since 1945, but generally is associated with the period of the late 1960s onwards. However, there was an active Scottish home rule campaign in the late 1940s in the form of the Scottish convention movement led by John McCormick. This culminated in a petition (the Scottish covenant) to parliament reputedly containing 2 million signatures (Kellas 1984). It demanded a Scottish parliament within the framework of Britain (i.e. legislative devolution), thus falling far short of the SNP's aspiration for complete independence. A somewhat similar movement was active in Wales from 1950 to 1956 (the Parliament for Wales Campaign), but it collected slightly under a quarter of a million signatures. Like the Scottish covenant, it sought to draw in all parties to the campaign.

217

Given that the major parties retain separate Scottish and Welsh organisations with separate conferences and manifestos, it is not surprising that they are the repository for national sentiment too. The Scottish Conservative Party, for example, dates from only 1965, having previously been the Scottish Unionist Party and owing its parentage to the Liberal Unionists of the 1880s. It has been argued that this enabled it to project a distinctive brand of Conservatism and to appeal to uniquely Scottish characteristics (Mitchell 1990; Seawright 1994). Encouraged by Churchill, the Scottish Unionists were opposed to the centralisation inherent in the postwar Labour government's programme of universal welfare and nationalisation, and the Conservatives were the first British party since the war publicly to commit themselves to the idea of an elected Scottish assembly in the form of Edward Heath's famous Declaration of Perth in 1965. Since then, the Conservatives have become increasingly hostile to elective devolution, on the grounds first that the 1974–79 Labour government's plan was simply bad and needed improvement, and then (since 1979) that the whole idea was bad and that the real answer was less state intervention in general. This sea change has coincided with the decline of the Conservative Party in Scotland and its increasing regard by Scots as an 'English' party.

The Liberal Party has consistently advocated devolved government, usually within the context of an overall federal framework, but did support the more limited measures for Scotland and Wales proposed by Labour since the Labour government of 1974. In the prewar era, the Labour Party gave sporadic support and sponsorship to home-rule measures for Scotland, but this agenda faded into the background in 1945 with the more pressing needs imposed by the construction of the welfare state, the nationalisation programme, crisis management of the economy, the onset of the cold war and the decolonisation of India. Labour's socialist programme was heavily centralist, and Scottish interests were supposedly accommodated within the cabinet by the secretary of state. While this model may have worked under Tom Johnston, the legendary wartime secretary, this was not really the case in the first postwar Labour government (Pottinger 1979). When Labour resumed power in 1964, the same basic arrangement prevailed, but this time with a far more powerful figure as secretary of state in the person of William (later Lord) Ross, and was extended to Wales with the creation of the WO (a campaign pledge by Labour).

According to Ross, the apparent efficacy of the system obviated any need for devolution, but when Labour returned to office in 1974, it was under circumstances of a minority government and the rapid growth of the SNP vote, which was perceived as a threat to Labour's majority in Scotland. Thus, there was an abrupt *volte face* on devolution in the summer of 1974 under the most bizarre circumstances: the party in London overturned a decision of the June meeting of Labour's Scottish council (its number depleted by a world cup football match) to oppose devolution for Scotland. A special conference of the Scottish party in August duly endorsed an elected assembly for Scotland, and devolution for Scotland and Wales became a centrepiece of the government's programme between 1974 and 1979.

The measures involved the SO's functions going to an elected Scottish assembly, which would have legislative powers, and the creation of an elected consultative assembly for Wales. Trying to get the Scottish and Welsh plans on to the statute books, however, proved to be exceedingly difficult. The first combined bill was dropped in 1976, and the successor bills took up the remainder of the parliament. A referendum clause was added, which was later amended to include a 40 per cent minimum of the turnout for a vote in favour (the Cunningham amendment), and fundamental issues remained unresolved. The most famous was the 'West Lothian question' posed by Tam Dalyell, Labour MP for West Lothian (later Linlithgow), which asked whether Scottish MPs at Westminster would retain the right to vote on English domestic issues while English MPs would be unable to vote on Scottish domestic issues transferred to the assembly at Edinburgh. Given that Labour depended on its majority in Scotland to keep the government at Westminster afloat, this was no small item.

The legislative process culminated in the referenda of March 1979 (table 5), which were both defeated (technically in Scotland and absolutely in Wales) and the subsequent vote of no confidence and fall of the government.

The division on the government side was clear during the referendum campaigns (less so among Scottish MPs) and during the passage of the legislation some English Labour MPs forced damaging amendments to the proposals. In these circumstances, it may have been expected that Scottish and Welsh voters would give increasing support to more radical options for change and to the nationalists. In fact, the reverse happened. The SNP peaked in 1976, and was split hopelessly by the devolution issue, falling prey to a lengthy period of internal factionalism after 1979. As the legislation progressed, there was increasing support for the status quo among voters, a trend which continued after the 1979 election, with support for outright independence and the SNP hitting a low in 1982. Subsequently, there has been a steadily rising level of support for devolution and independence

Table 5 Referendum results for Scotland and Wales Acts, 1 March 1979 (percentage of electorate)

	Voting yes	*Voting no*	*Not voting*
Scotland	32.5	30.7	37.1
Wales	11.8	46.5	41.7

Source: R. Levy (1995), Governing Scotland, Wales and Northern Ireland, in L. Robins and R. Pyper (eds), *Governing the UK in the 1990s*, London, Macmillan, p. 222.

again, with the latter option apparently being favoured by about half the population in 1991. There seems to be an iron rule that the less likely an option is as a real possibility, the more favourably it will be looked on. Thus Scottish voters are much less sanguine about the prospect of an assembly with extra taxation powers, as the Labour-backed Scottish constitutional convention has most recently proposed.

Despite the debacle of the devolution legislation, Labour in Scotland renewed its commitment to the principle of self-government after 1979. Indeed, deprived of power for so long and egged on by groups such as Scottish Labour Action and the Campaign for a Scottish Assembly, Scottish Labour propounded ever-more radical devolution plans – and radical means to achieve them – throughout the 1980s. Opposition to devolution among Scottish MPs and within the broader party membership effectively ceased because it was seen as a counter to the depredations of Thatcherism in Scotland. By accepting the idea of a Scottish mandate based on the sovereignty of the Scottish people, Labour's position became indistinguishable from that taken by the SNP in 1976 (Geekie and Levy 1989).

Latterly, Labour's chosen vehicle for advancing this agenda has been the cross-party Scottish constitutional convention (neither the SNP nor the Conservatives are represented in the convention), first convened in 1989. Its proposal, published on St Andrew's Day 1990, was a blueprint for the more or less complete transfer of all domestic and some foreign policy functions to a sovereign Scottish parliament funded by assigned revenues and income tax top-up. In reasserting the primacy of Scottish sovereignty, the plan represented a recipe for the indefinite extension of the parliament's powers, and thus complete separation of Scotland from Britain. Long-standing problems, such as the West Lothian question, remained unresolved. The convention plan published in October 1995 rectifies some of the more glaring anomalies of the 1990 scheme, but follows the same basic principles on sovereignty. Predictably, the SNP have described the proposals as a 'retreat' from 1990, while the secretary of state for Scotland has reiterated the government view that the plan will 'pave the way for the ultimate destruction of Scotland and the United Kingdom' (*Scotsman*, 18 October 1995).

In Wales, Labour was mostly opposed to the 1978 Wales Act (including such eminent MPs as former party leader Neil Kinnock) during the referendum. Subsequently, and essentially for the same reasons as in Scotland, many Labour MPs have changed their view and have supported the idea of an elected Welsh assembly with control over domestic matters. The all-party Campaign for a Welsh Assembly continued to argue for an assembly to ensure the greater accountability of the WO, and in the mid-1980s PC supported a plan for the creation of a 100-member elected senate with control over WO functions. In this sense, Plaid has been more pragmatic on the self-government issue than the SNP, which, until 1995, had maintained

Table 6 Support for devolution of various parts of Britain, by region (percentage in favour), 1995

	Devolution in all regions	Devolution to regions wanting it	Devolution to Scotland and Wales only	Devolution to Scotland only	Total (any devolution)
Scotland	14	8	15	28	65
North England	13	18	11	3	45
Midlands	16	16	14	4	50
South England	17	16	11	4	48

Source: ICM Poll, *Guardian*, 19 January 1995.

its policy of isolationism on the constitutional issue since its experiences supporting Labour's plans in the 1970s (Levy 1990).

Devolved government for the English regions is still an afterthought tagged on to the Scottish and Welsh questions, and Labour's 1992 plans for 'rolling devolution' have been abandoned through lack of interest in most areas (table 6). The position seems to be very little different in the mid-1990s to that of thirty years ago, although the north of England may be an exception. In the event of a Labour government, a group of Labour MPs from the region threatened not to vote for a Scottish parliament if the north did not get an assembly too (*Observer*, 19 March 1995).

Although nothing has actually happened yet, the proposals for devolved government for Scotland and Wales from Labour have generally grown bolder, and there is an acceptance among English voters that some change is going to happen if there is a Labour government. The Conservatives have assumed the mantle of the defenders of the union, and this is reflected in the title of their 1993 reform proposals, *Scotland in the Union: A Partnership for Good* (HMSO 1993), which amount to a series of very minor adjustments to the role of the SO, the Scottish committees at Westminster and bodies such as the Scottish Arts Council. Given the parlous state of the Conservative Party in Scotland, the renewed surge in support for the nationalists and the promises made by Labour in opposition, it is very difficult to see how the current status quo can survive a Labour government.

The government of Northern Ireland

In trying to normalise Northern Ireland since the onset of the troubles, successive governments have pursued three basic strategies: the reconstruction (since 1972) of some kind of self-government based on the consent of the constitutional parties on both sides, dual management of the province via an accommodation with the Irish government, and the military repression of paramilitary activity in the province and on the mainland. Conspicuous and lasting success has not been a hallmark of these policies so far.

Plans for a new system of devolved government for the province have to be seen in the context of the decision to impose direct rule in 1972 on a temporary basis, following the rapidly deteriorating security situation in 1971–72. An effective state of civil war had been reached in which bombings, shootings, internment without trial and wholesale intimidation were part of daily life. While the 1970s were probably the most violent period of the whole 'troubles', a horrendous catalogue of death and destruction continued up until the IRA and loyalist cease-fires of September 1994. It is not surprising that public opinion surveys in Britain have shown support for Northern Ireland remaining part of Britain at less than 30 per cent at least since 1981 (Cochrane 1994).

As Hadfield (1992) observes, the principles the government has followed have deviated little from those of the (failed) Northern Ireland Constitution Act 1973, which encapsulated both devolved government for the province and an intergovernmental dimension. The act provided for the replacement of Stormont by an assembly elected by proportional representation, the creation of a power-sharing executive drawn from the assembly and headed by a chief executive, and a constitutional guarantee of Northern Ireland's status, subject to the consent of the electorate in a referendum. Added to this was the provision to create an intergovernmental forum involving British, Irish and Northern Irish representatives. The problem with this scheme, as has been the case with all subsequent ones, has been the unionists' objection to power sharing and the link with the Republic, and the nationalists' objection to the majority veto over the province's future status. Elections for the assembly were held in June 1973 and a power-sharing executive subsequently created after pressure was put on some unionist politicians to participate. Talks were held between the British and Irish governments at Sunningdale in December 1973, where it was agreed to establish an all-Ireland Council of Ireland. This proved to be the catalyst that united the unionist community, and in the February 1974 general election anti-Sunningdale unionists won eleven of the twelve Northern Ireland seats. The Ulster Workers' Council general strike of May 1974 finally destroyed both the assembly and the power-sharing executive.

In May 1975, elections were held for a consultative constitutional convention, but the report produced by the convention proposing a return to the Stormont system was rejected by both the British government and the mainly Catholic SDLP. The convention was dissolved in March 1976. After a further inconclusive attempt to bring the two sides together in early 1980 (the Atkins conference), attention was switched to finding an intergovernmental solution bypassing the politicians in Northern Ireland altogether. This resulted in the creation of the British and Irish Inter-governmental Council in November 1981. In 1982, the government switched strategy back on to Northern Ireland with the Northern Ireland Act, which provided for 'rolling devolution' via an elected assembly that would gradually take back functions from Westminster. The assembly was boycotted by nationalist and republican politicians from the start, and was wound up in June 1986. Meanwhile, the New Ireland Forum (comprised of nationalist politicians from the north and representatives of the main parties in the Republic) published a report in 1984 outlining possible solutions, all of which were rejected by the British government (New Ireland Forum 1984).

The only enduring innovation from the period was the Anglo-Irish agreement signed at Hillsborough castle in November 1985, which gave the Irish government some consultative role in the affairs of Northern Ireland via the Anglo-Irish Intergovernmental Conference. Described by Cochrane as 'a devastating blow to the unionist community' (1994: 383), it symbolised the willingness of the British government to put cooperation with the Republic above the wishes of the unionist majority. In 1989, Peter Brooke, then secretary of state, launched another initiative to get the constitutional parties talking about devolved government, but these faltered in 1991. The intergovernmental route, however, did bear fruit finally in December 1993, when the British and Irish prime ministers signed the so-called Downing Street declaration, offering the right of participation in talks to all who renounced violence and laid down their arms. The British government, stating that it had 'no selfish strategic or economic interest in Northern Ireland', undertook to uphold the wishes of the majority either to remain in the UK or to become part of a united Ireland. Significantly, the Irish government also accepted that a united Ireland was possible only under the same conditions.

Given that these principles bore many similarities to proposals apparently agreed between John Hume of the SDLP and Gerry Adams of Sinn Fein in talks that had been going on at least since the summer of 1993, it was not surprising that they were rejected as a betrayal by Ian Paisley's Democratic Unionists, and greeted with scepticism by the Official Unionists. However, the declaration was probably helped along by Adams' failure to endorse it. The Provisional IRA announced a 'complete cessation of violence' from 1 September 1994, followed rapidly by a similar declaration from the Protestant paramilitaries. In February 1995, the much-leaked framework proposals were made public jointly by the British and Irish prime ministers. These included: a new ninety-member Northern Ireland assembly, elected by proportional representation, with executive and legislative powers; an all-Ireland body made up of elected representatives of the Northern Ireland assembly and Irish parliament, with legislative, executive and harmonising powers as designated by the British and Irish governments; the renunciation of the Republic's constitutional claim to Northern Ireland; a charter of rights for the whole of Ireland protecting civil, political and cultural rights; separate referenda in the north and the south of Ireland on any major constitutional change; and adjustments to British law enabling the people of Northern Ireland to choose their own destiny.

At the time of writing, all-party talks on the framework proposals have still to get off the ground because of a failure to secure agreement over the decommissioning of paramilitary (principally IRA) weapons. Unionists remain extremely wary about the all-Ireland elements in the plan, a sentiment epitomised in the election of David Trimble (generally regarded as a hard-liner) as the new leader of the Official Unionists in September 1995. With the ending of the IRA cease-fire in February 1996, the province faces an uncertain future. However, the prospects for Northern Ireland staying a part of Britain are perhaps less now than at any time since partition in 1920. Should the framework proposals ever be used as a basis for devolution elsewhere in the UK, then Ukania may well be only history early in the next millennium.

References

Almond, G. and Verba, S. (1963), *The Civic Culture: Political Attitudes and Democracy in 5 Nations*, Princeton, Princeton University Press.
Audit Commission (1988), *The Competitive Council*, London, HMSO.
Aughey, A. (1995), The political parties of Northern Ireland, in L. Robins, H. Blackmore and R. Pyper (eds), *Britain's Changing Party System*, London, Leicester University Press.
Balsom, D. (1979), *The Nature and Distribution of Support for Plaid Cymru*, Glasgow, Centre for the Study of Public Policy.
Balsom, D. (1985), The three Wales model, in J. Osmond (ed.), *The National Question Again: Welsh Political Identity in the 1980's*, Dyfed, Gomer.
Banks, J. C. (1971), *Federal Britain?*, London, Harrap.
Birch, A. H. (1978), *Minority Nationalist Movements and Theories of Political Integration*, Princeton, Princeton University Press.
Birrell, D. and Murie, A. (1980), *Policy and Government in Northern Ireland*, Dublin, Gill and Macmillan.
Bogdanor, V. (1979), *Devolution*, Oxford, Oxford University Press.
Bowyer Bell, J. (1993), *The Irish Troubles: A Generation of Violence 1967–1992*, Dublin, Gill and Macmillan.
Brand, J. (1978), *The National Movement in Scotland*, London, Routledge.
Brand, J. (1992), SNP members: the way of the faithful, in P. Norris, I. Crewe, D. Denver and D. Broughton (eds), *British Elections and Parties Yearbook 1992*, Hemel Hempstead, Harvester Wheatsheaf.
Bulpitt, J. (1983), *Territory and Power in the United Kingdom: An Interpretation*, Manchester, Manchester University Press.
Butler, D. (1995), *British General Elections Since 1945* (2nd edn), Oxford, Blackwell.
Cochrane, F. (1994), Any takers? The isolation of Northern Ireland, *Political Studies*, 42:3, 378–95.
Connolly, M. (1990), *Politics and Policy Making in Northern Ireland*, London, Allen.
Crewe, I., Sarlvik, B. and Alt, J. E. (1977), Partisan de-alignment in Britain, 1964–74, *British Journal of Political Science*, 7, 129–90.
Dalyell, T. (1977), *Devolution: The End of Britain?*, London, Cape.
Edwards, O. D. (ed.) (1989), *A Claim of Right for Scotland*, Edinburgh, Polygon.

Elis Thomas, D. (1991), The contribution of Wales, in B. Crick (ed.), *National Identities: The Constitution of the UK*, Oxford, Blackwell.

Geekie, J. and Levy, R. (1989), Devolution and the tartanisation of the Labour Party, *Parliamentary Affairs*, 42:3, 399–411.

Hadfield, B. (1992), *Northern Ireland: Politics and the Constitution*, Buckingham, Open University Press.

Hanby, V. (1976), The renaissance of the SNP: from eccentric to campaigning crusader, in L. Maisel (ed.), *Changing Campaign Techniques: Elections and Values in Contemporary Democracies*, Beverly Hills, Sage.

Hechter, M. (1975), *Internal Colonialism: The Celtic Fringe in British National Development 1536–1966*, London, Routledge.

Hechter, M. and Levi, M. (1979), The comparative analysis of ethnographical movements, *Ethnic and Racial Studies*, 2:3, 260–74.

HMSO (1993) *Scotland in the Union: A Partnership for Good*, cmnd 2225, Edinburgh, HMSO.

Jowell, R. (ed.) (1992), *British Social Attitudes: The 9th Report*, Aldershot, Gower.

Jowell, R., Witherspoon, S. and Brook, L. (eds) (1988), *British Social Attitudes: The 5th Report*, Aldershot, Gower.

Keating, M. and Midwinter, A. (1981), *The Scottish Office in the United Kingdom Policy Network*, Studies in Public Policy paper no. 96, Glasgow, Centre for the Study of Public Policy.

Kellas, J. (1973), *The Scottish Political System*, Cambridge, Cambridge University Press.

Kellas, J. (1984), *The Scottish Political System* (3rd edn), Cambridge, Cambridge University Press.

Levy, R. (1990), *Scottish Nationalism at the Crossroads*, Edinburgh, Scottish Academic Press.

Levy, R. (1994), Nationalist parties in Scotland and Wales, in L. Robins, H. Blackmore and R. Pyper (eds), *Britain's Changing Party System*, London, Leicester University Press.

Levy, R. (1995), Governing Scotland, Wales and Northern Ireland, in R. Pyper and L. Robins (eds), *Governing the UK in the 1990s*, London, Macmillan.

Mackintosh, J. P. (1968), *The Devolution of Power*, Harmondsworth, Penguin.

McAllister, I. (1979), *Party Organisation and Minority Nationalism: A Comparative Study in the UK*, Glasgow, Centre for the Study of Public Policy.

McLean, I. (1970), The rise and fall of the SNP, *Political Studies*, 18:3, 357–72.

Midwinter, A. (1984), *The Politics of Local Spending*, Edinburgh, Mainstream.

Midwinter, A., Keating, M. and Mitchell, J. (1991), *Politics and Public Policy in Scotland*, London, Macmillan.

Miller, W. (1981), *The End of British Politics: Scots and English Political Behaviour in the Seventies*, Oxford, Oxford University Press.

Miller, W., Brand, J. and Jordan, M. (1980), *Oil and the Scottish Voter 1974–79*, London, Social Science Research Council.

Mitchell, J. (1990), *Conservatives and the Union: A Study of Conservative Party Attitudes to Scotland*, Edinburgh, Edinburgh University Press.

Mughan, A. and McAllister, I. (1981), The mobilization of the ethnic vote: a thesis with some Scottish and Welsh evidence, *Ethnic and Racial Studies*, 4:2, 189–204.

Nairn, T. (1977), *The Break-Up of Britain: Old and New Nationalism*, London, New Left Books.

Nairn, T. (1988), *The Enchanted Glass. Britain and its Monarchy*, London, Vintage.

New Ireland Forum (1984), *Report*, Dublin, Stationery Office.

Newman, S. (1992), The rise and decline of the Scottish National Party: ethnic politics in a post-industrial environment, *Ethnic and Racial Studies*, 15:1, 1–35.

Parry, R. (1981), Scotland as a laboratory for public administration, paper presented to the conference of the PSA UK Politics Group, Glasgow, September.

Pottinger, G. (1979), *The Secretaries of State for Scotland 1926–76*, Edinburgh, Scottish Academic Press.

Pulzer, P. (1972), *Political Representation and Elections in Britain* (2nd edn), London, Allen and Unwin.

Rhodes, R. A. W. (1988), *Beyond Westminster and Whitehall: The Sub-Central Governments of Britain*, London, Unwin Hyman.

Rose, R. (1982), *Understanding the United Kingdom*, London, Longman.

Rose, R. and McAllister, I. (1986), *Voters Begin to Choose: From Closed-Class to Open Elections in Britain*, London, Sage.

Ross, J. M. (1981), *The Secretary of State for Scotland and the Scottish Office*, Studies in Public Policy paper no. 87, Glasgow, Centre for the Study of Public Policy.

Royal Commission on the Constitution (1973), *Report*, cmnd 5460, London, HMSO.

Royal Commission on Local Government in England (1969), *Report*, London, HMSO.

Royal Commission on Local Government in Scotland (1969), *Report*, London, HMSO.

Scottish Constitutional Convention (1990), *Towards Scotland's Parliament: A Report to the Scottish People*, Edinburgh, Scottish Constitutional Convention.

Scottish Constitutional Convention (1995), *Scotland's Parliament: Scotland's Right*, Edinburgh, Scottish Constitutional Convention.

Seawright, D. (1994), *The Decline of the Scottish Conservative and Unionist Party 1950–1992*, PhD thesis, University of Strathclyde.

Smith, T. (1979), *The Politics of the Corporate Economy*, Oxford, Martin Robertson.

Stewart, J. and Stoker, G. (eds) (1989), *The Future of Local Government*, Hampshire, Macmillan.

Studlar, D. and McAllister, I. (1988), Nationalism in Scotland: a post-industrial phenomenon?, *Ethnic and Racial Studies*, 11:1, 48–62.

Travers, T. (1989), Community charge and other financial changes, in J. Stewart and G. Stoker (eds), *The Future of Local Government*, Hampshire, Macmillan.

Whyte, J. (1990), *Interpreting Northern Ireland*, Oxford, Oxford University Press.

12

The technological 'revolution' in government

John Street

In the beginning...

Fifty years ago, there was only one computer in the world. It was called ENIAC (Electronic Numerical Integrator and Computer) and was housed at the University of Pennsylvania. The first British computer came into operation in 1948, at the University of Manchester. These new machines occupied whole buildings, consumed vast quantities of electricity, broke down regularly and were of very limited practical value. Now, half a century later, computers are to be found in offices, schools, universities, libraries; they are used to run factory production lines, to operate super-market check-outs; they analyse data for the police, create mailing lists, compile bills and so on. It would be hard to underestimate their ubiquity and their importance. And, of course, politics and the business of government has – like everything else – felt the effects of the information technology (IT) revolution. Writing in 1985, David Howell reflected upon his career as a minister and upon the effect of IT in government. For him, its use was raising profound issues:

> It makes questions about the proper role of governments, its functions and status, still more unsettled than in the past – more fluid, more provoking of disagreement and very probably more acrimonious. It creates, in short, a revolutionary political process which must be understood if it is to be channelled constructively. (Howell 1985: 76)

If the impact of IT seemed to threaten major changes in 1985, our current predicament promises yet more dramatic developments.

Parties now use computers to target voters for direct mail. Voters can use the Internet to contact Whitehall, and politicians make (albeit vague) references to the emergence of 'electronic democracy'. Government departments, like every other large organisation, rely upon computers to conduct their daily business. Changes in policy and practice are also led by changes in technology. Military and security technology based on IT developments have been acquired by government, just as new medical uses of IT have become part of the National Health Service. These deliberate adoptions of

227

the new technology have been accompanied by the need to cope with its unintended effects. The environment in which governments now operate has been transformed by the use of IT, most obviously through the use of electronic communications, which have eroded national borders and speeded up change. There are those, for example, who will claim that dramatic fluctuations in the stock market, with their consequent political crises, are partly the product of a system that is run by computers and not by people.

But just as it is difficult to underestimate the changes that IT has engendered, it is equally possible to exaggerate them, particularly in extrapolating to the next fifty years. Twenty years ago, when the IT revolution first appeared as a topic of public concern, all manner of extravagant claims were made. The optimists talked of the emergence of a leisure society in which all dull and dangerous jobs would be done by robots and computers. This new order was to be run by a state in which the hierarchies of old were replaced by an egalitarian network (Evans 1979). The pessimists, by contrast, spoke gloomily of the creation of a divided society, in which the majority were made permanently redundant by the new technology, while any threat they might pose was being monitored by another application of the same technology (Hines and Searle 1979). Neither of these predictions has proved to be accurate, although it is possible to see elements of both in the world we currently inhabit. The truth is both more mundane and more complicated. In this chapter I look at the different ways in which IT has impinged upon the British system of government, seeing what changes have been wrought and trying to assess their implications for the conduct of government.

The informed state

It was fashionable in the mid-1970s to talk of the crisis of overload in British government. The idea, most cogently expressed by Anthony King (1975), was that government's reach had exceeded its grasp, that it promised far more than it could deliver. There were many reasons for this state of affairs, but one was the growth of 'interdependence'. Governments (of whatever political colour) were caught in a complex web of dependency relationships, and any attempt to change policy or respond to problems was made impossibly difficult. The world was too complex. One response to this predicament was – as the new right advocated – to reduce the size and ambition of the state, and to curtail citizens' expectations for it (see chapter 2). But another response was to address the problem of complexity through the use of computer technology. Government departments, following the line taken by other such organisations, began to 'automate' the office in the same way that manufacturing had been automated in previous eras. This was not just a matter of introducing word processing, but of replacing antiquated forms of data collection (file cards and filing cabinets) with electronic forms. By the 1990s the government was spending £2 billion a year on computing facilities.

Storing data on computer was not only easier and cheaper, it also made possible far more complicated tasks of coordination and correlation. When data were stored in filing cabinets in offices throughout Britain they were very difficult to search. Much depended on the filing system – searches were only as effective as the categories and cross-referencing used. And it was virtually impossible to compare or match up data stored in separate locations (and stored for different purposes). With the use of computers that were capable of full text retrieval, all data were entered and retrieved electronically. This eased access because you could now define your categories after you had stored the data, and you could change them as and when you needed to. It also eased compatibility: data stored in one place could now be matched up with data in another. The enhanced ability to handle and use data made it possible to devise policies that had previously been inconceivable.

The present social security system, for example, could not exist without the computers that currently organise the Department of Social Security. In 1977, the British government created an operational strategy for the Department of Health and Social Security (DHSS) (as it then was). By 1985, according to David Lyon, the DHSS was heading the 'biggest computerisation programme in Europe', organised around a central index which meant 'that information on almost every citizen of the United Kingdom is available to a wide variety of agencies and people, structured around a "whole person concept"' (Lyon 1994: 94).

Early in 1996, the government announced that the computerisation of Whitehall was to receive an added boost (*Guardian*, 30 January 1996: 8). This would, it was claimed, save £9 billion, mostly through a cut in the wage bill as civil servants were shed and replaced by computers. But attached to this proposal was a plan to increase the links between a number of government departments: benefits, tax, passports, student loans, driving licences and so on. The government represented this as creating an 'electronic post office' that eased access and increased opportunity for ordinary citizens.

Local government too has been affected by IT. This is perhaps most dramatically represented in the bid that Norwich City Council and Norfolk County Council made to the Millennium fund in 1996. The idea was to wire up the whole county, to turn Norwich into an 'information city', and to create an entirely new range of services and facilities through the application of telematics. Included in the bid were proposals for a 'virtual library', making available library and archive material at the touch of a button; a 'digital city' to help regenerate business in the region; an 'exploratory' to promote tourism; and 'an agora', to provide information about retail outlets and leisure activities.

While such changes at local and national government seemed to some to represent a more efficient and effective way of collating and distributing information, others detected in these same developments the creation of a 'Big Brother' state.

The surveillance state

A decade ago, Duncan Campbell and Steve Connor predicted that by the year 2000, there will be 'a government central computer network recording the name and number, current address, date of birth, sex, identity number, family relationships and many other particulars of virtually the entire population' (Campbell and Connor 1986: 88). Some would argue that their prediction is already with us – together with the fears that lie behind it.

Credit and direct-debit cards may be very convenient ways to pay for goods and services, but to some they represent part of a sinister trend. Every transaction records the time and place in which it occurs. Our consumer habits leave an electronic trail that can easily be followed. When we subscribe to magazines or give to charity, our name goes on to a list that may then be sold to other organisations, and hence the junk mail we receive. But this inconvenience disguises, it is argued, an important intrusion upon privacy. Our name and our interests now circulate without our having any control over their movements. And organisations can, as a result, target us. These intrusions may seem trivial, but they can be seen as symptoms of a more pervasive disease. While the information we divulge through consumption may be voluntarily assigned, there is other information that we are obliged to record – in paying taxes or licensing our car or whatever. The information given to state organisations (or *Next Steps* agencies) can then be used in other contexts to monitor us. It is very difficult for people to know what data are held on them, because – despite the provisions of the Data Protection Act 1984 – the information is hard to check, and the speed of its collection may far outstrip our capacity to monitor it (Pearce *et al.* 1988). The fear of this monitoring is further heightened by the use of databases such as the National Police Computer or that used by MI5 (British Society for Social Responsibility in Science 1985). Lyon (1988: 95) estimated that in Britain there were 113,141,000 individual files held on computer. When it was proposed that Britain introduce an identity card, these fears surfaced, if only because the number on the identity card was to be people's national insurance number, which is the same number that MI5 use in recording information on their computer. Computer technology allows for the easy correlation and collation of such data, and thereby enhances the possibilities for, and powers of, surveillance.

These developments are also linked to the introduction of closed-circuit television in public places. These devices, which can also be used to read car number plates (and to identify the owner by referring to the Driver and

Vehicle Licensing Centre), allow for the surveillance of citizens as they conduct their daily routines. As Lyon (1988: 95–6) writes:

> Drivers on the M1 motorway (and other routes) have their licence plates scanned by a computerized TV camera placed on a bridge. By the time they reach the next bridge, the police have received sufficient information on specific vehicles to alert them as to which should be ignored, watched or intercepted.

While these cameras have been used to discourage crime and identify criminals, critics argue that these gains are made at considerable cost, most especially to the civil liberties of the rest of the population.

The democratic state

In stark contrast to those commentators who herald the arrival of the surveillance state, others celebrate the arrival of a democratic one. There are several strands to this claim. First, rather than seeing the acquisition of data on citizens as a device for controlling them, it is seen instead as a means of ensuring that the state is responsive to the needs of citizens. The more that is known about citizens the more easy it is to devise policies that are aimed directly at their needs. Second, the new forms of data storage are seen as destroying old hierarchies, sustained by monopoly control of information, and replacing them with networks, in which relations are equalised and secrecy is undermined. Traditional bureaucracies sustain themselves by controlling access to information. With the advent of the computer, such controls become much harder to operate. Computers are seen as intrinsically democratic technologies. Third, new forms of data storage are complemented by new forms of communication. What this means is that access to knowledge and its use allow for greater participation by ordinary citizens. Departments of state can already be contacted through the use of e-mail and the Internet. It is a relatively small step from this to direct public participation in decision making through the use of interactive link-ups.

Much of the talk about 'electronic democracy' is highly speculative. Britain has, as yet, nothing to rival the experiments in participation that have been tried in the USA and elsewhere in Europe (Arterton 1987; McLean 1989). Indeed, it lacks the basic infrastructure (in particular, nationwide cabling) of the kind that exists in France. But the opportunity to participate is hampered by more than technological gaps. The strictness of Britain's secrecy laws, and the very limited steps taken towards open government, make talk of push-button democracy a future possibility rather than a present probability. Nonetheless, IT has increased our access to information, if only by the simple expedient of putting *Hansard* on CD-ROM or by the use of the Internet to post government press releases.

Where the change is most apparent is in electioneering and pressure group politics. While Britain has yet to reach the sophistication of the USA, where campaign organisers claim that no one can win an election without using the Internet and means such as direct mail and telephone targeting, in Britain the changes have been more modest. Nonetheless, it is evident that parties and interest groups have learnt to deploy IT in targeting potential supporters (Kavanagh 1995; Smith and Webster 1995). But these changes in political campaigning are less a case of 'empowering' citizens, of giving them access to parties and groups, and more a matter of getting access to them. It is perhaps significant, however, that the Labour Party's 1995 policy statement on the Internet, *The Net Effect*, refers to the possibility of electronic participation in decision making.

The globalised state

Just as computers enable government departments to communicate more easily, they also ease communication between nations. Arguably the most dramatic change engendered by IT is a global communications system (McGrew and Lewis 1992). This is evident in a number of areas of contemporary life. Most recently, attention has focused upon the Internet, and the promise of the 'information superhighway', which allows communication across the globe and provides for new forums for discussion and sharing information. But it is perhaps the direct application of this technology that is most significant, in particular the global connections between the money markets of the world, which allow money to be moved rapidly across time zones and land masses. Such developments have been accompanied, through the use of satellites, by a parallel televisual communications system that allows for news and images to be transmitted rapidly and, more significantly, without reference to national borders. Shirley Williams (1985: 212), one of the few British politicians to address themselves seriously to the impact of IT, wrote: 'The communications revolution tends not only to fragment political parties and enhance awareness of local issues, but also to make national borders irrelevant.' The significance of these developments lies in the way they affect the autonomy of states. Decisions made within national borders may count for nothing if the location of power and the source of change lies elsewhere.

The deregulation of broadcasting in Britain in the 1990s was largely a product of political ideology and political interest, but it was also the product of technical change. Whatever the driving force, the effect was to create a situation in which the state could exercise less control than before over what its subjects watched or heard. New forms of communication diminished national sovereignty.

The altered state

Technical change has also had a profound impact upon other aspects of British politics, most obviously through its impact upon employment and wealth creation. The world of work has a major effect on politics. Work (and its absence) is vital to the way in which wealth is distributed within a country, the way interests are identified and to the way social, educational and technology policy is designed. Information technology has dramatically altered the structure of employment in Britain and the set of incentives and of pressures operating on government (Kaplinsky 1984; Gill 1985).

The government has responded to the development of IT in a number of ways. Education policy, for example, has reflected the view that society has to adapt and change to cope with the new technology. So it is that IT has become a key component of the National Curriculum. It has also led to changes within higher education, where again the need to develop and use IT has caused a shift towards training and research in this area. Equally, there have been developments in industrial policy. These extend from involvement in such initiatives as ESPRIT and the Alvey project, both of which aimed to encourage research into and adoption of IT (Street 1992). In the early 1980s, through the National Enterprise Board, the government supported the creation of Inmos, a company that was to develop British microprocessors. Inmos was subsequently privatised.

Information technology has had other effects upon the operation of government. It has altered the patterns of employment in Britain. This is most dramatically represented by the growth of the Thames Valley corridor into which many high-technology companies have located, and the decline of traditional northern heavy industry. This is not just a fact of demography; it also has important political consequences. In a liberal democracy with limited state powers, the distribution of wealth and resources is influenced by economic bargaining power. The changing economic structure and the creation of new skills have altered the structure and strength of political interests in Britain. At the same time, these initiatives can be seen as part of a larger struggle to maintain Britain's position in the world economy and to retain some element of national sovereignty in the face of the growth of transnational corporations.

Whatever the forces driving the change, it is argued that there have been real and awkward political consequences with which governments have had to deal. The problem is neatly summarised by Bill Jordan (1981: 37): 'a decreasing number of people will receive wages and salaries, and an increasing number will have to claim on the state for subsistence.' There are profound difficulties, within a liberal democracy, of justifying permanent levels of unemployment – that is, unemployment that is not transitional or cannot be redescribed as education (for the young) or retirement (for the old). Why should those in work subsidise those unemployed, given that there is no expectation that work will be found for them? It is no surprise that the major political parties are reluctant to concede in public that Britain will never return to full employment, although they may acknowledge this fact in private.

And the next fifty years?

In reflecting upon the changes wrought by IT on government, there is a danger of seeing the process as an inexorable one, driven by the inescapable logic of technology. Change is presented as something that *has* to happen. Indeed, this is the impression created by the way the government itself addresses the issue. In the early 1980s, when Kenneth Baker was minister for information technology, he adopted the slogan 'There's no future without IT.' But this idea of inevitability is mistaken. Though technology does change and though we adapt to it, it is not simply the product of some irresistible force. The production and implementation of technology are themselves the product of political decisions, which can be detected in science policy, in industrial subsidies and in regulations. All these contribute to the pace and impact of technical change, and explain why countries and governments vary in the extent to which, and the way in which, they are affected by technology.

For this reason, we need to be wary of grand or gloomy promises for the future, or at least ones grounded only in terms of what technology may or may not do. The evidence of our reaction to the first years of the IT revolution is that most predictions are, at best, only partially correct. We should, therefore, be sceptical of those who predict the coming of electronic democracy and those who predict the emergence of an all-seeing, all-powerful surveillance state. Technology will continue to help change the character and conduct of government, but the ways in which it will do this cannot be read simply from the makers' specifications or the advertisers' grandiose prose. It might *look* as if having more information more readily available is a key to better government; equally it might *look* like a basis for complete surveillance. It may be that, in fact, an excess of information simply reduces people to a state of confusion and paralysis. The answer cannot be assumed. It depends on the political conditions that frame the world in which IT operates. If we want to predict the future, we need to start by looking more carefully at the past.

References

Arterton, C. (1987), *Teledemocracy*, London, Sage.
British Society for Social Responsibility in Science (1985), *TechnoCop: New Police Technologies*, London, Free Association Books.
Campbell, D. and Connor, S. (1986), *On the Record*, London, Michael Joseph.

Evans, C. (1979), *The Mighty Micro: The Impact of the Micro-chip Revolution*, London, Gollanz.

Gill, C. (1985), *Work, Unemployment and the New Technology*, Cambridge, Polity.

Hines, C. and Searle, G. (1979), *Automatic Unemployment*, London, Earth Resources.

Howell, D. (1985), Information technology and relations between government and the public – some hopeful reflections, *Catalyst*, 1:4, 75–85.

Jordan, B. (1981), *Automated Poverty*, London, Routledge.

Kaplinsky, R. (1984), *Automation: The Technology and Society*, London, Longman.

Kavanagh, D. (1995), *Election Campaigning: The New Marketing of Politics*, Oxford, Blackwell.

King, A. (1975), Overload: problems of governing in the 1970s, *Political Studies*, 23:2, 283–96.

Lyon, D. (1988), *The Information Society: Issues and Illusions*, Cambridge, Polity.

Lyon, D. (1994), *The Electronic Eye*, Cambridge, Polity.

McGrew, A. and Lewis, P. (eds) (1992), *Global Politics*, Cambridge, Polity.

McLean, I. (1989), *Democracy and the New Technology*, Cambridge, Polity.

Pearce, P., Parsloe, H., Francis, H., Macara, A. and Watson, D. (1988), *Personal Data Protection in Health and Social Services*, London, Croom Helm.

Smith, C. and Webster, C. (1995), Democracy and new technology, in J. Lovenduski and J. Stanyer (eds), *Contemporary Political Studies 1995*, Exeter, PSA.

Street, J. (1992), *Politics and Technology*, London, Macmillan.

Williams, S. (1985), *A Job to Live*, Harmondsworth, Penguin.

Conclusion: end-of-century Britain

Bill Jones and Lynton Robins

In the time span of fifty years Britain has developed into a more diverse, complex and unsettled society, barely recognisable from what it was when the war came to an end. The old international certainties that characterised foreign policy in 1945 have been replaced by controversy over Britain's role in the world, while the postwar dreams of building the new Jerusalem, long put to one side, have been replaced by ambitions to reconstruct much of society past. Abroad, the eventual loss of empire and embracing of Europe, which should have resulted in Britain playing a less demanding and more clearly defined regional role, found Britain unable to handle the new realities, much as Dean Acheson spelled out in his painful quip concerning the problems of international adjustment. It is argued that Britain has no role within a deeply federal European Union, while it is also recognised that being left on the margins of such a development would also be damaging to Britain. Britain, always a reluctant member of the only feasible option, faces a new-century challenge of negotiating the optimum variable-geometry involvement with its partners that keeps it at the heart of Europe while standing to one side. Nimble footwork will be necessary to outmanoeuvre the increasing numbers of politicians willing to consider British withdrawal from Europe in favour of what Harold Wilson once mocked as the 'GITA' option – that Britain should 'go it alone'. Without trace of political embarrassment, end-of-century Little Englanders are arguing that Britain went alone in 1939 and should do so again.

At home, the nature of British society has changed beyond what any sane person in 1945 could have ever envisaged. Britain has become an oil-producing nation, with a geography transformed by developments in transport, the mass media and information technology. Technological change has been accompanied by social change, with what might have been judged as excessive affluence from the puritanical perspective of 1945. A multi-cultural society as well as an economy that can employ women part time rather than men full time would also distinguish between now and then. Discussion of concepts such as 'deindustrialisation' then 'globalisation' would mark the transformation of the political culture from one receptive to popular socialism to one celebrating popular capitalism. The vocabulary of state ownership and nationalisation has been superseded by the language of privatisation, deregulation and market testing. Alongside the growing affluence of the majority exist the insecurities and deprivations of an uncared for poor. Karl Marx, never adopted by Labour and eventually rejected by the Soviets, may be forgiven a posthumous smile as politicians who fully embraced market forces find they are drinking from a poisoned chalice. For while corporatism and welfarism were costly servants to employ during the 1960s and 1970s, unrestrained capitalism is proving a devastating master in the 1990s.

In his book *Audit of War*, a study of the illusion and reality of Britain as a great postwar power, Corelli Barnett wrote of Britain's descent from its seemingly assured place as one of the 'big three' in 1945 to:

> the place of fifth in the free world as an industrial power, with manufacturing only two fifths of West Germany's.... As that descent took its course the illusions and the dreams of 1945 would fade one by one – the Imperial and Commonwealth role, the world power role, the British industrial genius, and, at last, New Jerusalem itself, a dream turned to a dank reality of a segregated, subliterate, unskilled, unhealthy and institutionalised proletariat hanging on to the nipple of state maternalism. (Barnett 1986: 304)

This view might seem overly pessimistic but if council housing is any yardstick, he has a point. As recently as 1979 less than a third of families housed by councils came from the poorest 20 per cent, with as many as 10 per cent drawn from the richest 20 per cent. By the 1990s, however, the poorest accounted for a half of council tenants and the richest virtually none. Figures also show that only half of male heads of household on council estates were in employment compared with the national figure of 85 per cent. The bleak picture of run-down council estates, with boarded over windows, rubbish in the gardens, teenage vandalism and drug dealing is becoming commonplace in end-of-century Britain. The view that poverty has increased since the dawning of the Thatcherite age is challenged by those who argue that this is only the case when a relative measure is applied, and that the poorest of the 1990s enjoy a lifestyle far beyond that of most Britons in 1945. Others might counter that the poverty of most immediate postwar Britons was restricted narrowly to material and techno-logical goods, and that in terms of spirit, morale and aspirations they enjoyed riches as never before and, as yet, never since. It is for this reason that prime minister John Major's nostalgic view of a back-to-basics Britain, never delivered, remains an attractive idea in British politics. It is the stuff of much of our popular culture: well behaved children playing in the sunshine, their fathers playing cricket on the village green, wives gossiping over the sandwiches, the warm beer that awaits, church bells, and so on.

It could be 1950 in the collective memory of middle England. It is an attractive, if unrealistic, vision of the past which politicians are being urged to recreate half a century on. It is easy to understand why. The contrast with the vandalised, crime-ridden, drug-plagued urban wastelands in which many Britons now live is stark indeed. While some see the answer to threats posed by the underclass in terms of creating islands of gated security, others debate ideas of how to reconstruct a new society based on much from the past. Communitarianism, stake holding and various manifestations of citizenship form the language of this romantic project.

Unemployment and a changing labour market need not have a corrosive effect on wider society, but it is the case that they have done so in the 1990s. In his analysis, *The State We're In*, Will Hutton (1996) discerns a 30/30/40 society, in which 30 per cent of adults are marginalised, another 30 per cent work in insecure forms of employment and only 40 per cent have tenured full-time jobs (see chapter 8). Elsewhere he argued:

> Two-thirds of new jobs created since 1992 are part-time. Where jobs are full-time, three quarters are offered only on short-term contracts. And once a full-time job is lost the chance of regaining full-time employment is negligible; the unemployed move into semi-employment and back again. These are hard times. (*Observer*, 2 June 1996)

John Major's dilemma was that he was never able to realise his dream of back-to-basics Sunday-afternoon Britain and populate it with low-paid, casualised, flexible and part-time workers worried about their future.

Along with tougher times has come a new attitude towards fellow citizens. The sense of national togetherness and common purpose evident in the immediate postwar years was replaced by individual advantage being given greater priority. The electorate became ever less willing to vote for high welfare spending and, as economic success eluded Britain in the 1970s, so altruism gave way to greater defence of self-interests, understanding of the poor and disadvantaged by anger at their weakness, and tolerance of diverse opinions by a narrow authoritarianism. Whether Margaret Thatcher provoked or reflected the changing mood of the British electorate, her arrival marked a decade in which most of what remained of citizens' concern one for another was swept away by the pursuit of personal gain. Certainly the eponymous ideology legitimised personal greed and, whether quoted within context or not, her view that 'there was not such thing as society' formed a fair expression of British-style new right politics.

If the debate concerning the nature of contemporary poverty is put to one side, that Britain is a more divided society at the end of the century than at the end of the war remains beyond contest. A study by the Child Poverty Action Group found that between 1979 and 1993 the poorest 10 per cent of the population experienced an 18 per cent fall in real incomes after housing costs, compared with a rise of 37 per cent for the population as a whole and a leap of 61 per cent for the richest 10 per cent of society (Oppenheim and Harker 1996). In similar vein, a report from the Organization for Economic Cooperation and Development confirmed that the distribution of male earnings is now wider that at any time in this century for which there are reliable records. Levels of individual wealth, as recorded by the *Sunday Times* annual survey of the richest 500 people in Britain, reminds a divided nation of how very plump the so-called 'fat cats' have grown: for example, Viscount Rothermere, the media tycoon, is worth £650 million; David Sainsbury, owner of the supermarket chain, £2,520 million; the Duke of Westminster, property owner, £1,500 million; and Richard Branson, self-publicising entrepreneur, £725 million. To some commentators the immediate and continuing success of the national lottery, established in the mid-1990s, resulted from the absence of all other forms of mobility that might enable the poor to escape from their poverty and join Britain's growing legion of millionaires.

The current situation in Britain can be summarised by the following points (taken from *Social Trends 1996*).

- The most wealthy 1 per cent own 18 per cent of all wealth.
- The most wealthy 10 per cent own 49 per cent of all wealth.
- The most wealthy 50 per cent own 92 per cent of all wealth.
- Average weekly earnings before stoppages:
  waitress – £157,
  caretaker – £220,
  bricklayer – £261,
  nurse – £316,
  primary school teacher – £391,
  doctor – £746.
- Average tax bill according to income:
  £10,000 – £1,670,
  £20,000 – £4,250,
  £39,000 – £7,370.

While free markets invigorate, promote individual enterprise, create riches, elicit effort from those who, without market discipline, might be tempted by idleness, they also corrupt and undermine. Declining cultural standards (from the excesses of tabloid journalism to pornography), drugs and crime are all delivered by the workings of the marketplace. Neither are market forces any respecters of tradition or institution. The monarchy's fall from grace together with the declining relevance of other ancient institutions in national life; the internal divisions that have plunged the Conservative Party into prolonged crisis; the decline in standards from education to health care; not to mention the decline in standards of public life: all these have in common in one way or another market forces as a contributory cause. Of all social change, it is the rise in the pattern of crime that most alarms the public. A recent British Crime Survey found that more people were more worried about becoming victims of crime, particularly burglary and rape, than about losing their job, serious illness in their family or being injured in a road accident. Many are concerned about the rising level of violence that accompanies much crime and, albeit rarely, atrocity, the likes of which had no counterpart in the immediate postwar decades.

In the pages of this book, political scientists have described and attempted to explain the processes that have shaped Britain's postwar politics. Future scholars may provide alternative accounts of this turbulent half century: they may discover some alchemy that converts governments concerned about national security into ones willing also to provide social security; a novel analysis of voting behaviour may yet reveal a generational impact that has eluded contemporary psephologists; or they may pinpoint some idea, already articulated but not judged worthy of mention by these contributors, as being crucial in shaping the new orthodoxy as it emerges during the next half century. Whatever, the challenges facing political scientists in providing what remains still a fairly 'rough draft' of history have grown in complexity during the last forty or fifty years. Nor does their task look any easier in the next half century.

References

Barnett, C. (1986), *The Audit of War*, London, Macmillan.
Hutton, W. (1996), *The State We're In*, London, Vintage.
Oppenheim, C. and Harker, L. (1996), *Poverty: The Facts* (3rd edn), London, Child Poverty Action Group.

Index